The American West

Problems in American History

Series editor: Jack P. Greene

Each volume focuses on a central theme in American history and provides greater analytical depth and historiographic coverage than standard textbook discussions normally allow. The intent of the series is to present in highly interpretive texts the unresolved questions of American history that are central to current debates and concerns. The texts will be concise enough to be supplemented with primary readings or core textbooks and are intended to provide brief syntheses to large subjects.

Published

Jacqueline Jones *A Social History of the Laboring Classes*
Robert Buzzanco *Vietnam and the Transformation of American Life*
Ronald Edsforth *The New Deal: America's Response to the Great Depression*
Frank Ninkovich *The United States and Imperialism*
Peter Onuf and Leonard Sadosky *Jeffersonian America*
Fraser Harbutt *The Cold War Era*
Donna Gabaccia *Immigration and American Diversity*
J. William Harris *The Making of the American South: A Short History, 1500–1877*
Anne M. Butler and Michael J. Lansing *The American West: A Concise History*

The American West

A Concise History

Anne M. Butler and Michael J. Lansing

© 2008 by Anne M. Butler and Michael J. Lansing

BLACKWELL PUBLISHING
350 Main Street, Malden, MA 02148–5020, USA
9600 Garsington Road, Oxford OX4 2DQ, UK
550 Swanston Street, Carlton, Victoria 3053, Australia

The right of Anne M. Butler and Michael J. Lansing to be identified as
he Authors of this Work has been asserted in accordance with the UK Copyright,
Designs, and Patents Act 1988.

First published 2008 by Blackwell Publishing Ltd

2   2009

Library of Congress Cataloging-in-Publication Data

Butler, Anne M., 1938–
he American West: a concise history / by Anne M. Butler and Michael J. Lansing.
p.   cm.—(Problems in American history)
Includes bibliographical references and index.
ISBN 978-0-631-21085-6 (hardcover: alk. paper)
ISBN 978-0-631-21086-3 (pbk.: alk. paper)
West (U.S.)—History.   2. West (U.S.)—Civilization.   3. United States—Territorial
pansion.   4. National characteristics, American.   I. Lansing, Michael.   II. Title.

F591.B94 2008
978—dc22
2007009756

A catalogue record for this title is available from the British Library.

Set in 10/12.5pt Sabon
by The Running Head Limited, Cambridge, www.therunninghead.com

For further information on
Blackwell Publishing, visit our website:
www.blackwellpublishing.com

For our students – past, present, and future

Contents

List of illustrations		ix
The Authors		xi
Acknowledgments		xiii
	Introduction	1
1	First Wests, Many Wests	11
2	Inside Native Wests	47
3	Enforcing an American West	81
4	Imperial Wests	115
5	A Diverse, Urban, and Federal West	150
6	Mythic West and Modern West	182
	Suggested Readings	216
	Index	229

Illustrations

1.1 Map of the American continent in the 1770s   13
1.2 Abandoned ruins at Mesa Verde   18
2.1 Rosebud winter count   52–3
2.2 *Bison Bulls* by Titian Ramsay Peale   70
3.1 German Jewish immigrants with Kiowa Indians   98
3.2 Chinese miners in an underground tunnel   107
4.1 Dakota Indian burial teepee with wrapped bodies   119
4.2 African American family on a porch in Denver   141
5.1 Tejana/os standing by a broken car   170
5.2 Japanese American woman crocheting in front of a
     needlework exhibit   175
6.1 Indians on the dock at Alcatraz Island prison   202
6.2 Map of the metropolitan areas of the West, 1990   209

The Authors

Anne M. Butler, Trustee Professor, Emeritus, in the Department of History at Utah State University, served as associate editor, co-editor, and the first woman senior editor of the *Western Historical Quarterly*. She is the author of *Daughters of Joy, Sisters of Misery: Prostitutes in the American West* (1985), and *Gendered Justice in the American West: Women Prisoners in Men's Penitentiaries* (1997), and co-author (with Ona Siporin) of *Uncommon Common Women: Ordinary Lives of the West* (1996). The recipient of numerous awards for teaching and scholarship, she has published extensively on the West, especially concerning race and gender. Currently she is completing a monograph about Roman Catholic nuns in the American West.

Michael J. Lansing is Assistant Professor of History at Augsburg College. His research focuses on gender, nature, and space and place in the North American West and his essays have appeared in the *Western Historical Quarterly*, the *Utah Historical Quarterly*, *Ethics, Place and Environment*, and the *Journal of Historical Geography*. Winner of the Montana Historical Society's Burlingame-Toole Award (1997), the Oscar O. Winther Award for the best article published in the *Western Historical Quarterly* (2001), and the Dale L. Morgan Award for the best scholarly article published in the *Utah Historical Quarterly* (2005), he also serves on the editorial board of the University of Arizona Press' monograph series, "Western Women's Voices."

Acknowledgments

In the production of this book, we appreciate the support of Blackwell Publishing, especially Emily Martin and Deirdre Ilkson in the United States, and Carole Drummond of The Running Head in the United Kingdom. Ken Provencher deserves the credit for determining that a volume about the West would be included in the Problems in American History series. We thank him for his constant encouragement and gentle compassion in the face of various calamities and delays. Special thanks also to Peter Coveney, whose multi-faceted expertise, solid advice, and unflagging graciousness infused every aspect of the publishing process. As authors, it has been our good fortune to be affiliated with such outstanding editors as Ken and Peter.

Photo curators in several repositories facilitated our search for images and we thank them all. An extra nod is due to the photographer Michelle Vignes. We thank our many colleagues in western history for providing the provocative scholarship that enriched our thinking and informed our work. As the authors, we accept full responsibility for the content herein and assert that any error rests solely with us.

At the outset, most books appear to be an easy undertaking. Only later will a devilish array of time-consuming tasks complicate the project – more research, more pondering, more revisions. With co-authored texts, these pesky obstacles grow exponentially. While we wrestled with organizational matters and shifting deadlines, our partners watched plans and months slip away. Many companions acquit themselves well during the unwieldy and vexing efforts to harness a manuscript, but none do so better than Jay Butler and Nina Clark. The authors acknowledge that, individually and jointly, we owe these two an enormous debt, and thank Jay and Nina for cheering us on to the finish line.

Introduction

As president, George W. Bush loved the West, especially as he found it in Texas. A former governor of the Lone Star State, he was fond of all 261,914 square miles of scrub pine, high plains, and chaparral that fell under his gubernatorial responsibility. No place amidst the tumble weeds, mesquite, meandering rivers, and grassy sod, however, was quite so special to Bush as his vacation hideaway, far from any urban centers. For Bush, the best Texas was a more or less 1,600-acre ranch near Crawford, a hamlet just about spitting distance – by frontier measure – from that quintessential western glory spot: the Texas Ranger Hall of Fame.

Tucked away on his rambling western estate, attired in a work shirt, blue jeans, and boots, the president could roll up his sleeves, grab a chain saw, and clear a few feet of tangled Texas brush. Dust flew, the saw motor revved, the president broke his concentration for a quick, quirky grin, and cameras clicked, as reporters, present by invitation, captured this moment of the world's most powerful leader enjoying the chance to get down close and dirty with the land. Thanks to this carefully staged "photo-op," images of the out-of-doors, physically fit president flashed about the world with a professionally orchestrated message – George W. Bush was not simply a president, he was an American, a Texan, a westerner; accordingly, he was not just a man, he was a rancher, a son of the frontier.

The Bush clan, arguably one of the most powerful of political families in all of American history, traces its heritage to prominent citizens of early New York, Rhode Island, and Connecticut. Even the modern branch of the family is rooted in the East. George W. Bush was born in New Haven, Connecticut. Though he passed some of his childhood in Texas, he attended high school at the prestigious Phillips Academy in Andover, Massachusetts. Following graduation, he headed back to the city of his birth for college. There, in New Haven, he took his degree at Yale University. When casting about for a graduate program, he chose another venerable educational institution of the East, Harvard University in Cambridge, Massachusetts.

George W. Bush, the politician, wanted Americans to forget this social and educational high-brow history and early grounding in the patrician arenas of America.[2] Bush sought to cast off his eastern political and industrial insider roots and redefine himself as the emblematic "outsider." Nothing could do this better, nothing create a sharper "other" image than a spacious but modest ranch with deer and armadillos, jack-rabbits, and cattle.

Give that Yankee-bred lad, scion of wealth, a pair of boots, a cowboy hat (white, of course), and a pick-up truck and the Bush Texas ranch became the stage on which this ersatz cowboy convinced the American people that he was not of the eastern establishment, not of the "inside the beltway" crowd, and not of the Brahmin elite, although he was of all three. On the ranch, surrounded by the symbols of nineteenth-century western life, he joked about "swagger" just being the way a Texan walks, or used "Old West" jargon like "bring 'em on" and "wanted dead or alive." Gone were the ivy-covered halls of Phillips, Yale, and Harvard; gone were the green university commons and the narrow, crooked streets of Andover, Cambridge, and New Haven. They were replaced with the tart lingo of white pioneers, the swirling dust of cowboys, the machismo of livestock herding, and the purple-shaded horizons of the West.

The interior of the Bush ranch house was not used much as the setting for press conferences and photo shoots. Public events were held outside in the sweltering summer heat or nipping winter chill, with presidential guests standing awkwardly behind out-of-place podiums. Reporters shouted their questions over the drone of the locusts or the rustle of leaves, as the president hurried his official visitors into the welcoming escape of the house.

There were no lush magazine spreads of the Bushes entertaining foreign dignitaries or relaxing before a huge stone fireplace. There were no grand shots of a fabulous kitchen, complete with hanging copper pots, subdued lighting, and colorful Mexican tiles. The plans for a "modest ranch" and the cost of the house, built while Bush was governor of Texas, were kept hush-hush. The house was to be a private, not public space. No need to sully the ranch with talk about all the public dollars it took to create luxurious comfort in the midst of a wickedly uncomfortable terrain. After all, Texas and, by extension the West, is not about money, it is, in its laconic, leathery-faced, steely-eyed way, about values and toughness, and guts.

Why was it so important for George W. Bush to style himself in boots and cowboy hats and to take on the hues and voice of a westerner? Why did he want a Texas hideaway that reeked of the nineteenth-century frontier? Was it because his actual personal authenticity, grounded in the academic and political institutions of the moneyed Northeast, lacked appeal? Was he astute enough to realize that over the past 40 years the West – especially the Southwest – had emerged as a major force in national elective politics? How convenient that a ranch, located in a remote and bleak rural spot, could create such powerful regional identity for a transplanted, very wealthy, eastern politician.

In Crawford, Texas, George W. Bush found an effective way to market himself to the national and international media. It did not matter from where he had sprung or where lay his elitist roots. Here, in the West, Bush could persuade Americans and himself that he had found his American soul and identity. The Crawford ranch allowed Bush to "talk the talk and walk the walk" of the West. It worked out well for him that the country so readily agreed – the West is where men, especially presidents – find identity. That the country accepted such obvious guile with ease said something about the broader importance of the West in American life and American history. After all, George W. Bush did not invent the various western images that he exploited so successfully. Frontier images and western themes have been important in our national culture for a long time. Other presidents – notably Theodore Roosevelt, Lyndon Baines Johnson, and Ronald Reagan – grasped the way western verve authenticated a political personality. Nonetheless, Roosevelt was a vacationing New Yorker, Johnson a provincial country boy, and Reagan a savvy Hollywood actor. Bush, however, appeared to believe in his faux western image to a degree that others did not and in that aspect, he represented perfectly the way the West, for good or ill, marked the modern American mind.

The United States created and retains its national identity in the West. Accordingly, the West exerts a powerful influence on the thinking of Americans, who tend to have intense feelings – positive or negative – about the legacy this one region has bestowed on the entire country. Despite its turbulent past and complicated present, the West remains a central element in the history of America.

Yet, asked to define the essence of that ingredient, most Americans stumble over a few hackneyed and ill-defined phrases: the West allowed men and women to be "open" and "free;" the West was where "people stood up for themselves," where Americans "conquered" and "tamed" the land; in the West, a man was judged by what he could do and not by who he was, he righted the wrongs done to him and got satisfaction by "taking the law into his own hands." Peculiar that Americans have clung to such phrases, especially since persons of every color in the West have been judged by rigid racial and economic standards, rather than by personal character or talent. Peculiar since most persons of all hues generally do not care to live close to free-wheeling neighbors who will maim and murder over real or imaginary personal grievances, or exploit the riches of nature for their own ends.

The reality has been and continues to be that the West produces and is the product of wide-sweeping cultural conflicts, deeply entrenched racism, violent confrontations, scrambled race relations, and oppressive behaviors. At the same time, the West is important in the broad story of America because it reveals much of the lived experience of many different cultures and peoples, even as it highlights the mercurial economic and political maturation of the nation. Clearly, western history has turned on factors and events that are exciting, as well as vulgar, enthralling, as well as unattractive, inspiring, as well as chilling. In other words, the West opens onto a maelstrom of American humanity and nature. To understand American history, it is necessary to understand the many forms and faces of the West, at their best and at their worst.

This is more easily said than accomplished. No matter how much scholarship has been produced about the West, Americans cling tenaciously to a set of outmoded clichés about the region. There continues to be national chatter that revolves around the stereotypical language of "cowboys and Indians," "pioneer wives and mothers," and "schoolmarms and dance hall girls."

For instance, many Americans stubbornly hold to ideas of the West as portrayed by the actor John Wayne, a performer who carved for himself a larger-than-life western image through movie stereotypes, becoming a frontier icon for Anglo society. Americans' knowledge of the West is quite often drawn from such Wayne films as "Stagecoach," "The Alamo," "True Grit," "The Cowboys," and "The Searchers." For over 35 years, John Wayne, along with other studio-fabricated cowboy actors, produced movies that encouraged Americans to feel enthused about the West, which they apparently did, without question or thought. Images of John Wayne's West, as Americans wanted them to be, appear to be deeply embedded in the nation's collective thinking. Carefully stored in the country's sense of self, these images are paraded across our modern stage as reassuring historical certainties in a world that wants to applaud its heritage without scrutiny. That realization led the authors to this book: a narrative of the American West that illuminates the multi-cultural, multi-structured, and multi-contradictory elements in regional life, as well as the power of race, gender, and corporate capital in shaping society and landscape.

Accordingly, there are three goals for this book. First, we hope to create a readable and concise history of the West, helpful for those unfamiliar with the region's past. One of the West's most intriguing characteristics is that the region itself has been a constantly shifting terrain, with no agreement in any era as to what land actually constitutes "the West." Perhaps that is one reason why when Americans speak about the West they do so with vague generalities, if not outright confusion.

We define this book as a chronicle of how and when various parts of North America came to be regarded as the American West. Although readers may think of western history as a story of the "frontier," the trajectory here is somewhat different. Much of this text is informed by the thinking of the historians Jeremy Adelman and Stephen Aron, who said the frontier was "a meeting place of peoples in which geographic and cultural borders were not clearly defined." For Adelman and Aron, with frontiers viewed as "borderless lands," one is able to appreciate that "inter-cultural relations produce mixing and accommodation as opposed to unambiguous triumph."[3] With those ideas as a guide, this narrative is closely linked to the ways the United States government extended its sovereign reach through territorial expansion and emphasizes that the West was and is tightly woven into the fabric of the whole nation. Throughout, we have thought to keep five western history themes before the reader: the convergence of cultures that led people to compete for power and agency; the role of the West, especially in its environment and natural resources, as a center for emerging capitalism; the place of the federal government as an overseer of expansion and regulator of resources; the importance of violence in many forms as a constant in western history; and the continued attachment to a mythic West, despite the incontrovertible evidence to the contrary. Accordingly, devotion to a linear chronology may on occasion give way to the importance of theme. We trust this will not be confusing, but rather a reminder that history did not occur in tidy segments, set off by the bookends of years. Overall, the text examines the West as a primary element in nation building, and recognizes its eventual consolidation into a clearly defined region, as one of the powerful forces in modern America.

In addition, the terminology and language choices in this work have been influenced by the changing uses among scholars of color. Accordingly, we stress the terms preferred by the authors Sucheng Chan, Douglas Henry Daniels, Mario T. García, and Terry P. Wilson in *Peoples of Color in the American West*. Readers will find the following: African Americans, blacks, Asian Americans, Mexicans, Mexican Americans, Latina/os, Tejana/os, Chicana/os, Natives, Native Americans, Indians, Anglos, whites, European Americans. Clearly, the language of race evolves over time and some of these terms may be discarded by future scholars.

We acknowledge that these definitions and usages may not satisfy everyone. This short text is not an all encompassing portrait of the West. Every explorer, every treaty, every historical celebrity will not be here. Rather, the reader will find patterns of western history, as reflected in selected narratives. For information about longer treatments of the West, readers should turn to the section "Suggested Readings," found in the back pages of this book. There for consideration are a number of important and sweeping studies of the West that explore the range of western history in detailed ways.

This account will guide readers, especially students, along western events and examples, with the particular intention that these will complement the US history curriculum. This short volume covers, in an abbreviated format, western history from the pre-colonial era to the present day. Within these pages, students will see how the forces and changes within western history did not occur in a vacuum, but added to and drew on social, economic, and political events in other parts of the country. It is hoped this will enhance appreciation for the role of a region in national development, but also suggest a clearer picture of the West as a linchpin within the general context of US history.

A second goal for this book is to produce a volume that draws on the current scholarly work in the field of western history. In the 1980s and 1990s, this discipline found new energy in the work of historians who pursued what was called the "new western history." Essentially, this group of historians challenged a long-held view of the West as the uncontested domain of Anglo men or one that promoted shrill patriotism at the expense of national integrity and human decency. These scholars questioned a history that mourned the death of George Armstrong Custer but cheered the murder of Sitting Bull, one that commemorated the Alamo dead, but ignored the Mexican sovereignty at stake in the war over Texas. In addition, the new wave of history took issue with the earlier invisibility of women in the story of the West. This scholarship brought to center stage a larger cast of characters, especially people of color, and considered the events of western history from the eyes of those participants.

In these works, Native Americans, Mexican Americans, African Americans, Asian Americans, and women of every culture stepped forward as more than complacent background figures, who affirmed the superiority of Anglo European male conquerors, championing through rifles and wars, power, and death. The "new western history" changed the discussion about the environment, questioning the long-term abuse of western eco-systems for short-term corporate gain. Thus, these scholars debated the very essence of the discipline, reconfiguring the definitions of place and language, people and experience. These historians wrote about agency in the lives of individuals and the actions of communities, giving voice to those long silent or slighted in the written record. Thus the "new western history" showed the complexities of power and the force of race, class, and gender in the American West.

Exciting as many of these studies have been, more than 20 years have passed since the dynamic and often controversial scholarship rippled through western history. The "new western history" is older and ready for reconsideration. Current scholars, many of them from communities of color, have further re-organized the discussion, particularly by seeking the voice of the "other." They increasingly questioned existing notions of what constitutes the West, who is a westerner, and what it means to live in the West.

Previously, scholars – mostly from the cohort of educated white middle-class males – tended to place themselves at the edge of the Atlantic Coast and gaze nostalgically toward the Mississippi River and beyond. They told their rousing stories from that vantage point, one that seemed adventurous and successful, but which led western history to its narrow male-centered celebration of physical antics and conquest as the markers of superiority and dominance.

Today, historians stand in the West and face east; they stand there as indigenous people looking at their homes and their neighbors. They ask "Where and for whom was the story of the West one that told of the bold and the victor? By whose definitions has the West been so described?" Their gaze takes in the lives of ethnic and minority people; they find the active rather than the passive; their language discards such vocabulary as "savages," "massacres," and "conquest." Rather, they look to racialization, economic power, land use, and gender models for their understanding of the West. This work employs a standard chronology, but it seeks, where applicable and available, to incorporate the concepts and the ideas of these scholars with their recent scholarship in western history.

A third goal for this book has been to utilize several forms of research. We did not try to invent a new story of the West, or to delve into unused manuscripts. Rather, we have sought ways to use primary sources buttressed by the current secondary literature. In the main, we have looked to the public record and newspapers. These have been and continue to be informative, accessible, and interesting ways to look into the past.

We specifically sought to employ electronic and online sources for documentation. As historians, we value the experience of searching the collections of public and private repositories. As educators, we agree that the electronic library is growing as a valuable instructional tool. Students, who may think of history research as a dusty matter relegated to dark archives, can understand that the technology in their lives – particularly the rapidly expanding reach of the internet – is, in fact, a useful way for historians to conduct exciting and important research.

Nonetheless, electronic sources can prove elusive – many a website address has disappeared from computer screens. We have used resources located at robust sites, ones that suggested permanence, or at least as much stability as the internet can provide. That websites evaporate is a reminder of how much electronic research replicates the uncertainty of working with paper documents. More than one historian has opened a county court transcript and discovered the packet sleeves empty, turned a diary page and found the desired passage excised, unfolded a yellowed newspaper and seen only crumbled remains. This is the nature of historical research – enthralling, enticing, deteriorating, and sometimes frustrating.

This book targets the uninitiated in western history, but also those who are willing to read about the West with a fresh eye and a new thought. However students choose to pursue history – whether with paper or computers – it is our intention that this book will help them to think more and in critical ways about the American West. Ultimately, we hope it will convey the rich histories of the many peoples who have left a mark on the magnificent and varied terrain of the West.

Consequently, this book argues that across time the West has been a shifting landscape of critical national importance in both individual and collective ways. In its various forms and locations, the region offered great opportunity and excitement for some, great loss and devastation for others. This book seeks to portray these multiple, overlapping, and contradictory realities.

Perhaps those accounts will prompt readers to reflect again on George W. Bush and why his ranch was so important to the president's national and personal stature. For that matter, why has the country, like George W. Bush, found its sense of self in the history of the West? Why does a hardscrabble mythic nineteenth-century West, with its water pumps, stagecoaches, and lonely ranches seem more powerful and more valid than a twenty-first century West with its hydro-electric power, suburban sprawl, and nuclear warheads?

We urge readers to ask themselves what they have believed about the West. How, if at all, has the West shaped their thinking as Americans? How has the West manufactured "patriotism," but inhibited responsible citizenship? Where is the West? Who is a westerner? How have languages influenced life in the West and how

are languages evolving as a future force? How does western history frame race, gender, and class relations across landscapes of
extremes? How will Americans negotiate the ongoing conflicts of
land usage and environmental management? What is the divide
between appropriate resource distribution and indiscriminate ecological destruction? How will western regional identity be explained
in the future and who will provide that explanation? How will the
West fare in the continuing economic and political rivalries between
and among the regions of the United States? How will these issues
touch Americans, as they confront the challenges of the West in a
new century? The following pages offer some possible ways to
explore these complicated questions as individuals and as a society.

NOTES

1 Frank Bruni, "The 2000 Campaign: The Weekend Retreat; Bush Finds
   Comfort Zone in a Remote Texas Ranch," *New York Times*, National
   Desk, July 22, 2000, <www.select.nytimes.com/search/restricted/article?
   res=F50F10F73F5EOC718EDDAE0894>.
2 Other scholars have noted the connections between George W. Bush, the
   eastern establishment, and the American West. For example, see Dan
   Moos, *Outside America: Race, Ethnicity, and the Role of the American
   West in National Belonging* (Hanover: Dartmouth College Press, 2005),
   1–2.
3 Jeremy Adelman and Stephen Aron, "From Borderlands to Borders:
   Empire, Nation-States and the Peoples in Between in North American
   History," *American Historical Review* 104:3 (June 1999): 814–41,
   quotes 815–16. Alaska and Hawai'i, areas of growing interest within
   western history, are treated lightly herein.

Chapter 1

First Wests, Many Wests

And We do hereby strictly forbid, on Pain of our Displeasure all our loving subjects from making any Purchases or Settlements whatever, or taking Possession of any of the Lands above reserved.[1]

In the fall of 1763, as chilly nights settled on the Appalachian mountains and autumn colors tinted the dense woodlands of the Atlantic East, an assortment of humans – Native American women and men, British colonists, indentured servants, Africans, runaway slaves, renegades, and outlaws, European immigrants, traders, and military personnel – milled through and about this land, claimed by Indians as birthright but demarcated by white society as the western reaches of the English colonies. Wary of each other generally and specifically from the recent carnage of the French and Indian War, these folk looked out on a region that faced an uncertain future with but one guarantee: a cacophony of political and economic goals articulated in many languages and by differing cultures portended of more conflict among foes than commonality in friendship, more death by violence than life with harmony.

The rolling, verdant landscape was homeland to many eastern tribes – Shawnees, Senecas, Mohawks, Delawares, Hurons, Oneidas, Iroquois, and to the south the Cherokees, Creeks, and Choctaws – who had defined their political spaces, cultural values, and economic relationships through social patterns, diplomacy, or warfare long before the European incursions. Indians of each tribe had

clear expectations for how the region should be managed and for
years the woodland people had manipulated their contact with
European emissaries and traders to their advantage. Indians had
conferred with Europeans in local communities and delegations
had traversed the Atlantic, hobnobbing with the elite and moneyed.
Natives negotiated alliances, playing off the international rivalries
of the moment amongst the French, English, Spanish, Swedish,
or Dutch to secure the best economic and political positions for
tribal areas. They had juggled peace and war, each a linchpin in
their efforts to retain traditional land, while drawing off the most
desirable commodities and diplomatic advantages to be extracted
from white society. At least one colonial governor recognized the
critical importance of these alliances with Natives, writing to England, "The concerns of this Country are so closely connected and
interwoven with Indian Affairs, and not only . . . [for] our trade,
but even the Safety of this Province . . . depend upon our continuing in Friendship with the Indians."[2] In 1763, however, various
Native men and women perceived that with the British defeat of
France, came a shift in European power that might jeopardize such
friendships and the interests of Indians.[3] The war had cost Natives
heavy losses, raising critical questions among Indians about their
future with whites. For example, economic bargains made with the
French were not necessarily going to be as attractive with the English, who, indeed, offered low quality trade items. Further, with
resentments over burned lands, lost crops, death, and disease, Indians wanted to know why the French and English did not fight and
die in their own countries, instead of bringing their disagreements
to North America. Natives knew the answer to that question was
that the battle occurred on turf the Europeans ultimately coveted
for themselves.[4]

As for "our loving subjects," also known as British colonists, they
were not blind to the full enormity of their king's declaration. Settlers, already well past the front line of the Appalachians, heard that
not only was their westward progress halted by a mandate from
Great Britain, but also they were to turn themselves, families, and
animals back to the eastern parts of the colonies. Colonists were
to stop traveling along the Allegheny River to the Monongahela,
making use of the easy water transport and portage, then slipping
through the Cumberland Gap, searching out the best of the fertile, well-watered soil. This was more than annoying to backwoods

Figure 1.1 This Jonathan Carver (1710–80) map from 1778, although not entirely accurate, reveals there was depth and breadth to the diplomatic and geographic knowledge available for competing societies in the eighteenth century. *Source:* Courtesy, Library of Congress, Geography and Map Division.

people, those nascent expectant capitalists who defined opportunity by the ease with which they could acquire western land.

For more than 20 years, eastern investors had egged these axe and gun pioneers to continue their advance into and over the mountains. Land speculators knew settlement of white communities could only add to their own wealth, advance the empire interests of England, and secure the back country for colonial governors. Never mind that wealthier colonists had amassed their huge grants through corruption and graft, influencing colonial legislatures to pass land laws that favored the well-to-do. Frustratingly for the speculators, the European military contests had slowed the push into the back country. Now, just on the cusp of success, the western free-for-all, a boon to the rich and the less-than-rich alike, by command of the crown, was to stop. *why?*

In the colonies, it was the small farmers and settlers who felt the weight of the king's order, prohibited, as individuals, to purchase land, negotiate trade, or simply steal land from Native people. The irascible Thomas Cresap, who repeatedly challenged Philadelphia over its Maryland border, had nosed about the forks of the Ohio River as early as 1750 and three years later Christopher Gist led families along the Potomac River as far as Redstone Creek in Pennsylvania. Now, according to King George III, these people were ever to remain British colonials, setting aside the lure of western settlement, land-grabbing, and maverick politics, always so common in an unregulated territory.

These were all galling bits of news for the Americans, fresh from defending the British king's turf during the grueling seven years of the French and Indian War. From 1756 to 1763, that conflict had revealed the ineptness of the British military when confronted with guerilla-like fighters on foreign soil. British generals in the field, especially the infamous Edward Braddock, relied on aristocratic swagger and European tactics to convince Indians in the Ohio Valley of England's power over them and their French friends. In a blizzard of responses, the Indians, backed by French Canadians, dashed the British hopes for a quick solution to the hostilities. The English army collapsed in the face of withering unexpected attacks that humiliated the British, cemented French and Indian alliances, and left American settlers along the western phalanx of all the colonies fleeing for the safety of any nearby fort.

After several discouraging years for the British colonies, the French, in a series of defeats, revealed they were, indeed, vulnerable. Indian warriors reassessed their positions and backed away from their French alliances, several groups joining the British forces. Then, in an improbable move that undid the French, James Wolfe and his soldiers scaled a shear cliff of rock outside Quebec, stunning the forces of Marquis de Montcalm on the Plains of Abraham, a broad field high above the old city of Quebec.

After this bloody fight in Canada, there were other diplomatic details to be concluded, among them significant issues concerning the balance of power in Europe, but in North America, the French loss rekindled the western fever of British colonists. With the defeat of King George's enemies in North America, formalized through the

[handwritten marginalia: "they just join who will help keep their land 'safe'"]

Treaty of Paris of 1763, those who had endured the bitter years and fought for the distant monarch anticipated appreciation and generosity, especially in the tangible form of western lands. In addition, as their pack animals lumbered along the rough terrain toward the East, the sweating, disgruntled colonists muttered about other pronouncements from the king, ones that regulated negotiations for Native land and granted religious freedom to the French Catholics, living to the north in Quebec. Loyal British subjects certainly had not bargained for political considerations for their recent foes – the "heathen" Natives and the hated French of Quebec and the Ohio Valley.

This unhappy royal decree, known in history as the Proclamation of 1763, aimed to affirm the king's authority over a conglomerate of populations, dramatically delivered to him following protracted conflicts with the French. No longer the overseer of 13 coastal-hugging colonies, King George now saw his royal flag flutter along the Mississippi River from the Gulf of Mexico north to the Great Lakes. Given the tumultuous circumstances, the great distance between the governor and the governed, the long festering ill-will of the French, and Indian resistance, it must have seemed a sound strategy to offer these latter two groups some balm, something to deflect their simmering anger over the outcome of the French and Indian War. Perhaps King George could reduce his problems in North America by good faith action, promising Native Americans a halt to the British settlers flooding into the western regions of the 13 colonies and quelling the restlessness of New France, chagrined that its mother country had utterly failed to protect the Canadian colonies.

Of course, the proclamation also was centered directly on the king's more immediate colonial interests. Drawing some boundaries for the colonists appeared to be the sensible way for the mother country to keep watch over her frequently unruly subjects, whose wandering ways complicated the collection of taxes for the crown. The suggested displeasure of King George, should his American subjects choose to ignore this proclamation, proved slight compared to the surliness that flared among the colonists, who grumbled the document conveyed more rights to "savages and Papists" than to British subjects.

Poor King George with his imaginary boundary line that arced across the Appalachians from Nova Scotia to Florida, and his nod to the French and their staunchest Native allies who managed to ignite the fires of unity among the notoriously fragmented and feuding colonists from Savannah to Boston, from Charleston to New York. Thus, King George, or more correctly Great Britain's Privy Council, succeeded in what no patriot voice had yet managed and pointed the cantankerous colonists toward common banners – their distaste for the French, scorn for the Indians, anger toward Great Britain, and lust for more land.

King George may only have hoped to exert some order over his disparate and widely scattered subjects, so recently come under his domain in North America. But the Proclamation of 1763 actually contained more than an affront to the restless interests and wounded pride of land-hungry colonists. With its references to assurances for Native peoples, governance in French Quebec, as well as boundaries of Spanish West Florida, King George wrapped into one short package a North American declaration that encompassed the long and complicated history preceding 1763. It was a history, in one way or another, grounded in notions of "homeland," "frontier," "invader," "invaded" and constantly seasoned with cultural conflicts, economic dislocation, and brutal warfare. It was a history composed of many elements, all of a much longer and diverse lineage than the events that led to the Proclamation of 1763.

Native peoples of North and South America, as well as the islands of the Caribbean, constructed political, economic, social structures far before recorded history or the disquieting arrival of Europeans. Indeed, the earliest footprints of Native people could have marked the western hemisphere anywhere from 25,000 to 40,000 years ago. Scholars point to a series of migrations across a once solid land bridge in the Bering Straits or epic voyages over the Pacific Ocean as reasonable explanations for the populating of North and South Americas.[5] Small bands, driven out of Asia by hunger, war, or curiosity followed a series of hunting corridors, dropping south along the Pacific Coast into Central and South America, moving west to east through Canada, before trekking down the Atlantic seaboard. Some groups perished, defeated by harsh climates, unexpected calamities, group illness, or war. Others pushed on, adapting to the new environments, adding technologies, and exploiting food supplies that they encountered over many generations.[6]

As a result, across thousands of years, human communities in the Americas entered into the process of civilization building and cre-

very self-sufficient

ated unique societies. Some, in harsh arid areas, hunkered down in little bands, struggling to maintain themselves. They scratched out an existence in areas with extreme temperature swings and few natural resources, especially water. Some took shelter in high warren-like caves, until impelled by unknown forces, their communities drifted away, abandoning their rock-like cities to give silent witness to their lives.[7] Others, in loosely affiliated family groups, adopted a marginal nomadic life, perpetually hunting and gathering in the daily search for food. The constant and uncertain struggle for nourishment kept the bands small and the standard of living scant. But where climate and water were salubrious, populations grew and more complex societies were born influenced by planting and harvesting seasons, combining a sedentary life with a nomadic one. For example, by 1000 BC, the southwestern Mogollons had added farming to their traditional hunting and gathering life. Their crops included maize and beans and their influence spread from the southern edge of present-day New Mexico, north through Arizona, having a direct impact on the ancestors of the Pima and Papago Indians. Among the striking remains of early desert people were a complicated irrigation system and an extensive network of underground storage rooms known as kivas, both of which bolstered their agricultural productivity.[8]

In the archeological remnants of the Moundbuilders, so-called for the thousands of huge burial hills they constructed, was found a culture that influenced a stretch of territory from the Southeast around the Gulf of Mexico through the lower Mississippi Valley and north towards Canada. The sophistication of the Moundbuilder society underlined the multi-faceted ways that Native communities throughout the western hemisphere had adapted and altered over time, showing that indigenous people did not live in static societies.

In this culture, domestic arrangements included small camps and fortified semi-permanent villages. The largest, Cahokia, situated in modern day Illinois, supported a population of at least 20,000.[9] Proximity to the several rivers of inland America aided travel, diplomacy, and communication. Plants and seeds were important parts of the diet, increasingly supplemented by game animals and fish. For hunting, groups often ranged across many miles, returning to a home base in time to harvest large gardens. Constantly adding to tools with chipped stone points, axes, and small

Figure 1.2　For approximately 100 years, these ruins at Mesa Verde in Colorado were home to the ancestral Puebloans, skilled artists and craftsmen, who built a network of buildings deep inside the sheltering cliffs. *Source:* Courtesy, Denver Public Library, Western History Collection, Jesse L. Nusbaum, N-293.

vessels, they increased the crops they raised and traded tools, utensils, food, maize, and game along an extensive river network. By approximately 1000 AD, some traditions of these Mississippians had spread into the river valleys of the Plains. People along the Missouri River planted corn, beans, and squash and began to adopt the practices of their woodland neighbors to the east and their pueblo-dwelling neighbors to the drier southwest.[10]

Perhaps most singular in culture were the tribes that settled along the Northwest Coast. Factors of geography kept those Natives separated from much of the intense cultural and material exchange that marked the emergence of their neighbors to the south. They, however, enjoyed other benefits. Where many first peoples were challenged by an uneven supply of water or dry soil, the Northwest communities enjoyed an abundance of natural resources and food supply. Along the coastal areas, life centered on the ocean, where the bounteous fish, especially salmon, became a dietary mainstay. Freed from the pressures of continuous hunting and gathering, the Northwest peoples had time to develop an elaborate culture, notable for its intricate carved art forms and social mores that employed a complicated gift-giving through ritual meals and ceremonies called potlatch.[11]

Nearing the end of the fifteenth century, shortly before the arrival of Christopher Columbus in 1492, perhaps as many as 65 or 70 million people inhabited the North American terrain. In many areas, urban complexes, organized by a division of authority grounded in gender and supported by an agricultural economy, flourished. Prosperity promoted societal continuity and encouraged the expansion of all aspects of life, as well as extensive interaction and exchange from tribe to tribe. Thus, political protocols, cross-tribal diplomacy, economic arrangements, cultural symbols, religious ritual, group decision-making, and social custom were highly stylized, diverse, and sophisticated among Native people from coast to coast.

The pre-European centuries created an exclusive environment, where Native peoples honed their relationships with the land and each other. The indigenous peoples of North America pursued political, social, and economic lives as fluid and dynamic as those of Europeans across the ocean. During these halcyon days for Native development and growth, perhaps as many as 550 different tribes ranged across North America. Among them, there were at least 300 languages, which had evolved from extremely complex linguistic structures.[12]

The continent was, of course, not a "frontier" to Natives. Rather, it was "home." Group identities took shape over hundreds of years, until tribes across the continent had a present form and a past heritage. By politics and trade, by custom and language, by deed and diplomacy arose the myriad Indian names that filled the many corners of North America – the Creeks and the Catawbas, the Navajos and the Apaches, the Pequots and the Pawnees, the Cheyennes and the Susquehannocks, Blackfeet, Sioux, Lumbees, Zuñis, Delawares, Seminoles, Winnebagos, Crows, Kiowas, Assiniboins, Choctaws, Tlingits, Shoshones, Osages, Gros Ventres, Miwoks, Papagos, and Mandans. Each of these communities, as well as hundreds of others, entered into a new experience once Europeans began regular and ongoing contact with North America.

The coming of Spanish explorers in the 1500s set the unfortunate tone for the future of Indian relations with Europeans. Setting out in many directions, conquistadors, intent on the search for wealth in

any form, plunged into North and South America, launching waves
of expeditions that continued for several decades. Among those who
joined the search for precious metals, exotic spices, human conquest, and new travel routes, Hernando Cortés led more than 500
men on a 1519 expedition into the Valley of Mexico. In less than
two years, the Aztecs had fallen to the Spanish and Cortés and his
associates moved to plant the Spanish flag in other locations. Within
20 years, Hernando de Soto led his party ashore on the west coast of
Florida, setting out for the Mississippi River; other Spanish marched
among the Zunis and the Pueblos, sailed on the Gulf of California,
saw the Grand Canyon, or scouted along the Rio Grande, Colorado, and Arkansas rivers.

In 1528 Pánfilo de Narváez made landfall off Tampa Bay –
among the men in his expedition was the Moroccan Esteban.
Esteban, destined to explore thousands of miles and live by his
wits, before dying among the Zunis in the 1530s, was the first
known African to set foot in North America. He would not be the
last. Spanish expeditions typically called for a supply of black servants or slaves, including a few women. The tramp of Spanish boots
echoed across the nooks and crannies of the American Southwest
and pounded north deep into the Midwest, sounding out the changing rhythms of the race relations that would mark the West in all its
corners.[13]

With those sounds came the vicious subjugation that showed the
all-encompassing sweep of these invaders. As the Spanish explorers
swept north out of Mexico, as far as the coast of northern California and into present-day Kansas, uncivilized treatment of civilized
communities, wanton destruction of property, suppression of local
religious practices, transformation of the countryside, and lust for
gold dominated their behavior. The distances between small Indian
clusters played to the advantage of the intruders, who were not
inclined to understand the matrilineal clan structure, but saw only
the vibrant agriculture as an indicator of other forms of wealth.
Initial cultural contacts that would have best been carried out by
skilled ambassadors, who acted on the precepts of a thoughtfully
planned program of respect and understanding, instead were left
to the helter-skelter random behaviors of militaristic and culturally uninformed soldiers of fortune. The land had become a world
of undulating borders with Natives standing on one side and Europeans on the other; while Indian people saw homelands under

"conquest & mentality" → cultural differences
aquisition

invasion and lines of authority disrupted, Europeans saw horizons for conquest and opportunities for riches.

The presence, mandated by the Spanish crown in the 1520s, of Roman Catholic friars did nothing to better early contacts or to smooth international relationships. Franciscan friars, spiritual sons of thirteenth-century Italy's famed Francis of Assisi, were the usual companions to the conquistadors. Impelled by a Franciscan ideal that sought purity in spirituality, these monks were a natural choice for missionary work in the hinterlands of an unknown continent. Dismissive of personal property, bound to the wandering life of beggars, the Franciscans were eager New World travelers. In their rough robes and sandals, they cared naught for home and hearth, but found zeal in proselytizing among "pagan" people.[14] Their world view translated into a series of missions in Mexico, Florida, and New Mexico – small centers where captured Native people were expected to learn European work and convert to Catholic prayers. Given less to persuasion and more to coercion, the friars willingly risked the bloody uprisings of the aggrieved Natives, for a violent death on mission shores meant instant sainthood in the Catholic lexicon, honor within European church circles, and a glorious conclusion to one's personal sacrifices for faith.

Predictably, contention arose between the secular and spiritual representatives of the Spanish crown. These disagreements had little to do with issues of morality and justice and much to do with politics and power. The two groups squabbled over who would control the Indians, who could corral them for work, and how their land would be parceled out to their new overseers. This tug-of-war for the minds and bodies of the Natives took on bitter tones, while the subjects of the argument continued under abject conditions to plow fields, herd animals, construct buildings, prepare food, dig wells, or complete any labor the Spanish demanded.

The Europeans seemed to look down on the Indians around them without seeing into the spirit of Native people.[15] Priests and soldiers accepted the outward appearances of Indian conversion at face value, overlooking the internal tribal political and economic motives that may have fueled the move to Christianity. Whether Indian people fully embraced the new religion, added some facets of it to their own beliefs, or melded two faith systems, creating fresh theological concepts were not issues the Spanish considered deeply. Completely distracted by their own interests and their own conversations, the soldiers and the priests neglected the chance to understand Indian people in roles other than those of the subjugated.

Overall, the arrival of the Spanish – whether priest or soldier – meant that Indian people were killed, enslaved, or forced to accept Christianity. The efforts of Natives to deflect the attacks or negotiate better terms of co-existence were summarily dismissed or betrayed. The narrative is one of nearly unmitigated death and destruction for Indians. It was an epic, however, that brought more than just crass adventurers and black robed priests to Native lives.

The Spanish, movers and shakers in Europe, came with their own sense of confidence and intellectual correctness. Beyond the Americas, they had trafficked in African and Middle Eastern cultures. Their royalty, military, and church authorities had dealt with Catholics, Protestants, Jews, and Muslims. From years of European upheaval, they knew about attack and defense, aggression, and compliance. Clash and conflict, bred in the Moorish invasions and refined in the Inquisition's horrors, defined their experience. They saw themselves as "tough," whether in national or international, civic or religious affairs. Their fast-moving technology and burgeoning capitalism added to their assured manner and pushed them to a "winner takes all" mentality. Who were they, in their flashy armor and prancing horses, to be daunted by these Indians, who seemed not to understand place and power in a rapidly changing world?[16]

As if those factors were not overwhelming enough, Europeans brought their own animal husbandry and horticulture, dropping both upon a startled American eco-system. Alien animals and plants invaded with the same ferocity as the humans, pressing down on the land in totally new ways.[17] Who gave thought to the terrain, hosting foreign sheep and oxen, their feed and their excrement? Why would one care that a creeping vine overtook indigenous flora or notice the scale that formed on the leaves of a nearby bush? These matters of science were barely formulated and hardly the concern of brash explorers.[18] For certain though, as the Spanish explorers raised the lusty banner of "Gold, God, and Glory," they introduced ecological and cultural wars fated to rearrange everything they touched.

They also complicated those wars through their centerpiece and most glamorous gift to the New World – the horse. Native armies could fight with fury, but where in the world did the mounted warrior not best the foot soldier?

The horse, however, did not long remain the cherished advantage of the invaders. Native people immediately perceived the advantage and importance of horse skills, skills that the Spanish preferred to deny Indians. Such denial, of course, was futile. Indians acquired the horse through barter, gift, accident, and theft. As a result, a powerful horse culture spread north from tribe to tribe, changing forever the way of Indian life in North America. By 1720, the Blackfeet of the northern Plains were among the last of the Indians to encounter the horse. Like other tribes to the south, they mastered horsemanship quickly, enhanced their fighting prowess, and integrated the horse into an economy, politic, and culture centered on the buffalo.[19]

So, the Spanish contributed a tangle of cultural by-products to their hosts. Perhaps none was so important as the collection of European germs that unleashed a torrent of devastating disease among Native populations. Violent warfare everywhere took its toll, Spanish practices and commodities smothered local societies, but nothing struck with a deadly force to equal the merciless attacks of measles, smallpox, or venereal disease. Because the total population figure for pre-contact North America remains a matter of academic debate, there has been uncertainty about the numbers who died from European-borne germs. Yet, all agree that the physical well-being and general health of Native peoples of all ages were savagely undercut by various epidemics that killed scores and left survivors debilitated.[20]

In addition, the barriers of European versus North American languages worked an extra hardship for indigenous people. There was no common lilt between the tongue of the Indian and that of the European. Indeed, Indians, who had communicated successfully across linguistic groupings for years, must have felt there was a dizzying array of European languages, as conversely did the Europeans. Disparate groups grappled for words, learning "the this and the that" needed to communicate. Native women, as servants, captives, consorts, and wives of Europeans, emerged as cross-cultural interpreters, instructing the invaders in "survival" vocabulary and explaining the halting speech of the invaders to tribal members. The problems, however, far surpassed matters of translation, but enveloped the very core definitions and perceptions of words. Descriptions, agreements, negotiations – each meant quintessentially different concepts to the opposing sides.

Despite their murderous prowess, within less than 45 years, the Spanish on the Southwest borders were exhausted. They had extended themselves way too far into rough and arid land, about which they knew little and cared less. Their garrisons, or *presidios*, were hardly fitting of such a label, but the regulation of them was controlled by a cumbersome chain of command that wound its way out of the small settlements and forts, south to Mexico City, and over the Atlantic to Spain. When this system was followed, those in the Americas waited weeks for orders concerning the most trivial of local operations.

These directives, when received, reflected the social and political thought of the homeland and sought to replicate European Spanish society, rather than promote adaptation. The soldiers at these outposts, often the least desirable of the Spanish military, showed small aptitude for shifting their routines to fit local circumstances. In European pantaloons, helmets, and breastplates, the king's army sweltered in the dry heat, as is members stumbled about trying to recreate Spain in the American Southwest. The few Spanish civilian workers who had joined them cranked out a miserable existence. Both groups were displeased that great wealth and tractable Indians continued to elude them.

In every way, it was an off-balance world, one that brought only a few Spanish women to New Spain. Living in poorly run, often slovenly bachelor communities, the soldiers fell with ease into the worst behaviors of invading armies. Their associations with Native women took on all the expected negatives. Torment and rape were common. Casual sexual encounters also occurred, but increasingly Spanish men lived in long-term domestic arrangements with Indian women. The importance of relationships with women in Spain diminished. The inevitable requests of some to marry their Indian partners raised new issues of race relations for the government and the Catholic church. Matters of racial control, issues concerning laws of inheritance, and questions of how the bestowing of a religious sacrament concerned humanity became central in the lives of *mestizos*, those born of European–Native unions.

With this isolated and warped life, it still might have been possible for the Spanish to cultivate long-held rivalries between tribes to their own advantage. Rather than stimulating withering hatreds through their maltreatment of women and girls, the Spanish might have built coalitions with Native families. Spanish horses and weapons must have made at least some tribes think about forging an alliance with the Europeans against local enemies. But the conduct of the Spanish and their denial of access to their animals or tech-

lots of reasons why "neathens" were very self-sufficient

nology had lost them any allies they might have recruited among
Native people. Even the Apaches, known for an uneven relationship
with the sedentary Pueblos, shied away from aligning themselves
with the marauders from Europe.

In this evolving situation, Indians saw they must create new political and economic strategies for negotiating with the Spanish, but
the crush of so many aggravating factors made that difficult. No
one plan could have solved the many areas of contention, as dealing
with the Spanish had a certain mercurial quality. Personnel came
and went, as did the "rules and regulations" imposed by the Spanish
government. The few voices of Spanish reformers, such as Bishop
Bartolemé de las Casas, who objected to the enslavement of Indians, were not loud enough to bring about sustained change from
European administrators. Native policy, therefore, never took on
a single design, but assumed various forms. Whether using barter
and trade, religious acquiescence, or military cooperation, Indians
chose according to the exigencies and the leadership of the moment.
However, when the horrors of Spanish occupation reached unbear-
able levels, Indians showed the organizational abilities that allowed
them to coordinate armed resistance.

Native people used local wars in their attempts to throw off the
burdensome yoke of Spanish oppression. Actions to defend Indian
territory and repel Spanish oversight were sudden and intense, with
the Europeans caught by surprise. The results infused the Indians with a surge of confidence as they vanquished the soldiers and
missionaries around them. These were, however, small spurts of
success.

It was in the Pueblo Revolt of 1680 that Native people made a
long-term dent in the Spanish colonial world. All aspects of Pueblo
life had buckled under a variety of stresses that included several
seasons of little rain and poor crop production. Tribal relations
between the sedentary, agricultural Pueblos and the nomadic, pred-
atory Apaches, traditionally rather erratic, took a dramatic down
turn. The equally hard-pressed Apaches, known for their migratory lifestyle and fluctuating attitudes, abandoned any semblance
of peaceful trade and returned to their earlier system of raiding
Pueblo supplies and kidnapping Pueblo women. In this difficult
time of hunger, despair, and collapsing Indian diplomacy, the Spanish, unwisely, chose to intrude themselves and enforced regulations
against lingering indigenous religious practices. These circumstances

made the time right for an influential local leader who appeared in the person of Popé, a Pueblo holy man.

Under his direction, a carefully planned revolt led to a rout against the Spanish, who retreated to Santa Fe and then fled to El Paso. Among those who died were more than half of the missionaries, some who had lived among the Indians for several years. The Spanish who survived had to face the reality that much of the fervor of the violence centered on destruction of hated symbols of Christianity.

The Pueblo Revolt of 1680 restructured the character of New Spain. Although Spanish administrators might have expected their armies to subdue and punish the offenders, the opposite occurred. Other pueblos, inspired by the success of their neighbors, also ignited in anger. Mexico City proved too far away and too poorly staffed to mount an effective response. The Spanish sword of punishment plunged into any apprehended Indians only led in turn to more death for the Europeans.

It was 10 years before the Spanish found a diplomat and soldier with sufficient fortitude to retake the pueblos. Diego de Vargas, convinced of his own skills, made some inroads in securing Pueblo loyalties. However, in 1696 another significant Pueblo uprising reminded the Spanish that their relationships with the Indians had changed for all time. As the Spanish crept back cautiously into Pueblo areas, they adjusted some of their earlier restrictions, especially in the practice of religion.[21]

At the start of the 1700s, the Spanish could look over a nearly 200-year effort to control a land that Native people had lived in and nurtured for generations beyond counting. In the main, the results for the Europeans were highly questionable. The Spanish government increasingly objected to the treasury drain by New Spain. The Franciscans, while powerful at the missions and usually victorious in their clashes with the military and secular leaders of Spain, counted a high number of their priestly brothers martyred and their authoritarian control over local religious practices reduced. New Spain administrators adopted a tough stance, rattling sabers at other challenging nations and pronouncing the Indians "quelled," but with all the many problems throughout their empire, the reality was somewhat different. The mixed cultural and political outcome tangled into a political and social scenario never seen in earlier national interactions.

The Indians and the growing *mestizo* community adopted Catholicism, mixing it with various aspects of their traditional religion. Still, for nearly another 100 years, Native people in sudden and unexpected moments rose up as they had done in 1680 and 1696. The message appeared to be clear – the Spanish might have come to stay, but they would never truly "control" the indigenous peoples of the Americas. The price they paid for their haste and arrogance would be measured by the Indians. Ultimately, forces from within and without would push against the weakened foundations of New Spain and bring it to collapse.

Yet, even when that happened two results of the Spanish intrusions remained. First, the American Southwest took on a nearly permanent visage of conflict. The Spanish had destabilized an entire region, its people, as well as themselves and many of the disruptions that were produced by that process would not easily evaporate. Second, through Native and Spanish unions emerged new communities of people. Given the great swath of land over which the Spanish traveled and the long time of their residence, cultural mergers did not show homogeneous traits. Although there was a common joining of Native and Spanish people, there were not necessarily identical social and economic factors for all concerned. Tejana/o life in Texas, Hispana/o in New Mexico, and California/o in California, each with its own character, gave witness to the multiple cultural identities that would always be part of the Southwest and, in fact, would escalate with the passing of each year.

The confrontation of one culture by another, the collapse of local infrastructures, the scramble for exploitation of people and resources, the friction of borders rubbing against each other, the resistance of and accommodation by of indigenous populations, the creation of new policies within Native groups, the rearranging of gender spaces, and the melding and merging of language and lives, even in the face of nearly unmitigated hostility and violence, became the hallmarks of all the places in the American West that became the lands of contested borders.

To the north of the Spanish ventures, lay another world, quite different from the dry and desert Southwest. Here was rugged land that butted against the equally rugged Atlantic Ocean. Beyond the salty coast, numerous crashing rivers crisscrossed and plunged along cataracts through the interior. Four clear seasons marked the year, shown by the changing palette of thousands of trees, the cooling of early evening, and the crisp air that covered all. Each turn of the weather brought special resources to the Natives, but it was winter, with its bitterly low temperatures and heavy snows, that would be most challenging and rewarding for the Europeans with eyes set on northern booty.

Despite the image of the North Atlantic as a forbidding barrier to early explorers, French fishing ships had trolled the coastal waters of North America for cod, at least since the early 1500s. They came to know the region well and more than one group had ventured onto the rocky shores. Over time, these Frenchmen accumulated considerable knowledge about the region, and back in their home ports, they passed their information from one group of sailors to another.

Focused on pressures in Europe, the French government took a while to enter the romp of exploration, but the nation's interests and greed were no less than her Spanish counterparts. Although France had dallied in getting to the New World, she benefited from the knowledge of the area and the contacts with Natives that the fishing fleets had accrued over the years. Perhaps, the French reasoned, they would be the lucky ones to find the elusive water route to Asia or grab great mounds of gold and silver in the North, or, better yet, best their international rivals in the clamor for New World empires,

In 1535, after a number of failed French attempts to find the main passageway, Jacques Cartier finally sailed into the great St Lawrence River. Wide and broad, the lavishly beautiful river, complete with many islands, supported a range of flora and fauna. Fish, especially cod, were plentiful, but so were the hosts of birds and animals that lived along the banks. Grasses and flowers new to the Europeans flourished along with the thick stands of quality timber of many kinds. This vibrant waterway, that stretched nearly 2,000 miles from the Atlantic Ocean to the Great Lakes, functioned as a natural highway commanded by Natives and central to French exploration.

Nonetheless, it was not until 1608, when Samuel de Champlain stepped onto the land of present-day Quebec City, that the French permanently settled in this northern region. Champlain emerged as an influential and constant figure in the growth of New France, making him something of an anomaly in the annals of seventeenth-century history. Many Europeans, especially government administrators, found themselves unsuited for the complicated rigors of the New World and returned to their European homes with haste. Champlain, however, immersed himself in his surroundings. Champlain wanted to know about everything and everybody in this dramatic land and if Native people showed themselves reluctant to come into French settlements, then Champlain would send the French to the Natives. He dispatched men from his company to move among the Indians, gather geographic information, and learn local languages. At the same time, he did not neglect his contacts in France, returning more than once to publicize his efforts or shore up his backers. Thus, he kept a bridge, as it were, between mother country and colony.

With this initial appreciation for and curiosity about the area, it is not surprising that over the next 100 years, the French marked off large portions of Indian land, as various explorers trekked across the Canadian and American West. Taking advantage of the intricate maze of rivers and lakes that facilitated travel, French explorers set out in several different directions. Among Champlain's initiatives, he sent his protégé Jean Nicolet further west, in an expedition that scouted the area of the Green Bay of Lake Michigan. The Jesuit priest, Jacques Marquette, a student of Indian languages, driven by scientific interests along with missionary zeal, made several journeys before his death in 1675, at the age of 38. Others made their way to the upper reaches of the Mississippi Valley. By 1682, the French had so infiltrated western lands that the explorer and entrepreneur René-Robert Cavelier LaSalle, having reached the mouth of the Mississippi River, grandly claimed the entire valley for France, christening it "Louisiana," in honor of King Louis XIV.

During these contacts in the Canadian area, the Indians and the French pursued relationships distinctly different from those between the Spanish and Native people to the south. These Indians knew about Europeans and aggressively pursued business relationships with the French, convincing them to abandon their quest for gold and settle on an economic goal that would be beneficial to both groups. That goal concerned the profits each could amass from beaver pelts, ultimately bound for European consumers. Given their business nature, these commercial alliances and mutual entrepreneurial interests guaranteed an approach that diverged from the Spanish interaction with Native societies. In New France, Indians did not shrink from cultivating profitable opportunities for themselves and Europeans accepted the notion that they entered into an association of mutual need. As a result, the initial cross-cultural dynamics, so typically characterized by random bloodletting, assumed other characteristics.[22]

In the main, it was the powerful Hurons who first welcomed the Jacques Cartier expedition, enticing the explorers with generous gifts of pelts and enthusiastic promises of easy access to a great supply of beaver. In exchange, the Indians wanted hatchets, knives, pots, and cloth that would inflate their standard of living, and enhance their work as diplomats, hunters, domestic workers, and warriors. The French, who had hoped for precious metals, settled on other profits that came from the Indians – specialists in the chase, the kill, and the processing of animals. Thus, the two groups embraced each other, although at times in a prickly manner.

Unlike the Spanish, the French did not engage in wholesale slaughter of Indian villages, nor lock entire Native communities into an enclosed mission. Catholic priests, especially the Recollects and the Jesuits, generally called "Blackrobes," constructed an early presence in Canada. Some Natives complained bitterly about punishments and proselytizing by the missionaries, but others saw reasons to welcome the priests.

The French, standing on the banks of the St Lawrence and gazing around at as many as a thousand Indians, appreciated that they were in a vulnerable position, subject to disastrous attack should their economic partnerships with the Natives collapse, an anti-Christian faction strike, or debilitating illness, blamed on the Europeans, sweep through a tribe. For their part, Indians tempered their welcome with skepticism – the dangers of dealing with Europeans were widely known. Accordingly, the French, both the religious and secular newcomers, from the first days of Quebec, looked for ways to deflect Indian hostility, move into local settlements, establish commercial ties, learn Native skills, replace Native religious practices with Christianity, and develop fluency in Indian languages. The Indians sought to increase tribal wealth, demonstrate their power against neighboring foes, elevate their diplomatic status, and limit French control of the Native world.

The French, whose settlements generally had a majority of men, avoided the widespread coerced sex associated with military invasion. The Indians did not hesitate to punish sexual transgressors and, in part, graphic accounts of deadly reprisals against Europeans who misused women acted as a restraint. In keeping with the French effort to meet Indians on their ground, trappers and traders tended to seek marriage with Indian women, honoring tribal customs for matrimony and settling into traditional domestic arrangements within the community. These practices did not mean that sexual abuse and rape did not occur, but the willingness to enter into tribally recognized marriage softened the sexually violent image that Europeans had so deservedly earned.

In addition, finding and trapping the beaver was the provenance of Indian men, giving them an added cachet with the French. Native men excelled at canoeing through the tumbling rivers, finding the lairs of the elusive animals, and snaring the catch. French trappers relied completely on their Indian associates for wilderness survival and successful hunting. The days in the field placed the Indian in the role of knowledgeable instructor and the French trapper in that of unschooled newcomer.

Further, it was Indian women, in this matrilineal Huron society, who held much of the economic power and the French trappers and traders would have been utterly at a loss without those partnerships that crossed gender. Women, the farmers of Huron society, owned and worked the great corn fields. Their skinning and tanning tools made them property holders, whose abilities made it possible to ship pelts to distant markets. Within an Indian band, the wedding of a woman and a Frenchman promised economic dividends for the community, elevating marriage negotiations to the level of tribal well-being.

Matrimony introduced the trappers to local kinship arrangements, making them dependent on their wives in a variety of ways. Women acted as translators, protected their new husbands within Indian society, instructed them in the customs of daily life, shared their wealth as agriculturists, taught them the rituals and taboos of the tribe, guided them in developing their hunting skills, and provided them with the security of a home and family in an alien culture. The trappers, in fact, became students again, this time in the new home, embracing its landscape, learning about its values, engaging its cultural standards, and benefiting from its rich resources. Thus, the French had practical and personal reasons to desire close, even familial, relationships with both men and women of Native communities, reaching across gender divisions in an unusual way for early cultural interaction.[23]

These new lifestyles came with obvious positive results for the French, but they were not without their liabilities. It was not possible for the French to align themselves successfully with each and every Indian tribe. Long before the arrival of the French, a complex Indian–Indian diplomacy played out between and among the tribes. The Hurons and Algonquins could see in the French reinforcements that might help them in their hostilities with the powerful Iroquois. The Iroquois, another name for the confederacy of the Five Nations, ranged across a huge territory, reducing the holdings of other tribes and demanding tribute on a regular basis. The presence of Europeans further intensified friction between the Hurons and the League of the Iroquois, as the former aligned with the French and the latter with the Dutch in New York. Iroquois men began to trap huge numbers of beaver for their Dutch associates and to do so hunted deep into the territory of the Hurons, exacerbating their already contentious relationship. Iroquois women, powerful partners in tribal management, continued, as keepers of the wealth, to calculate the economic benefits from Iroquois domination of the fur trade.

In 1687, the French, allied with the Hurons, destroyed a number of towns of the Senecas, part of the Iroquois League. These attacks not only set the torch to the Seneca long houses, but also the cultivated land of the women. These episodes of violence and death cast a shadow across the future power of Seneca women, who, like their Huron neighbors, exercised authority over agricultural production and distribution of food.[24] While the fires were the outward manifestation of war, they were also a symbol of the changing gender dynamics that struck within all tribes confronting European invasion.

The French–Huron victory was brief and, in 1648–9, in a blistering war, the Hurons endured a major defeat at the hands of the Iroquois. Dispirited and split into two groups, the Hurons looked to the growing number of French immigrants as a way to shore up their fighting power against the Five Nations. The French, who suffered their own losses in the recent conflict, did not disappoint them, but in the process further solidified the enmity of the Iroquois League – not a propitious occurrence for the Europeans. The warring Iroquois were quick to apply the same standards to a captured Frenchman as they did to a captured Huron – a near murderous run down a gauntlet, followed by excruciating torture and slow death – trials faced, for instance, by the Jesuit priest Isaac Jocques in 1646.

Still, there were aspects of comradeship between the French and

the Indians. Perhaps the living and working together, under somewhat uneasy alliances, created a fresh experience for all concerned.
The building of families across racial lines suggested the possibilities
of mixing people of varying backgrounds in a positive way. Those
possibilities faltered in some ways; for example, the *métis* children
born of French fathers and Indian mothers did not always find a
warm reception within the culture of either parent. Still, Indian and
French lives began to intertwine and settle on the land.[25]

Quebec and Montreal took on a zesty air of their own. If for no
other reason, the bitter Canadian winters cut off regular intercourse
with others. Once the French ships deposited their cargo and fresh
immigrants, they made sure they had set their sails for home by
early autumn. While the disappearing sails might have caused those
French standing on a Quebec wharf to tremble at the long winter
ahead, there were advantages. The isolation from France gave the
little colony the freedom to develop its own lively personality.
Women, known as *les filles du roi*, sent by royal assistance to offset
the gender imbalance and become the wives of colonists, were
chosen from the more or less lower ranks in French society. Their
families were not those of the elite with close contacts in the government. So, these women had little interest in shaping New France
into a replica of a mother country that prided itself on gracious
living. All in all, the costly 10-year program subsidized by the royal
treasury, failed in its "domestic values" goal to bond the New
France community closer to its French origins.

Increasingly, life took on the flow of urban–rural patterns. The
young men who, dressed in the thick and distinctive garb of the
trapper, moved between the cities and the out-lands adopted a somewhat earthy and boisterous manner, happy to leave graffiti on the
city walls or bring their *métis* children to the center of town.[26] Trappers, traders, and Indians lived in the back country, but traveled
into town for business transactions, political news, or access to
government services. Those who lived in camps and Indian settlements departed upon the completion of their affairs, to be replaced
by another group. Inevitably, the city residents came to look upon
these peripatetic visitors as more nuisance than neighbor, more customer than citizen, more uncouth than cultured.

No lawyers were permitted in New France, so individuals learned
to advocate for themselves before the courts. Further, there was
no printing press in Quebec and thus a hearty oral tradition for

spreading and commenting on the news developed. Still, the colony was not devoid of social services. In 1639, three Ursuline nuns and three Hospitallers had arrived on the French vessel, the *Admiral*, to launch educational and medical services to the French and the Indians of and around Quebec. Their contacts with Native peoples were quickly compromised by the onset of a deadly smallpox epidemic in the fall. Yet, despite these setbacks and their own extreme poverty, the two groups, one located in the Upper City close to the fort, the other in the Lower Town near the river, successfully launched small facilities to serve French families.[27]

In 1674, the French government, aware that New France had assumed a rather piebald and raucous identity, moved to control its interests in North America, thus replicating the error of most foreign rulers who had slim understanding of New World peoples – either Native or newcomer. The royal plan, based on an earlier 1627 initiative that handed New France to administrators called the Company of 100 Associates, involved the granting of land to seigneurs or lords. These men, after securing a large parcel of land from the government, had the responsibility to develop the acreage. This they did by recruiting settlers from France, through promises of roads, mills, security, and community. In return, the newly arrived immigrants paid an annual tax to the seigneur. Those who became the landed farmers secured their laborers through contracts to *engagés*, men and women who traveled from France to serve as indentured servants under three-year contracts. It was intended to be an orderly system, one that would suppress some of the wilder aspects of New France, distribute land in an organized manner, provide a labor force, populate the colony, and keep the authority of the mother country as a presence in the minds and the hearts of the colonials.

Regardless of what was happening in New France and with Indian–French relationships, those who remained in France were increasingly distanced from the colonists. The interests of Parisians and colonists grew more and more dissimilar. The population of the colony was increasing – by the early 1700s there were perhaps over 20,000 residents – but more and more of these were Canadian-born and Canadian-raised. They had no personal knowledge of France, felt no emotional bond for the king, spoke a French more and more disdained by their co-nationals in Paris. New France, like colonial outpost communities in all locations, felt the pinch of becoming a debtor society. Hard cash proved elusive, as profits and wealth flowed across the Atlantic to France. The governing structure in New France, established by the mother country, clanked along in a more unruly manner than officials had intended.

The ties between Europe and New France buckled. They would bend to breaking limits by the strains of war and difficult economic days. The Canadian backwoods, with its own flowering culture and style, had diluted the loyalty of the French Canadians. The Indians had exploited the commercial interests of the French by binding them more closely to the Canadian landscape than to the shores of the mother country. France itself had not paid close attention, nor shown itself flexible enough with its colonial experiment in empire building. In the next century, those factors would bring changing patterns to New France.

While Spain and France struggled to find themselves a permanent place of power in the New World, England lurked in the background, watching and learning from the folly of her European rivals. Internal conflicts had kept the English from joining in the efforts to plant national interests in the New World. While England sent explorers to New World waters, not until 1607 did the Powhatan Indians of Virginia see the English patch together a permanent settlement at Jamestown.

Jamestown's story is well known for the shakiness of its beginnings, despite advance information that should have smoothed the way for the English. Instead, they floundered under the same mishaps as the Spanish and the French – a collection of soldiers and adventurers, some of whom were distracted by the lust for gold and failed to participate fully in the basic precautions that might keep one alive in a strange wilderness. Some among the men ignored the detailed instructions they had received from the crown, directives that among other things told them to "first build your storehouse . . . before any house be set up for any private person."[28] Alas, the work of common laborers, farmers, and carpenters held slight allure for those in the group who saw themselves on a dizzying quest for riches. Those first English soldiers of fortune paid the price for their haplessness and would have died to a man without the intervention of the local Indians.

But within 10 years the English in Virginia had reversed their original mistakes, confronting America in ways that increased their chances for success in the European contest for control of the New

World. Perhaps no year more than 1619 showed that the English would take the necessary crucial steps to solidify their position in Virginia and beyond.

First, the colony carved out a significant political advantage by establishing the House of Burgesses as a local governing body. The settlers learned it was impossible to wait for governance requests to pass through long channels of administrators in England. Their perilous situation in a foreign environment made them anxious to have speedy answers for immediate problems. Thus, they wanted to decide for themselves where local roads could be built or community latrines constructed. While the English Privy Council retained administrative power over matters of shipping and taxation, local officials assumed charge of local problems.

Second, the English stumbled onto a way to stabilize their labor force when a dozen or so Africans in chains came ashore at Virginia. It was the fate of those first enslaved persons, possibly literate Christians from West Africa, to become part of the Jamestown population. Their appearance, however, foreshadowed the ghastly slave trade that kept the English colonies supplied with African laborers through coercion and murder. Anglo settlers who had despaired of a strong agricultural future without a large labor force saw in Africans the workers they wanted for their labor intensive crops. Tobacco, cotton, rice, and indigo – crops destined to become the staples of southern farming – would succeed for a time, but at a human cost that could never be tallied. African people, torn from their homes, shipped thousands of miles, and whipped into submission propelled agriculture forward, solidified the economic base of the southern agriculturalists, and added further to the growing racial juggernaut that crippled the American West.

Third, in 1619 yet another ship docked in Jamestown. It carried, among other things, English women, recruited for the purpose of marrying the bachelor settlers. These women bore in their hearts and minds a cultural devotion that determined the future strength of a prevailing English identity. English women marrying English men guaranteed the rise of English social institutions – schools and churches for the education and edification of English children. Further, marriage within Anglo culture limited the practice of English men creating family units with indigenous women, as had been done by both the Spanish and the French. Thus, the English, although not entirely, avoided the friction and rivalry of having two separate kinds of families – one English–English and the other English–Native.

The arrival in 1620 of the *Mayflower* with the Puritans in Massachusetts Bay Colony further entrenched the all-English family. Although theologically at odds with the Anglican settlers in Virginia, the Puritans enthusiastically codified English values. Largely traveling in family units, they intensified the conviction that English weddings should involve partners of a common cultural heritage.[29] The Puritans, after all, believed themselves to be the chosen children of God. As such, they hardly cared to associate with, much less marry, any outside their select group – whether such a person should be Indian, French, or an Anglican. Those travelers aboard the *Mayflower* had not been called "Separatists" for naught.[30]

The combination of attitudes in the northern and southern English colonies led to a general domestic separation of Anglo settlers from Native communities. The John Rolfe and Pocahontas marriage may have been charming and romantic as its narrative was shaped and reshaped across the centuries, but Anglican clergyman debated whether the bride had a soul – if not, she could hardly be wed in a Christian church. To the misfortune of the Anglo community, the first settlements created an insulated environment in which English mores, laws, and rituals were little encouraged to mix with other cultures.

Despite their differences, English colonists in the North and the South prevailed, creating specialized worlds that would have an impact across the continent.[31] The history of both regions was marked by expansion from east to west. In the South, that expansion tended to be manipulated by wealthy speculators and the practice of settling land before government survey. In the North, the first extension into the back country followed a rigidly structured pattern that required a government contract of permission, survey before settlement, and the transport of entire communities to a new location.[32] After 1720, this system faltered and the northern settlement patterns replicated much of the land scramble of the South.

Those developments increasingly took on the tone of animosity as tensions grew between those living in back country areas and those representatives of the British crown governing the colonies in the East. Thus, the first significant regional hostilities in the British colonies did not organize across North–South interests but formed out of ill-will between tidewater and piedmont communities. The latter, generally of a common social class, felt that the former, of an aristocracy, failed to respond to their needs, especially improvements in transportation and protection from Natives. In the meantime, the tidewater officials fretted that they were losing control over back country residents – a worry that was not ill-placed.

By the time of the Proclamation of 1763, the back country was in turmoil. The northern areas had been marked by repeated Indian–colonist clashes. In 1637, the Puritans had effectively annihilated the Pequot Indians, a victory that invigorated the colonists' sense of Christian entitlement and imperialism, as well as their desire for more land. By 1675, these attitudes had encouraged the English to encroach further into Indian territory. In a bloody two-year war, King Philip led the Wampanoags and Narragansetts, former enemies now allied against their common foe, in a ferocious assault on the English. The English retaliated viciously, but also changed their attack strategies, using the guerilla ambush style common among the Natives, as well as destroying Indian agricultural stores. During the worst of the fighting, the colonists retreated toward the East, but once the Indians had been killed or enslaved, the settlers began a cautious re-entry to the back country. It proved to be the pattern that would characterize all future Indian–white warfare on American zones of clashing cultures. THIS!

Similar conditions of confusion existed on the southern front, which between 1763 and 1773 was racked by the Regulator Wars in South Carolina. The Scots-Irish and Germans there had already warred against the Cherokees. The struggle had been so intense that there was great insecurity throughout the piedmont, where almost 97 percent of all whites in the colony lived. The authorities in Charleston failed to address the economic instability and social disorder for people who were living without governing institutions but within the grasp of various corrupt political appointees. An assortment of marginal groups – hunters, debtors, poor settlers, mixed blood persons, and professional outlaws banded together with a common cause – the defeat of the planter class or so-called "respectable" people. Following a 1767 summer crime wave, this group rose up and, taking the name "Regulators," began a march on Charleston, where they demanded laws, jails, and circuit courts.

The Regulators quickly became more of a problem than their foes. They took to executing outlaws and then "correcting" the morals of other back country residents. In answer, yet another group arose in the back country. These were in the Moderator Movement and for a time a near civil war broke out between the Moderators and the Regulators. Essentially these were extra-legal or vigilante groups, the lessons of which were that such behaviors always occurred outside the law, sprang from highly conservative sentiments, involved the most powerful citizens as the "enforcers," and denied to other citizens the due process protections that would later be identified with the US Constitution.[33]

By the time the American colonists organized themselves for independence in 1776, all regions of the back country were in high disorder. Those who lived beyond the Tidewater had been disobeying colonial law for years, so defiance of the British king was nothing new. Further, their day-to-day concerns tended to be more immediate than colonists living along the coast, restricting the amount of time they had to devote to problems for the American army in Philadelphia and Boston. Of course, the British hoped to exploit the anger of Indian tribes, increasingly pushed back by advancing colonists. The Americans somehow thought they could convince the Indians to follow a policy of neutrality, although back country residents demanded more direct control of Native warriors.

all control — simply different strategies

The goals of the Indians were quite simple – they wanted to protect their trade, strengthen their position against any enemy tribes, and get a taste of revenge for the years of pain they had suffered from colonial intrusions and mistreatment. In their view, a victory for the British might mean tribes could reclaim lost turf. Many felt that the spirit of the Proclamation of 1763 pointed to the possibility that Great Britain would honor boundaries of Native land. And, given the power of the British navy and its ability to blockade colonial merchant shipping, the Indians knew they could rely on far better weapons and trade goods from the British, if such would be provided. These factors were sufficient to sway the Indian diplomats. As the American Revolution began, British colonists living on the contested outer regions found themselves surrounded by a ring of hostile Indians – Shawnees, Delawares, Cherokees, and to some degree, the Creeks. *← just trying to survive*

The victory of the Americans over Great Britain had enormous significance for the western areas of the colonies, where the war itself had not taken place. By the Treaty of Paris of 1783, the hostilities were declared suspended. In fact, in the western parts of the new country, the conflicts were just heating up. The enthusiasm for acquiring as much western land as possible surged through the Americans, who were fueled by their heady victory over Great Britain. The British, stung and angered, thought to separate America from her allies and yet hold to as much western land as possible. The French longed for revenge on the British, while the Spanish hoped to control the Mississippi River and strike for revenge against anyone. Native Americans, who had sided with the wrong nation, looked at western lands, now teeming with the enraged representatives of three major European nations and wondered how to rid themselves of these interlopers and still manipulate the beneficial aspects of doing business with white society.

Overlooked by all were the implications of the tangled interplay in the territories known as Spanish Texas, French Louisiana, and the southern Plains Indian regions of Apacheria and Comancheria. Here, removed from those places commonly highlighted in the narration of the Native introduction and response to European imperialism, another important story unfolded. This was a tale that, although long overlooked, deepened the nature of North American slavery, broadened the accounts of Indian tribal policy, and illuminated the dynamics of gender.

Indeed, the land that seemed so distant and romantic, so receptive to myth-building – French Louisiana and Spanish Texas – should have drawn the close scrutiny of the Americans.[34] There they would have seen that the Spanish moving north out of Mexico and the French moving south out of Canada and the Ohio Valley mingled with Indians in places that would be known as Comancheria and Apacheria. The overlay of cultures produced a world distinct from other regions of Native–European interaction.

After the French and Indian War, Spain gained administrative control of Louisiana. By this time, the French had added the Comanche and Wichita Indians to their earlier alliance with the Caddos. These Indian tribes came to a position of economic and political dominance across the region. A prominent component of these interlocking commercial relations included a vigorous trade in female slaves.

The armies of men see-sawed between military aggression and peace-keeping ventures. In the teetering back and forth, women and children of the foe became targets for capture. Within this environment, the most vulnerable of the enemy camp were actively pursued as captives. This system led to widespread occasions of human slavery, predicated not on race, but on gender.

Although a woman in a Native society often held carefully delineated economic and political power, when separated from her cultural community, a woman could find that her decision-making and personal agency evaporated. Instead, now held by an enemy camp, a woman became quite powerless, transformed into a slave to be used for forced labor – domestic, mercantile, or sexual. Often referred to almost benignly as "captivity,' the condition was, in fact, slavery, one in which women had no control over what happened to them.

In this unsavory circumstance, women were valued as war booty. Men were not seen in the slave trade, as they either killed themselves before capture or were murdered when apprehended. Women and children, however, might be captured as punishment against an offending tribe, such as when the Spanish carried off Apache women. In addition to inflicting emotional pain on the enemy, the Spanish anticipated the value of the captives as a trade item during peace discussions, which they assumed would materialize at some point. The women, however, had no idea how long their slavery might last or its outcome – sold off to a jobber for labor and death, given as a "gift' during peace talks, exchanged for female slaves held by their captors' foes, murdered, raped, or married.

The French moving south and west on the Plains during the eighteenth century more than dabbled in this slave trade, as they stoked the fires of their Indian alliances. Natchitoches and its nearby fort was a trade center, where the French acknowledged the most valuable goods were horses, pelts, and slaves. The trade in female slaves allowed men on both sides of the table to enhance their commercial and diplomatic ties.

In this swirl of several Indian tribes, Spanish administrators, and French traders, men of opposing sides cooperated in perpetuating the traffic in women, holding them in a bondage that was neither gentle nor brief. Women were an instrument to be used for the advance of masculine political and economic strategies. In the meantime, female captives changed the demographics of American slavery, forcibly held in western lands that were increasingly mythically regarded as a paradise of unfettered freedom. Such unattractive elements in western life, as this female slavery, were typically minimized or ignored.

In general, the territorial limits of all the new land that came to the United States after the American Revolution were not written with the greatest clarity. True, the Mississippi River was established as a boundary for the new United States, but nothing was very clear about the northern and the southern boundaries – a point not missed by France and Spain, whose claims in the West remained blurry.

In addition, was not a Mississippi River water boundary a rather porous dividing line? Would countries not jostle over the notion that all should have equal navigation rights? Would farmers and pioneers not glance across the wide waters at new land that beckoned? Would Indians not glide along from tribe to tribe, seeking alliances before the next great forward thrust of English settlers? Since the entire continent had already been a field of violence and conflict since the first days when Spanish, French, and British adventurers had touched the soil of the New World, why would that change for those who populated the area increasingly known as the American West?

Thomas Jefferson, a key figure in the Republic's formation and always alert to his own political standing, did not overlook these questions and felt that the distribution and management of western lands were of importance for the new nation. If as well these issues aided him politically, how fortunate. After all, the new leadership in America could see that it had inherited the problems of the Privy Council of Great Britain – persons living far from the center of government chafed under circumstances whereby they were handled as "colonials." By 1785, operating under the governing authority of the Article of Confederation, Thomas Jefferson, who wrote brilliantly on political theory, placed his distinctive stamp, not just on the newest territory the country controlled, but on all future land acquisitions of the United States.

Those troublesome back country folk raised their voices about breaking away from the older colonies, even before the end of the Revolution. Lawmakers in the East, uneasy about growing restiveness and constantly struggling with land company speculators who wanted to secure huge profits through the sale of western territory, sought a remedy that would settle the unruly, mollify the speculators, and give the government a procedure for dealing with western lands. It was Jefferson who, after a first sweeping failure to resolve the problems, saw that the western territories represented two distinct dilemmas: how should the land be divided for ownership and how should distant land be governed by eastern administrators?

By the Land Ordinance of 1785, all government lands were divided into townships and these into 36 sections. The lands were to be sold at public auction and one township section reserved for a school. It was a unique document in the history of country building, for it mandated survey before settlement and introduced an orderly system for the transfer of public land into private hands. A number of factors, including the wealth of land speculators and the locations of auctions in the East, close to moneyed people prevented the Land Ordinance of 1785 from attaining the egalitarian goals to which it aspired. Nonetheless, it was a crucial document in early American history because it resolved the procedures for land distribution, before the United States governed all the territory it eventually controlled.[35]

That innovative law was followed by the Northwest Ordinance of 1787, an even more original document. This legislation addressed the governance of newly acquired lands. In a historic moment, the Americans constructed a three-stage system by which western lands entered the Union "for the establishment of states . . . and for their admission to a share in the federal councils on an equal footing with the original states."[36] In one stroke, American politicians, turned aside a centuries-old European practice of treating newly acquired lands as colonies and their peoples as a subservient source of labor, resources, and profit for the mother country. While it might have seemed remarkable that eastern politicians would shower such largess on the West, base motives did fuel their decision.

Eastern seaboard states feared the size and potential power of large land areas to the west. With new attractive spaces, loaded with natural resources, opened for settlement, the eastern states faced a possible population drain, as land-hungry settlers and European immigrants headed west. Further, the proposed boundaries for new western states dwarfed the older Atlantic colonies. What power would the 13 original states retain, as western size and population overtook them? Clearly, the eastern grasp on the western lands was not so secure following the American Revolution. Foreign agents of many stripes agitated in the back country with regularity and who could say that settlers with thin allegiance to the patrician East would not duplicate the recent conduct of the eastern rebels themselves? The westerners had not contributed much to the war effort, but it seemed they represented "independence" and "freedom." Had anyone really investigated the lives of back country people, the absence of these two qualities would have been evident.

Even if Americans failed to examine closely the lands they so romanticized, they had concocted a good national tale for themselves and the new nation would need, among many other things, a patriotic myth to get the country launched. More than one such myth was just ahead.

NOTES

1 "The Royal Proclamation, October 7, 1763, By the King." Avalon Project, Yale Law School, <www.yale.edu/lawweb/avalon/proc1763.htm>.
2 Governor Glen, "The Role of the Indians in the Rivalry between France, Spain, and England, 1761," Documents for the Study of American History, <www.ku.edu/carrie/docs/texts/glen_on_indians.html>.
3 Colin G. Calloway, *The Scratch of a Pen: 1763 and the Transformation of North America* (New York: Oxford University Press, 2006), 22–4, 66–9.
4 Ibid., 50–1.
5 Peter Iverson, "Native Peoples and Native Histories," in Clyde A. Milner II, Carol A. O'Connor, and Martha A. Sandweiss, eds., *The Oxford History of the American West* (New York: Oxford University Press, 1994), 13.
6 Walter Nugent, *Into the West: The Story of Its People* (New York: Alfred A. Knopf, 1999), 19–20.
7 Iverson, "Native Peoples and Native Histories," 17.
8 Kathryn A. Abbott, "Indians of the Southwest," in Howard R. Lamar, ed., *The New Encyclopedia of the American West* (New Haven: Yale University Press, 1998), 540–2.
9 Daniel K. Richter, *Facing East from Indian Country: A Narrative History of Early America* (Cambridge: Harvard University Press, 2001), 3.
10 For a rich description of the Moundbuilders, see Charles C. Mann, *1491: New Revelations of the Americas before Columbus* (New York: Alfred A. Knopf, 2005), 252–67.
11 P. Richard Metcalf, "Indians of the Northwest Coast," in Lamar, ed., *The New Encyclopedia of the American West*, 538–40.
12 P. Richard Metcalf, revised by Ives Goddard, "Indian Languages," in Lamar, ed., *The New Encyclopedia of the American West*, 522–5.
13 Quintard Taylor, *In Search of the Racial Frontier: African Americans in the American West, 1528–1990* (New York: W. W. Norton, 1998), 27–32.
14 David J. Weber, *The Spanish Frontier in North America* (New Haven: Yale University Press, 1992), 92–6.

15 Michael P. Carroll, *The Penitente Brotherhood: Patriarchy and Hispano-Catholicism in New Mexico* (Baltimore: Johns Hopkins University Press, 2002), 39–40.

16 David J. Weber, "The Spanish–Mexican Rim," in Milner et al., eds., *The Oxford History of the American West*, 47.

17 Richter, *Facing East from Indian Country*, 59–62; Weber, *The Spanish Frontier in North America*, 27–9.

18 The seventeenth century saw a flurry of European scientific developments; in 1665, the Englishman Robert Hooke, using a primitive microscope, identified cells and has been labeled the "father of biology."

19 For a detailed explanation of the link between the horse and the buffalo for Plains people, see Colin G. Calloway, *One Vast Winter Count: The Native American West before Lewis and Clark* (Lincoln: University of Nebraska Press, 2003) and John C. Ewers, *The Blackfeet* (Norman: University of Oklahoma Press, 1958).

20 Richter, *Facing East from Indian Country*, 59–62; Weber, *The Spanish Frontier in North America*, 25–9.

21 For a full account of the Pueblo revolts, see Weber, *The Spanish Frontier in North America*, 133–41.

22 A major explanation for the ways in which early cultures interacted and exchanged is found in Richard White, *The Middle Ground: Indians, Empires, and Republics in the Great Lakes Region, 1650–1815* (Cambridge: Cambridge University Press, 1991).

23 Major studies that address the economic nature of the fur trade and the place of women in it include Harold A. Innis, *The Fur Trade in Canada: An Introduction to Canadian Economic History* (1956; Toronto: University of Toronto Press, 1999) and Sylvia Van Kirk, *Many Tender Ties: Women in Fur Trade Society, 1670–1870* (Norman: University of Oklahoma Press, 1983).

24 Joan M. Jensen, "Native American Women and Agriculture: A Seneca Case Study," in Ellen Carol DuBois and Vicki L. Ruiz, eds., *Unequal Sisters: A Multi-Cultural Reader in Women's History* (New York: Routledge, 1990), 52–3.

25 For a full discussion of the experiences between Natives and the French, see James Axtell, *The Invasion Within: The Contest of Cultures in Colonial North America* (New York: Oxford University Press, 1985), 1–127.

26 For an understanding of the dynamics of life for the *métis* in Canada, see Jennifer S. H. Brown, *Strangers in Blood: Fur Trade Families in Indian Country* (Vancouver: University of British Columbia Press, 1980) and Jacqueline Peterson and Jennifer S. H. Brown, *The New Peoples: Being and Becoming Métis in North America* (1985; St Paul: Minnesota Historical Society Press, 2001).

27 *Glimpses of the Monastery: Scenes from the History of the Ursulines of Quebec during Two Hundred Years, 1639–1839* (Quebec: L. J. Demers and Frère, 1897), 13–21, <http://www.canadiana.org/ECO/PageView/ 28997/0003?id=091f884c23f2df6c>.

28 "Instructions for the Virginia Colony, 1606." Documents for the Study of American History, <www.ku.edu/carrie/docs/texts/virginia_instruct ions.html>.

29 Classic studies of the New England experience include John Demos, *A Little Commonwealth: Family Life in Plymouth Colony* (New York: Oxford University Press, 1970) and Kenneth A. Lockridge, *A New England Town: The First Hundred Years, Dedham, Massachusetts, 1636–1736* (New York: Norton, 1970).

30 Jay Gitlin, "Empires of Trade, Hinterlands of Settlement," in Milner et al., eds., *The Oxford History of the American West*, 90–6.

31 An important work that realigned the settlement narrative was Francis Jennings, *The Invasion of America: Indians, Colonialism, and the Cant of Conquest* (Chapel Hill: University of North Carolina Press, 1975).

32 To understand the dramatic changes for all systems, see William Cronon, *Changes in the Land: Indians, Colonists, and the Ecology of New England* (New York: Hill and Wang, 1983).

33 The Regulator Wars continue to yield fresh interpretations. Two recent works are Marjoleine Kars, *Breaking Loose Together: The Regulators Rebellion in Pre-Revolutionary North Carolina* (Chapel Hill: University of North Carolina Press, 2002) and Wayne E. Lee, *Crowds and Soldiers in Revolutionary North Carolina: The Culture of Violence in Riot and War* (Gainesville: University Press of Florida, 2001).

34 This discussion is based on the scholarship of Juliana Barr, "From Captives to Slaves: Commodifying Indian Women in the Borderlands," *Journal of American History* 92:1 (June 2005): 1–27. Other works that deal extensively with this subject are James F. Brooks, *Captives and Cousins: Slavery, Kinship, and Community in the Southwest Borderlands* (Chapel Hill, University of North Carolina Press, 2002) and Alan Gallay, *The Indian Slave Trade: The Rise of the English Empire in the American South, 1670–1717* (New Haven: Yale University Press, 2002).

35 An essential work for understanding the distribution of lands remains Malcolm J. Rohrbough, *The Land Office Business: The Settlement and Administration of American Public Lands, 1789–1837* (New York: Oxford University Press, 1968).

36 Documents from the Continental Congress and the Constitutional Convention, Ordinance of 1787, American Memory, Library of Congress, <www.memory.loc.gov/ammem/index.html>.

Chapter 2

Inside Native Wests

Capt. William Clark and Mr. Lewis (private secretary to the President) [will] proceed through the immense wilderness of Louisiana to the Western or Pacific Ocean.[1]

While citizens of the newly born United States consistently imagined the lands west of the Mississippi River as an "immense wilderness," the Mandans and Hidatsas who lived along the upper Missouri River in what is now central North Dakota knew better. For decades, trade fairs at their long-inhabited villages had ensnared travelers from Native communities across the Great Plains in a dense web of corn, squash, bison meat, beans, furs and hides, shells, precious stones, and cultivating tools traded by Indian women. In the late 1700s, horses from Indian groups on the southern and central Plains, in combination with British and French firearms, pots, and blankets garnered from traders around the Great Lakes, joined the long list of commodities available to those who visited the river villages every year. Drawing on connections from across the continent, the Mandans and Hidatsas transformed their settlements into one of the most dynamic centers of commerce in North America.

advanced economic power.

And so by the early 1800s, Lakotas, Assiniboins, Kiowas, Crees, Arapahoes, Arikaras, Cheyennes, Crows, and a host of other Natives visited these communities year after year, fostering intertribal politics as complicated as any other transactions birthed in trade. Nomadic groups vied for each other's hunting grounds and engaged in a spirited exchange with the river villagers that ranged from pleasant barter to open raiding. European traders also made their way to this commercial nexus, hoping to profit from the complicated web of diplomatic intrigue fostered by simultaneous interdependence and competition between Indian bands. But now a new player on the continent wanted to enter the intricate mix and tap into the vast wealth concentrated in indigenous trading centers (like the Mandan-Hidatsa villages) that could be found across western North America.

No wonder then, that on September 23, 1803, residents of Boston awoke to thrilling news of an American expedition through the recently purchased Louisiana Territory. Preparation for the trip had been ongoing for some months – in fact, the planning began before the purchase – but, in an early example of news management by an administration, the information was new to most Americans. President Thomas Jefferson's interest in the commercial possibilities of the vast lands beyond the Mississippi River, already laden with imperial and Indian rivalries, overrode the niceties of international cordiality. Ahead of negotiations with the French, Jefferson directed his private secretary Meriwether Lewis to hasten to Philadelphia, America's center of science and learning, and there investigate what would be needed to carry out the highly secret journey. Lewis, a brilliant but mercurial chap, plunged into his assignment, becoming a familiar figure in and around the City of Brotherly Love as he gathered supplies and trade goods. Finally, he recruited an experienced soldier, William Clark, as his co-captain.

When the French offered to sell a Louisiana that they owned in name only to the United States for a mere 15 million dollars, Jefferson did not hesitate. The president hastily authorized the April 30, 1803 purchase, although even a quick glance at the US Constitution showed no such authority granted to the chief executive. Casting off the mantle of secrecy that had shrouded the planning, the government widely advertised the coming trip.[2] Those Americans who doubted the importance of such a venture were reminded by both politicians and journalists of the expedition's potential to "encourage settlements and establish sea-ports on the coast."[3] But the article in the *New England Palladium* no doubt sparked lively conversation, as Americans considered the prospects of a trip through unknown wilds and presumably into the haunts of equally unfamiliar Indians that would result in the extension of the United States across the continent. Not a few wagers must have been placed that day as to whether the Lewis and Clark expedition would ever depart and, more to the point, would ever return.

The three-year journey was destined to become one of the best-known and most studied episodes in the history of the American West. Over time, many Americans envisioned Lewis and Clark *[ignoring Spanish, French & Indian]* forging their way through unexplored and unpeopled wilderness, opening up the West for farmers and businessmen. The expedition's itinerary became common knowledge to generations of school-children: the keelboat trip up the Missouri River, the cold winter camp on the banks of the upper reaches of that great watercourse, the heroic crossing of the Rocky Mountains at Lolo Pass, the long descent down the Columbia River for an even longer winter stay at Fort Clatsop near the river's mouth, and the triumphant 1806 return of the expedition to St Louis, where Clark reported that the men "were met by all the village and received a harty welcome."[4]

[1st more tails ad for image] Even as this narrative reigned supreme, crucial details slipped into obscurity. For example, Lewis and Clark were not the first Euro Americans to enter the American West. British fur trader Alexander MacKenzie had crossed the Canadian Rockies in 1792. Nor were Jefferson's envoys the first whites to encounter the Lakotas, Mandans, Nez Perces, Chinooks, or the many other Natives they encountered. French fur traders first visited the Mandans in the 1740s. Lewis and Clark were not even the first Americans to trade with Indians at the mouth of the Columbia River. Robert Gray, a merchant from Boston, met with Natives there as early as 1792.[5] Most importantly, when Lewis and Clark set out in 1804, the West was by no means "American." For many years, European imperial powers had articulated overlapping and contradictory claims to lands actually lived on and controlled by Indians. Those many thousands of Native inhabitants called the region "home" – not "the West" – and they had no plans to cede it to any of their European acquaintances, let alone newcomers from the United States.

How then should Lewis and Clark be understood? Despite the assertions of the *New England Palladium*, overland commerce, not settlement, was the point of their travels. Lewis and Clark were the last – not the first – to enter a competition between and among European nations. These countries sought to engage powerful Native communities in a lucrative trade that stretched across the continent and around the world. In joining the fray, Lewis and

Clark ushered in a new relationship between the United States and the indigenous peoples of the western half of North America. Jefferson's explorers were the first Americans to enter an Indian world more dense with complex intrigue, politics, and economic competition than any European port or capital. Their legacy made possible the eventual success of the United States in its competition with Europeans and Natives alike. Commerce, confusion, collusion, and conflict – all hallmarks of the Lewis and Clark expedition – characterized the relationship shared by Americans with Indians, as an American West slowly materialized from complex and coinciding Native worlds over the next four decades.

Through Lewis and Clark, President Thomas Jefferson openly catapulted the United States into the imperial competition for the prized commerce with the Indians of the Plains, Rockies, and Pacific Northwest. By extension, he also looked to expand the American presence in the otter pelt and Chinese trade of the northern Pacific Ocean.[6] It was the 1801 publication of Alexander MacKenzie's account of his trip across the continent that finally moved the new president to organize an overland expedition.[7] Jefferson's instructions to the young army officers encompassed three concerns. First, they should seek "the most direct & practicable water communication across this continent." Special attention needed to be paid to the Missouri River's "course and communication with the waters of the Pacific Ocean." Second, the expedition was to make maps of the lands they traversed. "Your observations are to be taken with great pains & accuracy, to be entered distinctly & intelligibly . . . to fix the latitude and longitude" of landmarks encountered on the journey. Third, the president desired knowledge of the Natives. He hoped that close ethnographic study of "the extent & limits of their possessions; their relations with other tribes of nations; their language, traditions, monuments . . . and articles of commerce they may need or furnish & to what extent" would give the United States a trade advantage.[8] In sum, Jefferson's directives mandated that the expedition project the young nation into an already crowded Northwest.

For example, the president knew of Russian fur traders' arrival in Alaska in the 1740s. By 1800, they had established permanent trading posts in Alaska and slowly worked their way south along the Pacific Coast. The Spanish, wary of Russian expansion, entered California in the 1760s, establishing missions as far up the coast as modern-day San Francisco. The Russians confirmed Spanish fears through the establishment of Fort Ross, just north of San Francisco Bay, in 1812. Meantime, drawing from MacKenzie's report, British traders operating out of Canada began building fur trading posts across the Far West. Sea-going British merchants also engaged in a spirited maritime trade around Vancouver Island and Puget Sound in the 1790s. The otter pelts purchased there proved especially profitable in China.

Completing a trans-global circle, Europeans coveted the tea, porcelain, and silk acquired from trading otter pelts in Canton. Using Hawai'i as a warm weather base of operations allowed them to shuttle between China, the Pacific Northwest, and Great Britain year after year. Their American peers from the port of Boston engaged in a similar exchange and, by the 1790s, had taken over the bulk of the Northwest maritime trade.[9] Meanwhile, Russian traders faced Indians – such as the Tlingits who attacked Sitka, Alaska, a Russian commerce center, in 1802 and 1804 – armed with guns from trading sessions with Americans. Not surprisingly, imperial ambitions, dynamic change, and Native inclinations made for rivalries between and among all these competitors. Jefferson recognized that on the success of Lewis and Clark hung a crucial overland connection for the United States in this fast-paced contest for commerce.

Yet Jefferson's insistence on gathering information on Native peoples underscored the role Indians played throughout the region. *[disregard for their knowledge]* From Alaska to the Great Plains and from the Pacific Ocean to the Mississippi River, Natives capitalized on an ancient history of local, regional, and transcontinental trade and mobility. Indian identities depended on all these elements, as well as the stories they told about themselves. This dynamic past involved not only self-definition and intertribal diplomacy but also migration and cultural transformation. After 1500, the latter often accelerated because of contact with Europeans. As for the newcomers, Natives integrated European traders and the items they offered into long-established exchange practices. *[of their choosing, not forced.]*

Those practices held more than mere economic meaning. Trade proved a conduit for diplomacy, intertribal relations, spiritual renewal, and careful politicking, as well material wealth. Especially among tribes in the continent's interior, not only trade items but also foreign germs spread through Native communities long before Europeans themselves arrived.

Figure 2.1 Through the winter count, such as the Rosebud one here spanning 1752–1888, Natives on the Great Plains collected and preserved tribal history, using a pictorial calendar to record significant events both inside and outside their own culture. *Source:* Courtesy, Smithsonian Institution, National Anthropological Archives (Ms 2001-10).

Indeed, before Lewis and Clark set off on their journey in 1804, Indians fell prey to multiple waves of disease – most notably, the smallpox epidemic that swept the continent from 1779–83.[10] Furthermore, in the geopolitics of the Great Plains, guns, acquired from Indian neighbors of the Great Lakes and Canada, and horses, traded from the Spanish Southwest decades earlier, transformed Indian life.

Simply the effect of trade altered Indian culture.

Simultaneously disruptive and empowering, armed equestrian cultures forced changes in the relations between various Indian groups. In the swirling combination of these many factors, Lewis and Clark stepped into a world struggling with cataclysmic change in the immediate years before their arrival.[11] (Figure 2.1)

Those changes challenged Indians with a mix of opportunities and problems. In some encounters, such as those between the Aleuts and the Russian *promyshlenniki* in the 1700s in Alaska, Natives confronted grim odds. Russian traders' typical tactic was to surround Aleut villages, taking whole families ransom, enlisting women and girls as sex slaves, and forcing men to gather sea otter pelts.

In other Native–white dealings, Indians held the upper hand.

Among the Chinooks at the mouth of the Columbia River, British mariners and "Boston men" came ashore for brief and usually amiable trading sessions. The quality materials available from the whites were especially valuable for the trade of the coastal Indians with other Natives further inland. Chinooks strengthened their hand with neighboring tribes through trade with Euro Americans. By the 1770s, the Lakotas moved onto the northern Plains from the upper Mississippi River Valley and busily expanded their range and power over rival Native groups. They used to good advantage their growing expertise with the horse and European firearms, integrating both, most notably, in their buffalo hunts. The resulting improved standard of living, greater tribal wealth, diplomatic status, and subsequent military power meant that the Lakotas – not Europeans – held the key to any southern entry into the northern Plains trade.

Predictably, Lewis and Clark's first major contact with Natives as they headed upstream from St Louis came in present-day South Dakota when they came upon a band of Lakotas on the Missouri River shore. This particular band, under the leadership of Untongarabar had earned a reputation among St Louis traders for a curt and demanding personality. Jefferson himself noted that the Lakotas held "immense power" in the region even as the United States proved "miserably weak."[12] The Lakotas' ability to maintain that power on the northern Plains required they control all Plains traffic, including the comings and goings of Europeans to the nearby Arikaras, Mandans, and Hidatsas that practiced agriculture and traded in villages along the river to the north. All three traded the corn vital to Lakota survival in exchange for European goods the Lakotas purchased through British traders allied with the Dakotas to the east.

Understanding the uncertainty involved, Clark "prepared all things for action in Case of necessity."[13] With much posing from leaders on both sides but no adequate interpreter, the whites and Lakotas got themselves into a prickly showdown. While Lewis and Clark wished to ensure the safe passage of future American traders through the area – a must for any sustained commerce on the northern Plains – Untongarabar and other Lakota leaders carefully focused discussions on whether or not the Americans would proceed upriver. Lakotas and Americans alike had much at stake. Arrows, bows, and rifles at the ready, only the sudden appearance of a separate canoe filled with American soldiers forced the Indian warriors to back down. Two more tense days of negotiation ensued. After hours of ceremony and diplomacy, Untongarabar finally agreed to allow the expedition onward without incident. He likely saw it as a minor concession – one boat could not threaten Lakota power.[14] Meantime, failing to grasp the broader ramifications of intertribal politics, Lewis and Clark secured little more then the right to their own passage. No trade agreement had been reached. No accord over the future passage of American traders had been solidified. The expedition had failed in its first attempt to negotiate a sophisticated and complicated diplomatic and social world with many political voices.

Further along the Missouri, they spent a week with the Arikaras, agricultural villagers sometimes allied with the Lakotas. Relations there proved more amicable than they had with Untongarabar. Kakawissassa – one of many Arikara leaders – offered the captains passage through the area, agreed that intertribal peace made for more fruitful trading, and expressed interest in American trade goods from St Louis. The expedition leaders moved on believing that all was well, but intertribal politics ensured that any agreements could be short-lived. In fact, in the years to come, the Arikaras generally resisted American traders moving north on the Missouri River. Their continued reliance on the Lakotas proved more beneficial than the occasional appearance of Americans.

Nonetheless, the expedition fascinated the Arikaras. Notably, the African American member of the party – York, William Clark's slave – caused quite a stir among the villagers. The slave's keen hunting and scouting skills had already proved crucial to the American party.[15] York seized on the hubbub and in Clark's words "made him Self more terrible in their view than I wished him to Doe."[16] Because of his dark skin, the river villagers imagined York as possessing special powers – powers that some Indian men believed could be transferred to them through his sexual intercourse with their wives. According to the expedition's journals, York, who later lived as a free man, willingly cooperated with this notion, although none of the Americans seemed to understand the radically different ideas of human sexuality, gender, and power the incidents revealed. Clark simply complained that York was acting more independently than any slave should.

Moving on from the Arikaras, Lewis, Clark, and their men arrived at the Mandan-Hidatsa villages. Items of every sort from thousands of miles distant found their way to the middlemen and women along the Missouri. Its only rival as a seat of Great Plains commerce was a similar cosmopolitan center among the western Comanches to the south. Long-time diplomats and savvy traders, the Indians welcomed Lewis and Clark – the first Americans to arrive in the historic gathering place – as yet another source of goods and guns. The newcomers might offer items that could strengthen their hand against their sometime enemies, the Lakotas and Arikaras, and with their steady trading partners, the Assiniboins and the Crees.

With winter ice making the Missouri River impassable, the men built winter quarters and spent five months among the Mandans and Hidatsas. These five months passed with friendly negotiations. Despite generally positive interpersonal relations, Lewis and Clark failed to reach any agreement with the Mandans and Hidatsas that would make Americans their primary trading partners. Meantime, day-to-day encounters between Americans and Natives also included French and British traders already living among the villagers. One of them – Toussaint Charbonneau – found himself a job as an interpreter with the explorers, as they looked onward towards the Rockies in the spring. One of Charbonneau's two wives, a captured Shoshone woman whom the French trader purchased years before, joined him as they left the Mandans and Hidatsas, becoming one of the most famous members of the expedition – Sacagawea.

Departing from the river villages in April 1805, the augmented American party continued to follow the Missouri River to the north and then west, into modern-day Montana. Moving from the river to footpaths through the high passes of the Rockies required horses for the expedition's gear, food, and packs. As Lewis and Clark approached the headwaters of the Missouri, Sacagawea, the captains hoped, would be useful when the expedition met the Shoshones. Lewis believed the woman, traveling with her young son, would assuage Native worries of a possible military raid and hoped "for a friendly negotiation with the Snake [Shoshone] Indians on whom we depend for horses to assist us in our portage from the Missouri to the Columbia River."[17] Sacagawea, an early example of the important role played by Native women in what became the West, did provide the cultural and linguistic knowledge that encouraged friendly relations with the Shoshones and got the travelers the horses necessary for a safe passage through the mountains. In fact,

Sacagawea providentially "proved to be the sister of the [Shoshone] Chi[e]f Cameahwait."[18] Pleased with the reunion and eager for American firearms, Shoshones offered up horses – in return for guns and ammunition – and guides to lead the expedition over the Rockies. A few days later, Salish allies on their way to join the Shoshones *All* further enlarged Lewis and Clark's horse herd, again showing the *thanks* influence of Native decision-making in the success of the expedition. *to the Indians*

Leaving the Louisiana Purchase behind as its members slogged over Lolo Pass, the expedition soon stumbled into a camp of Nez Perces in present-day Idaho. As with the Shoshones, these mountain and camas prairie dwellers desperately needed firearms to hold off nearby Native enemies. Lewis and Clark seemed to offer a ready supply of guns. In turn, the Nez Perces drew maps of the Columbia River watershed, showed the Americans how to build dugout canoes, and provided Twisted Hair and Tetharsky to serve as go-betweens with the many Native peoples of the Columbia River valley.[19] Equipped with information, watercraft, and interpreters, the expedition traveled downstream on the Clearwater, Snake, and Columbia rivers toward the Pacific.

As the Americans moved closer to the ocean, they met Indians unlike those seen in the previous months. Fishing, not hunting, dominated these new cultures. Salmon was the principal food and trade item. Many of the riverside villages displayed an array of European trade items, accumulated through years of trade at the mouth of the Columbia.

These Natives – especially the Wishrams and Chinooks – were already major brokers in an extensive trade with Indians, as well as whites. Their experience offered Lewis and Clark yet another set of *so they* challenges, as the Americans often found themselves out-bartered. *did have* In a variety of combinations, but almost always depending on sign *intelligence* language and their Nez Perce guides, the Americans worked to describe their interests and explain their intentions. Initial encounters with the Wanapams, Yakimas, and Walla Wallas went well. Further on towards the ocean, relations with Natives shifted. Umatillas near the junction of the Snake and the Columbia feared the Americans. The constantly shifting Native attitudes and responses tended to keep the, by now trail-weary, Americans off balance.

East of the Rockies, the captains proclaimed American sovereignty – often ignored by Natives, since it existed only on paper – and promoted intercultural commerce. West of the Rockies, where the imaginary territorial claims of European powers overlapped, Lewis and Clark muted claims of land ownership and played up the economic and military power of the United States. Thus, they attempted to use multi-faceted diplomacy to secure the advantage for America with various groups of Indians.

By the time Lewis and Clark reached the Dalles, they faced difficult rapids and yet another distinct and complex set of intertribal relations. The Wishram and Wasco villages there were the preeminent meeting ground for coastal and interior tribes. During peak trading times, hundreds of Indians gathered around thousands of pounds of dried fish, firearms, beads, kettles, bear grass, and canoes.

Members of the expedition noted not only the European trade goods, but also a mixed race child whose presence indicated that "white Men trade among them."[20] That others traded here carried more weight than finding Europeans rivals on the Great Plains. There, the trafficking by French and British traders was well known. Seeing evidence of trade with whites here in the Northwest, however, signaled that not just trade items but also traders, likely British, had already left traces in the Columbia River watershed. By all accounts, it seemed clear that Lewis and Clark were not the first whites to see the Dalles. This was crucial information to take back to Jefferson.

Continuing downriver, the Americans began to notice what they imagined to be petty theft. Indians who helped Lewis and Clark and their men with the difficult portages from the Dalles to the Cascades surreptitiously took goods from the expedition's stores as the party worked towards the Pacific. For Indians, the so-called theft proved to be an acceptable response to the intrusion of this new group of whites. Natives believed the resulting discomfort would insure that the Americans shape more appropriate relationships with local residents. In other words, the Indians who lived along the lower Columbia River demanded that the expedition take note of its comparatively weaker position, even as it received food and aid. Such expectations and understandings made no sense to Lewis and Clark, who complained about theft from the Dalles to the Cascades. Because they depended on Indians for food, however, the captains did little but scribble about the distraction in their journals, a response that affirmed the Indians' assessment of the whites' vulnerable position.[21]

Both groups viewed the other as inferior.

Meanwhile, the closer the Americans got to the ocean, the more European goods they saw. Among the Skilloots in early November 1805, less than a hundred miles from the Columbia's mouth, they heard the linguistic evidence of that constant contact with British and American traders along the coast. The trade jargon of the area included English language words and phrases. Nonetheless, negotiations broke down quickly. The Skilloots feared replacement as the trade "go-betweens" and tensions mounted on both sides. A bit of shared language could not offset the political power of the coastal traders. The exhausted Americans retreated to the river, where they waited in their boats until well past sundown before landing to make camp. Three days later, a fog-drenched, worn-down but relieved William Clark effused that the Pacific Ocean was in view: "O! the joy."[22]

A long, anxious, wet winter ensued. The expedition readied winter quarters by December 30, 1805, and christened the structure Fort Clatsop. Soured by the experience with the Skilloots, the party remained suspicious and wearied of local Clatsop and Chinook visitors. Over the damp winter, Lewis and Clark faced top-notch Native traders whose skills had been honed with British and American sailors in the sea otter exchange. Conditioned over the years to understand whites as people who traded a host of goods for otter pelts, Indians initially wondered about the strange ways of the overland party and its focus on swapping for food, not furs. Nonetheless, as able traders, the Clatsops soon adjusted.

In turn, the Americans' dependence on the Clatsops for food led to resentment and constant haggling. Four months of rain, moldy fish, and clammy bedding further dampened spirits and led to the expedition's low point – the theft of a Clatsop canoe. Most of the men simply now longed to return to St Louis as soon as possible.

Their chance to head east finally came at the end of March 1806. Moving upstream on the Columbia, the party again flirted with potential violence during strained moments at the Cascades and the Dalles. Thankful to reach the friendly Nez Perces, Lewis and Clark moved towards the Continental Divide. Running low on goods to trade for horses and food, and resorting to the former for the latter, the party fell into new depths of hardship. Held up by heavy snows, they finally crossed the Rockies in mid-June.

On the east side of Lolo Pass, the captains decided to split up the party. Lewis would take one group north, to the Great Falls of the Missouri, to meet with the Blackfeet. Clark would continue on overland to where the Yellowstone and Missouri rivers met. Reuniting there, the group would then float down the Missouri River to St Louis.

Meriwether Lewis did indeed meet the Blackfeet, learning that a British trader lived among them. Disappointed by this bad news, the American told the Indians that the Nez Perces and Shoshones – enemies of the Blackfeet – not only were allied together, but also would be the beneficiaries of firearms and technologies from America. Inadvertently causing intense consternation in the Blackfeet camps, Lewis' group suddenly found itself the object of a real Indian effort at thievery. The Blackfeet moved to take the Americans' guns and horses as a retort to this bold announcement of gains for their Indian foes. An altercation ensued, two Blackfeet warriors died, and Lewis' men barely managed to escape. Lewis' ill-advised declaration of the rearrangement of intertribal power on the northwest Plains ruined Blackfeet–American relations for decades to come.

Connects to future

Lewis reunited with Clark at the Yellowstone–Missouri junction, and the combined party headed south as quickly as possible. Stopping at the Mandan-Hidatsa villages, they learned about the limits of their earlier diplomatic attempts. Despite efforts to promote peace and trade two years earlier, Mandan and Hidatsa war parties were already moving against Lakotas, Arikaras, and Shoshones. The captains had been unable to dictate diplomacy or unilaterally rearrange intertribal politics. A brief respite at the Arikara villages further downriver met with another rejection of real diplomatic change. Dashing for St Louis, the expedition arrived on September 6, 1806.

Clearly, an inability to fully understand Native geopolitics frustrated the expedition's many attempts to ensure the persistence of American commerce. Nonetheless, political and economic power brokers with widely diverse motives and goals crashed into each other and something new emerged. Individual Native communities, each with a unique outlook, political desires, economic concerns, and set of rivalries, needed to be negotiated as carefully as flatboats on the Missouri or canoes on the Columbia. Though in the parlance of Europe and America the United States owned some of those lands, Lewis and Clark had been unable to cement American claims in the face of powerful Indian presences.

This disappointing outcome did not mean that the expedition was a total failure. Much the opposite. Mutual interests often resulted in Natives and Americans accommodating one another. Lewis and Clark could not have succeeded in the physical part of their journey without Indian allies. More broadly, the party's experience foreshadowed the future of Indian–American relations – and thus the track of western history – over the next 30 years. *connects to future*

Commerce undergirded nearly every endeavor. Lewis and Clark sought trade agreements with each Indian community they encountered. Unsuccessful in securing lasting treaties, commerce resulted nonetheless, as the explorers traded for food, for knowledge, or for diplomatic imperatives. In fact, trade proved integral not only to intertribal economics but also to basic diplomacy. Confusion often resulted from cultural misreadings on the Americans' part. Lewis' missteps with the Blackfeet, in ignorance of intertribal realities on the northwest Plains or the so-called Indian thievery along the Columbia River, showed the mix of misunderstandings that plagued the captains at every turn. Collusion between Natives and whites was possible where their interests intersected. Both Shoshones and Nez Perces stood as much to gain from an alliance as did Lewis and Clark, and their aid ensured the expedition's survival. Conflict – especially the tense clashes with the Lakotas in 1804 and the Skilloots in 1805 – flared when glaring confusion, poor communication, and large stakes overlapped.

Finally, Lewis and Clark's safe return – along with the many plant specimens, ethnographic observations, and geographic wherewithal, all detailed in the expedition's amazing journals – gave Americans information they needed for entering into the lands between the Pacific and the Mississippi. The ethnographic and scientific information gathered by Lewis and Clark provided the United States with more and better knowledge than any European competitor. The collected knowledge was the greatest and most enduring legacy of the Lewis and Clark expedition, making Thomas Jefferson's vision of an "empire of liberty" possible. ↓ *connects to future*

Not surprisingly, the US government continued to sponsor explorations in the service of future commerce and empire. Even as the captains made their way down the Columbia River in 1805, American officials organized other parties to examine lands and peoples west of the Mississippi and even the Louisiana Purchase. St Louis was not only the gateway to the Northwest.

The city also offered an inviting route to Santa Fe, the Spanish capital of New Mexico. Looking southwest and led by Zebulon

Pike, an expedition followed up on previously unsuccessful attempts
by small businessmen to find new markets and goods in Santa Fe.
Pike set off in July 1806. With orders to make contact with the
Comanches in west Texas and locate the headwaters of the Red
River, the lieutenant proceeded over the dry, dusty shortgrass plains
of today's Kansas. When the 23 men arrived at the Arkansas River,
Pike turned them west and, in November, arrived at the flatirons in
front of the Rocky Mountains. Naming Pike's Peak for himself, the
lieutenant then turned south over the Sangre de Cristos and reached
the Rio Grande in late January. Within the month, wary Spanish cavalry captured Pike and marched him and his men to Santa
Fe. Pike lost his papers and journals to his captors. Nonetheless, he
memorized the Spaniards' troop dispositions throughout the area
and retained much of his new geographic knowledge of the southern
Plains. Spanish authorities released Pike, who returned to St Louis
after stops in Chihuahua and San Antonio.

Pike's 1810 report characterized the southern Plains – which sustained thousands of Natives – as "sandy deserts." In so doing, his
writings shaped a longtime vision of the prairie west of the Mississippi as a place without trees and water, a place unfit for white
agriculture and settlement. Travelers, however, who braved the
great sweeps of grass could profit. Pike intimated that money
might be made by enterprising Americans who charted a course for
Santa Fe.[23]

Spanish administrators, anxious to keep the commerce of Santa
Fe connected to the rest of northern Mexico, looked to keep Americans out and hoped that the arrest and detainment of Pike might
send a signal to any Santa Fe seekers. The United States did not
know that the governor of New Mexico, Fernando de Chacon,
failed in four forays to intercept Lewis and Clark, hundreds of miles
to the north. Furthermore, military patrols out of Nacogdoches and
smaller posts along the Red River continued to keep Americans
out of the Southwest.[24] As in the Northwest, imperial jostling commenced as the United States announced its presence and economic
interest through military expeditions.

These intrusions meant that Natives across the interior West
met American fur and hide traders for the first time. Fulfilling the
promise of Lewis and Clark, St Louis-based trader Manuel Lisa
promptly seized on the commercial opportunity the captains created. April 1807 – just six months after the captains' return from

Fort Clatsop – saw Lisa and a small party, guided by one of Lewis and Clark's men, head north and west along the Missouri River. Deftly escaping near-battles with the Lakotas and Arikaras and passing through the Mandan-Hidatsa villages, the group of Americans ascended the Yellowstone River and established a trading post at its junction with the Bighorn River. Permanent establishments – not a yearly trip upriver – would make trade more profitable and stable for whites and Indians alike.

From there, Lisa sent out contract traders in every direction, looking to firm up the economic returns that Lewis and Clark's diplomacy made possible. Bands of Shoshones and Crows welcomed Lisa and his men, but they faced violent confrontations with the Blackfeet – who responded as might be expected, given that the Americans armed their enemies. Some conjectured that in sending his men to the south and west of his new fort, Lisa looked to connect himself with Spanish traders out of Santa Fe who occasionally ranged all the way north to the Green River. If successful, he could circumvent both American and Spanish authorities.[25] While his attempt to stretch the trade south to Santa Fe failed, Lisa continued to be a major partner in most fur trade ventures through the 1810s.

As Lisa made his way up the Missouri, a New York capitalist named John Jacob Astor spent time with peers in Montreal, learning more of the lucrative exchange in the Northwest. Inspired by these Canadian traders, Astor, like Lisa, decided that fixed trading posts offered the biggest return on any investment in the fur trade. He planned to build such a permanent post where the Columbia River met the Pacific Ocean. Eyeing Lisa's success on the Bighorn River, Astor believed that the Natives would welcome his men and the steady, regular trading that their permanent presence offered. Although entreaties to President Thomas Jefferson for official government sponsorship failed, the chief executive encouraged the ambitions of the wealthy New Yorker and later noted in a letter to Astor that the project was "the germ of a great, free, and independent empire on that side of our continent." As late as 1816, Jefferson suggested that any American claims to the Northwest relied on "Astor's settlement near the mouth of the Columbia."[26]

The resulting enterprise – known as the Astorians – commenced in 1810. One party left New York City on September 6, aboard a large ship, bound for the mouth of the Columbia via Cape Horn. Stopping in Hawai'i for rest, refitting, and resupply, Astor's men hired 12 Hawai'ians to join their company, dramatically expanding the personal horizons of a dozen islanders. In March 1811, the Astor company finally reached the long-sought river. The treacherous sandbar at its mouth claimed the lives of eight men before the ship safely arrived on the Columbia's south shore. With great hardship, the surviving Americans and Hawai'ians built a full-blown fort with multiple buildings, extensive gardens, livestock, and a blacksmith's forge. Surrounded by a sturdy stockade on a height above the river, Astoria loomed large and permanent and embodied eastern capital invested in western territory.

It attracted Clatsop and Chinook traders immediately. They likely appreciated the new political as well as economic power that access to trade goods granted. In fact, they discouraged other Indians from trading at Astoria, so that they might enjoy a monopoly with the Americans. The white traders, however, plotted to reach out for inland posts that would serve a greater number of Indians and bring more people into the trade.[27]

A second party of Astorians, traveling overland, fared poorly. Leaving St Louis in March 1811 and heading up the Missouri towards the river villages of the Arikaras, Mandans, and Hidatsas, the group narrowly avoided conflict with the Lakotas. Then the travelers turned west and cut across what is now Wyoming. Crossing the Rockies near the Tetons, they worked their way through the Snake River Valley. Exhausting stretches of whitewater and food and water shortages met them at every turn. Only the aid of Shoshones, still acting on memories of Lewis and Clark, managed to get that expedition to the Columbia River. After 11 trying months, the second wave of Astorians arrived at Astoria in February 1812.

The attempt by Astor to plant a clear American claim in the Northwest otter trade fell on hard times soon thereafter. News of war between Great Britain and the United States – the War of 1812 – did not reach Astoria until January 1813. Another troubling report followed quickly; a British flotilla was on its way to the Columbia's mouth to seize Astoria. Astor, the absentee entrepreneur back in New York, attempted to secure an American warship to protect Astoria, but to no avail. A distracted federal government was not about to rush to the aid of a far-off business venture.

In the meantime, along the Columbia, the Astorians made plans to abandon their establishment. By June, British traders arrived at Astoria, but because their allied warships had not yet arrived, a practical deal was struck, splitting up the region's trade for the season. These traders then allowed the Astorians to flee the Northwest in spring 1814. But another, larger contingent of British traders arrived in October, and offered to buy out the Astorians before the Royal Navy arrived. Facing a number of disagreeable scenarios, Astor's employees accepted the terms and hunkered down for the winter; the Union Jack soon flew over the post. Astor himself, safely home in New York, did not learn the fate of his western enterprise until October 1814.[28]

To the south, Santa Fe caught the eye of American entrepreneurs. From St Louis, numerous businessmen pushed their way into the southern Plains and Texas. In 1812, three Americans completed the long trek to Santa Fe, but inhospitable Spanish officials immediately threw them into jail. In 1815, some American trappers tried the road to Taos, where, after a brief welcome from locals, the visitors found themselves behind bars. Still, the area remained enticing to American businessmen, who anticipated healthy profits from the Southwest. National controversy about slavery in the newly acquired territories west of the Mississippi, however, threatened to undo any potential business ventures.

The Missouri Compromise of 1820 determined the illegality of slavery in the new territories west of the Mississippi north of Arkansas' northern border (with the exception of the new state of Missouri). With the contentious question settled, the US government was ready to fund another southwestern expedition staffed with scientists to examine routes to northern Mexico. Under the command of Stephen Long, a topographical engineer, the Americans journeyed west from the Missouri River to find the headwaters of the Red and Arkansas rivers. Within three weeks, they reached the Rocky Mountains. After a month examining the soil and plants along what became known as Colorado's Front Range, Long split his party for the return trip to St Louis.

The first group turned east carrying the expedition's many scientific and geographic observations. The second headed south to locate the still elusive headwaters of the Red River along the US–Spanish border. Disaster struck both companies. Three men from the first group simply disappeared one day, with all the scientific data, never to be seen again. Food ran low for the second group, and they received negligible help from local Natives. Finally, Long's divided men successfully reunited and returned to St Louis.

Stephen Long's published account of the fractured expedition, even without much of its precious data, added greatly to the United States' knowledge of the Southwest. Long, however, accentuated Zebulon Pike's vision of the Great Plains as a grim wasteland unfit for agricultural development by white farmers. Intentionally or not, his work helped commerce trump settlement west of the Mississippi before 1840.

American attempts to penetrate southwestern markets got a boost when indigenous revolutionaries overthrew the Spanish colonial government of New Spain and declared themselves masters of a new nation – Mexico – in 1821. The new government welcomed trade with Americans, especially in and around Santa Fe. Hispana/o merchants eagerly sought links to American firms. These business connections allowed them to turn a dependent and enfeebling relationship with authorities in Mexico City into an independent and profitable relationship with US citizens. Within months, businessmen from St Louis and Santa Fe blazed a freighting road between Missouri and New Mexico. On this famed Santa Fe Trail, for the next 20 years, wagons moved manufactured goods from Missouri to New Mexico and departed Santa Fe loaded with hides, textiles, livestock, and silver anxiously awaited in St Louis.[29]

A few Americans found more lucrative, if dangerous, work through tapping into long-standing trade systems among the Mexicans and Utes, Comanches, and Apaches. Others pursued beaver in northern Mexico's mountains (present-day Utah and Colorado). In 1824, they found themselves censured by the Mexican government, who looked to protect its own complicated commerce in goods, guns, horses, and captives with those Native peoples.[30] The Mexicans decided Americans would be allowed into Santa Fe, but restricted them from dealing in northern Mexico's many Native markets and beaver pelts.

Circumventing the law, American businesses looked to the rivers, mountains, animals, and Indians of the territory north of Santa Fe. There St Louis traders hired trappers to snare beaver pelts used in the production of high quality hats. These trappers were less interested in trading with Natives than in securing furs themselves, an indicator of how Euro American mountain men absorbed the wilderness knowledge of Indians and appropriated it as their own, maneuvering to cut their former Indian allies out of the action.

Jedediah Smith proved the most famous among these independent laborers. Moving to St Louis in the early 1820s, the young man, always reputed to be a Bible-carrying, non-drinking, straight-laced fellow, found himself in a battle between US soldiers and trappers and the Arikaras in 1823. Later that year, he led a group of traders to the Crows in the Bighorn Mountains. There they wintered among the Indians, a sojourn that brought many benefits from their hosts. Because these Americans continued the tradition of supplying rifles and goods that helped the Crows resist their rivals – Blackfeet and Arikaras – these agreeable Indians confided to Smith that many beaver might be found around the headwaters of the Green River. They also pointed him towards South Pass, the easiest passage through the Rockies. Smith's trip through the pass was of pivotal importance, not only to trappers, but also to settlers and travelers for many years to come. American trappers and traders were now poised to range across the interior West and compete with British and even Mexican rivals for Indian alliances.

American diplomats followed quickly behind the trappers. In 1825, a large military expedition moved up the Missouri River, securing treaties with the Poncas, Lakotas, Cheyennes, Arikaras, Hidatsas, and Mandans. Attempts to coax the Assiniboins and Blackfeet to the table failed. The Crows also turned their backs on the American terms. But just 20 years after Lewis and Clark, many of the Natives who rejected the invitation of those Americans formally acknowledged – on paper – the United States' right to regulate trade across the northern Plains and Rocky Mountains and send traders and trappers into those areas with promises of safety. Such assurances of American sovereignty marked a crucial turn for the United States government. White traders and trappers prospered when safe and, in turn, so did their eastern financial backers. Dependence on Indians could take more than one form – and the 1825 treaties pointed to that directly.

While these political matters swirled about, Jedediah Smith and other fur company employees ranged through the Central Rockies and Great Basin, encountering Paiutes, Mojaves, and in November 1826, Mexican officials in California. Ejected soon after his arrival by wary Mexican authorities, Smith moved east, barely surviving the Sierra Nevadas and the vast deserts that surrounded the Great Salt Lake. Smith returned to California and, after another detention, moved north along the Oregon coast. Angering Indians allied with British traders based on the Columbia River at Fort Vancouver,

Smith lost most of his furs. Still, the British welcomed Smith at that post in August 1828, hoping to benefit from Smith's vast geographic knowledge. Indeed, traders there helped Smith to recover his furs from the Umpquas. By the time Smith finally returned to St Louis in 1830, he knew more of the intimate details of the continent than any other American. Shifting his attention to the money to be made shuttling goods between St Louis and Santa Fe, Smith turned to the New Mexico trade. His sudden and somewhat mysterious 1831 death at a waterhole on the Santa Fe Trail abruptly ended his career. His passing limited the dissemination of his vast knowledge among Americans.[31]

Smith's legacy persisted, however, in the general reorientation of economic exchange by the 1830s. Just as the material wealth of New Mexico formerly went south into the heart of Mexico but now flowed east to St Louis, American traders and trappers slowly pulled the animal wealth of the Rockies and Plains to the same entrepot.

The beaver-chasers that came into the Rocky Mountains alongside Jedediah Smith entered into American legend as one of the most powerful and romantic symbols of the American West – the mountain man. Their lives reflected little of the glamour that attached to their memory. Alone for long periods of time, far removed from western centers of intellectual inquiry and learning, they were certainly little interested in the American concepts of democracy and freedom, ideals routinely connected with their life style. More often, they simply hoped to make money.

Living year-round in the peaks and valleys of the Rockies from the early 1820s through the 1830s, these men trapped their own pelts and relied on Indian hospitality – not Indian labor, as most whites before them had done. Sometimes marrying Native women, mountain men enjoyed a network of Indian support at every turn, but one that could be unpredictable. A few among them were African Americans, free men who had put many miles between themselves and the slave states of the South. They set off alone for hunting and trapping or to hire out for the various mountain skills they had acquired in order to avoid the deep-seated racism found in more settled areas.[32]

All trappers risked much and earned little. The hazards of living in remote areas were extreme. Severe weather and prowling animals demanded careful attention. Accidents and death were always a possibility, as was the threat of thieving competitors who might make off with one's cache of pelts. Furthermore, trappers needed to stay alert to Indian rivalries and alliances, understanding that their association with one tribe might guarantee them the enmity of another. Due to Merriwether Lewis' diplomatic *faux pas* all those years before, for instance, the Blackfeet continued to envision Americans as enemies.

Their dangerous enterprise contributed to a rapidly expanding regional economy. Yet the bulk of the profits went to the St Louis-based companies that organized and outfitted trappers at rendezvous, chaotic and colorful annual gatherings that attracted hundreds of people, especially in Cache Valley or along the banks of the Green River. The first few days were devoted to drinking, debauchery, gaming, and fighting. With the trappers physically and emotionally spent, traders opened their wagons of wares – knives and pots, coffee and sugar – for the bargaining, offering as little as possible for the premium pelts. At the end of rendezvous, the men, pelts sold and already in debt for yearly supplies they had purchased, set off alone for another year of trapping. So it was that at least one contemporary saw little romance in the mountain men's lives, arguing to a friend that the trapper was little more than "a mere slave to catch Beaver for others."[33]

Another complication quickly developed in this mountain business – indiscriminate over-trapping. Within little more than a decade, the mountain men trapped out most of the beaver in watersheds across the Rocky Mountains. Beavers' low birth rate and sedentary life made their populations especially vulnerable to collapse when pressured by continuous harvests. Thus the mountain men undermined their long-term prospects with short-term greed. *like this line.* With each passing year, the quality of the beaver declined, as did the poor income of the trappers. With the disappearance of the best animals and with a change in European fashion that substituted silk for beaver felt in fine hats, the Rocky Mountain trade faded almost as quickly as it materialized.

Less likely to be remembered but much more significant were the denizens of fixed fur trading posts along the upper Missouri River who traded directly with Indian men and women. Here traders, with their stores of manufactured goods, prodded Natives to harvest bison robes, valuable when transformed into durable leather belts to power the machinery of industrializing New England.

This trade fit into Indian lives quite well. Bison-centered cultures

Figure 2.2 European and American artists traveling with western expeditions produced visual images of the West, trying to record what they saw and also capitalize on western themes as a means to accrue popularity and profit. *Source:* Titian Ramsay Peale sketches, *Bison Bulls*, February 1820, watercolor 65. Courtesy, American Philosophical Society.

along the Upper Missouri already pursued buffalo hunting with vigor. That white traders now wanted tanned bison hides simply broadened the buffalo's importance from culture-sustaining animal to culture-changing conduit. The seamless merger of American and Indian interests in the Upper Missouri hide trade resulted in generally friendly relations through the 1830s. More ecologically stable then the Rocky Mountain beaver industry, the bison trade nonetheless came at a gradual environmental cost that would be paid decades later.

Using keelboats to navigate the Missouri River through the 1820s, and larger, more efficient steamboats in the 1830s, fur companies based in St Louis supplied posts on a regular basis. That nearly every hide trading center stood on the banks of the river pointed to the importance of the watercourse itself in this exchange. The Missouri served as the basic artery by which trade goods reached the posts and furs and hides returned to St Louis.

This regular shuttling via boat meant that the fur trade on the Upper Missouri relied on permanent American posts, reducing the role of the vagabond trapper. This shift from traveling traders and trappers built on an earlier tradition of resident French and British traders in the region, as well as the efforts of Manuel Lisa. With their stores restocked every year, the American fur trading posts involved more people and required more careful organization and coordination than previous fur trade enterprises. Furthermore, the permanent posts employed a wider variety of employees – Natives, mixed-heritage peoples, African American, French Canadians, Scots, Americans – in a wider variety of occupations – laborers, bookkeepers, blacksmiths, hunters, interpreters, as well as traders. As a result, an American presence much larger and more diverse than ever before dominated the Upper Missouri.

Even the posts themselves – storage depots, living quarters, social centers, and centers of commerce – seemed more permanent. Square timber stockades surrounded bunkhouses, warehouses, and workshops. Mimicking hundreds of years of Plains Indian village agriculture, gardens surrounded these riverside stockades, where the ground and water groaned under the weight of the environmental challenges.

The largest and most important of the fur and hide trading posts included Fort Union, at the junction of the Yellowstone and Missouri rivers, Fort Clark, near the Mandan-Hidatsa villages, Fort Pierre, in modern-day South Dakota, and Fort Cass, at the junction of the Yellowstone and Bighorn rivers. Geography played a crucial role. Fort Union lay astride one of the most important river junctions in the entire West. Sometimes Americans erected posts to take advantage of already existing Native commercial centers – such as Fort Clark's carefully selected location next to the Mandans or Fort Pierre's careful placement near the Lakotas. In other cases, Indians demanded that posts be erected to better serve their communities. For example, Crows who wearied of long travels to Fort Clark, negotiated with the Americans to build the much closer Fort Cass in 1832.

The fur trade society that grew up around these posts relied on Natives as much as on boats from St Louis. Most notably, the bison trade of the Upper Missouri required the crucial presence of

Indian women in both commerce and intercultural complicity. Plains women cemented the collusion between Americans and Indians that produced a profitable trade for both. Through the early 1700s, as corn growers and hide tanners, Native women had been the primary traders in pre-contact exchange. But with the arrival of horses and guns on the Plains in the years immediately before Lewis and Clark, trading responsibilities slipped away from Indian women. With the establishment of permanent American fur trading posts, they regained much of that role, and bolstered shared Indian–white interests.

Women did more than transform raw hides into finished robes. Lucrative kinship relations between Plains tribes and white traders developed when Native women married fur trade employees. As Indian women acquired status in their own communities and at trading posts through their interracial relationships, the fur and hide companies made them instruments of extraction. Both parties, in some sense, got what they wanted. The trade goods and those who trafficked them benefited Native women and their kin. Fur traders, in turn, could count on a steady supply of furs and bison hides.[34] They also enjoyed the personal comforts, sexual opportunities, dietary advantages, and cultural connection offered by these partnerships.

By the mid-1830s, Indians still controlled the bulk of what would become the American West. They had weathered – with difficulty – epidemic disease and the changed intertribal relations that resulted from the imperial designs of far-off governments in Mexico City, London, Moscow, and Washington, DC. Woven into world economies and distant commercial centers such as Canton in China, Santa Fe in northern Mexico, and St Louis in the United States, Natives seemed to be holding their own. Newcomers of many stripes had been met and treated with the courtesy and curiosity that each Indian community, negotiating a complicated web of politics and economics, could spare. *high intelligence! (U.S. took adv. but*

Ominous storm clouds, however, lingered. So, even as they gained *disrg* new wealth and power through trade, some Natives looked east and sensed that their worlds stood poised at the brink of fresh and less easily navigated challenges.

One force came from an unexpected quarter. Brought on by commerce, confusion, and collusion, the resulting conflict – a gradual, often violent process of transforming Native homelands into the American West – was further spurred before 1840 by burgeoning scientific knowledge. The collection of data that followed the establishment of permanent posts grew exponentially. It was organized and used in ways that favored the Americans who assembled their new information within a context that fit their own educational vision.

Information about the interior West – first collected for Americans by Lewis and Clark – came from intellectuals as well as explorers. With the 1825 treaties that secured safe passage for Americans along the Missouri River, a bevy of gentleman scientists scrutinized the northern Plains and foothills of the Rocky Mountains in the 1830s. Hosted by American traders at the Upper Missouri fur and hide forts, these men of leisure and learning, often with large retinues, studied western nature. Adding to the Euro American knowledge of the natural world involved more than collecting data and adding specimens to natural history collections. Placing local flora, fauna, and Indian peoples into a comparative process of collection and classification, these men advanced knowledge that aided whites in their eventual seizure of western lands. If knowledge was power, whites gained more and more every year. They also conflated Natives with animals and landscapes. Their ethnographic study that seamlessly overlapped with naturalist collecting actually served to dehumanize Indians, who became "specimens" alongside, grasses, animals, birds, and trees. superiority.

Two men – one, an artist, the other, a naturalist – made particular contributions to this process. George Catlin left his law practice to become an artist of Indian America after seeing a contingent of Winnebagoes at a museum of natural history in Philadelphia. In his paintings of Indians, whom he thought would soon be extinct due to inroads made by trade and diseases, he wanted to "fix and preserve" what he saw as their "wild" essence.[35] Catlin arrived on the Great Plains in 1830 and for six years carefully engaged in both written and artistic observations of a variety of Indian communities. Through portrait and landscape paintings, he tried to capture as much ethnographic information as possible.

After returning east, Catlin charged admission to thousands of visitors eager to see his "Indian gallery." In 1839, he began a tour of Europe, showing his vision of Native America to people around the world. The publication of his written journals in 1841 furthered his fame. The public's fascination with his paintings, however, faded, and by the 1850s the bankrupt Catlin tried unsuccessfully to resurrect his reputation through paintings of South America.

Prince Maximilian of Wied won less fame among the general public but more among naturalists. A German prince, he fought against Napoleon in the Prussian army and studied natural sciences at the University of Göttingen. In 1815, with a passion for zoology sparked by his education and his friendships with leading European scientists, Maximilian traveled across Brazil. Soon after, he turned his attentions to North America, most notably on a trip to the Upper Missouri from 1832 to 1834. Scientifically cataloging everything from Native vocabularies to the area's meteorology to local birds and plants, the prince returned to Europe and published *Travels in the Interior of North America.* Its compilation of climate patterns and linguistic data, along with full color prints of Indians, plants, animals, and landscapes, rendered by the Swiss artist Karl Bodmer, excited scientists across the continent and left a unique ethnographic record.

The finished products of both expeditions testified to the processes for the making of natural histories and subsequently their relation to Euro American imperialism. Neither Catlin nor Maximilian took up permanent western residence. They seemed more interested in bringing the Indian West back to fellow ethnographers, naturalists, and the public than in becoming westerners. Through paint, brush, and canvas, or specimen collection, or scientific instruments, they worked hard to make the particular animals, plants, and Indians of the Great Plains part of an understandable and larger whole. Both expanded knowledge by studying the local world they encountered – living or not – and recording or reproducing what they saw. This work translated the objects at hand into recognizable objects for others from America and Europe to examine, adding to the international education and scientific imperatives of the early nineteenth century.

Exporting the tiny, quantified bits of the local – species names, journal entries, temperature readings, portraits of Indians, physical specimens, landscape paintings – to centralized locations such as London, Paris, Berlin, Philadelphia, or New York allowed Euro-American culture to understand more places and peoples in one sweep than any indigenous person could do at that time. In a single building equipped with specimen cases, portrait gallery, and library, a white scholar could travel to far-off continents and peoples in a moment. Those who never ventured beyond the metropolitan centers of Western culture literally held the rest of the globe – including parts of the Indian West – at their fingertips. Catlin and Maximilian and others insured that the West became part of this exponential increase in world knowledge. They funneled the Indian West into endpoints of a collecting network that ultimately fostered European and American imperialism.[36]

Although proponents of European knowledge systems promoted Indian images and culture through learning outside the American West, inside the region disaster lurked. Microbiological invaders attacked Indians as no humans had done, wreaking demographic havoc. Viruses and bacteria borne by Indians and whites alike traveled through Native communities. 1837 saw a new wave of the vicious smallpox sweep across the West. Already pummeled by a series of epidemics that swept Indian homelands from the 1600s on, Native communities struggled to grapple with yet another punishing outbreak of fatal disease. Most directly affecting Mandans, Hidatsas, Lakotas, Pawnees, Blackfeet, and Assiniboins, nearly 20,000 Indians died in a two-year period.

Spread from Europe to North America in early 1837, the smallpox virus, which claimed whites but in lesser numbers, followed Lewis and Clark's original route north and west from St Louis along the Missouri River. Carried by a passenger on a steamboat used to resupply the hide-trading posts of Fort Pierre, Fort Clark, and Fort Union, smallpox spread across the Great Plains in the summer of 1837. Infected passengers disembarked at the Council Bluffs Indian Agency, which served the Omahas and the Pawnees. Further upriver, Indian agent Joshua Pilcher returned to his post at Fort Pierre, unknowingly bringing the disease to Lakotas, who fled to avoid the sickness. Three Arikara women, exposed to the virus on board the ship, carried smallpox to Fort Clark and the surrounding Mandan and Hidatsa villagers.

By the time the steamboat reached Fort Union, employees looked to nip the blossoming epidemic in the bud. Desperate to stem the mounting deaths, save their Indian families, and maintain their local control, whites at Fort Union tried to inoculate the Native women who lived with them in the fort. All the women died. Death soon spread uncontrollably – including among Blackfeet and Assiniboins visiting the fort. These Indians returned to their bands, where smallpox soon raged.[37]

Francis Chardon, the head trader at Fort Clark, graphically described the smallpox's spread among the Mandans – who lost about 90 percent of their population to this especially virulent siege. At the height of the epidemic, the long-time fur trade employee saw "Several Men, Women, and Children . . . lying dead in the lodges, some out side of the Village, others in the little river not entered, which creates a very bad smell all around us." Some of the dying committed suicide, or murdered wives, infants, and children in futile attempts to spare family members the horrific death caused by the pox.

Native social organization unraveled. In the ensuing chaos, Indian anger mounted. Those not yet in the last stages of the disease claimed that "it was time to begin to Kill the Whites, as it was them that brought the small pox in the Country." Chardon realized he and his white companions remained "badly situated, as we are threatened to be Murdered by the Indians every instant." Fulfilling that prophecy, an Arikara man killed one of Chardon's employees. The lethal smallpox slew the rest of the angry Natives before they could carry out their threats.[38]

The long-standing trade center on the upper Missouri collapsed as the Mandans died in droves. What had brought them great wealth – working as middle-men and women in a trade that stretched across the continent for almost a century – now turned against them by bringing a microscopic invader into their midst. Devastated, within two months after the smallpox disaster, the surviving Mandans fled their village and Fort Clark for refuge among nearby Hidatsa villagers. With smallpox sweeping the continent and killing the very people critical to economic exchange, Fort Clark and the broader hide trade teetered on irrelevancy.

Yet, previous experiences of Indian–white collaboration mitigated tensions among the survivors. For example, a group of Arikaras moved into the abandoned Mandan village within a year, likely attracted by benefits to be accrued from the proximity of Fort Clark. Like other survivors across the Plains, they redoubled their involvement in the trade, leaning on it more and more to overcome the demographic calamity that threatened tribal extinction.

Nonetheless, coming epidemics of cholera and influenza in the 1840s and 1850s darkly foreshadowed more Indian–white conflict. The pre-1840 diseases that weakened Native peoples, robbed them of their leaders, sapped their potential to rebound in numbers or spirit ensured that of the four dynamics introduced when Natives first met Lewis and Clark – conflict, collusion, confusion, and commerce – conflict would dominate.

The 1837 smallpox epidemic coincided with a financial panic that spread, virus-like, across the United States. Economic growth, sustained by the rapid expansion of cotton cultivation and canal construction, buoyed the young nation through the early 1830s. Cotton exports to Europe soared. Hauling cotton and other agricultural commodities to market required roads and canals. Known in the parlance of the time as "internal improvements," securing public support for the creation of a transportation infrastructure proved problematic. Connecting markets and populations in the East to the broad and rich lands that many hoped would someday become an American – not a Native – West, this growing transportation infrastructure incurred major debts. States rushed to build capital-intensive connectors to points west as it became politically untenable for an increasingly divided federal government to do so. Financed on credit or through rampant speculation, new companies also looked to build canals that could move people and goods ever westward, towards the Mississippi. In the boom, inflation grew, and financial instability expanded with it.

The bubble burst in May 1837. Fur traders and trappers felt economic pain, but the exchange with Natives rebounded quickly as demand for pelts and hides transcended devalued currencies. Other economic sectors – especially real estate and banking – collapsed entirely.

The six-year long depression that followed the panic, complete with rampant unemployment, did not last indefinitely. Yet it did shape the future. The dislocations caused by the Panic of 1837 dampened the nation's enthusiasm for expansion – just as smallpox and a growing Euro American understanding of the interior West eroded Native sovereignty and sustainability on lands west of the Mississippi. From the wreckage of the panic came financial and political openings for privately-built and controlled railroad systems, which soon rendered canals obsolete. Those railroads would eventually stretch across plains and mountains alike.[39]

The Panic of 1837 briefly cooled the expansionist ardor of the United States even as it pointed to the West's future. In the short term, Americans of every stripe and background agreed that the nation needed a transportation infrastructure to match its land

holdings east of the Mississippi. They simply disagreed about
how to pursue such ends. In the long term, an east–west network
offered direct access to the economic riches of lands west of the
Mississippi.

As the 1840s dawned, Native peoples reflected on the transformations of the previous 40 years – rearranged political alliances, an
expanded understanding of international diplomacy, and in some
cases, the accumulation of great wealth and power. Indians contem-
plated these matters, however, while reeling from pandemic diseases
that left them weakened in every way. Ahead lay future challenges
as the ungenerous Americans readied themselves for another major
push into the West – this time with unprecedented military might.

reference to the future.

NOTES

1 *New England Palladium* (Boston, MA), September 23, 1803.
2 James P. Ronda, ed., *Thomas Jefferson and the Changing West: From
   Conquest to Conservation* (Albuquerque: University of New Mexico
   Press, 1997).
3 *New England Palladium* (Boston, MA), September 23, 1803.
4 Gary E. Moulton, ed., *The Lewis and Clark Journals: An American
   Epic of Discovery, The Abridgement of the Definitive Nebraska Edi-
   tion* (Lincoln: University of Nebraska Press, 2003), 375.
5 James R. Gibson, *Otter Skins, Boston Ships, and China Goods: The
   Maritime Fur Trade of the Northwest Coast, 1785–1841* (Seattle: University of Washington Press, 1992), 36–61.
6 Alan Taylor, *American Colonies* (New York: Viking, 2001), 444–77.
7 Donald Jackson, *Thomas Jefferson and the Rocky Mountains: Explor-
   ing the West from Monticello* (1981; Norman: University of Oklahoma
   Press, 2002), 121–5.
8 Donald Jackson, ed., *Letters of the Lewis and Clark Expedition with
   Related Documents*, 2 vols (1962; Urbana: University of Illinois Press,
   1978).
9 Gavan Daws, *Shoal of Time: A History of the Hawaiian Islands* (Honolulu: University of Hawai'i Press, 1968), 1–60. For the prominence of
   Americans in the seaborne Pacific Northwest trade in 1800, see Tables
   1 and 6 in Gibson, *Otter Skins, Boston Ships, and China Goods*,
   299–302, 313.
10 Elizabeth Fenn, *Pox Americana: The Great Smallpox Epidemic of
   1775–1782* (New York: Hill and Wang, 2001).
11 Calloway, *One Vast Winter Count*, 426.

12 Quoted in James P. Ronda, *Lewis and Clark among the Indians* (Lincoln: University of Nebraska Press, 1984), 30.

13 Moulton, ed., *The Lewis and Clark Journals*, 47.

14 Ronda, *Lewis and Clark among the Indians*, 35.

15 Quintard Taylor, *In Search of the Racial Frontier*, 27–32.

16 Moulton, ed., *The Lewis and Clark Journals*, 55. See also Robert B. Betts, *In Search of York: The Slave Who Went to the Pacific with Lewis and Clark* (Boulder: Colorado Associated University Press, 1985).

17 Moulton, ed., *The Lewis and Clark Journals*, 135.

18 Ibid., 185.

19 Ronda, *Lewis and Clark among the Indians*, 161–2.

20 Moulton, ed., *The Lewis and Clark Journals*, 228.

21 Ronda, *Lewis and Clark among the Indians*, 172.

22 Moulton, ed., *The Lewis and Clark Journals*, 236.

23 Zebulon Montgomery Pike, *An Account of Expeditions to the Sources of the Mississippi and through the Western Parts of Louisiana* (Philadelphia: C. and A. Conrad, 1810), Appendix to Part II, 8.

24 Weber, *The Spanish Frontier in North America*, 294–6.

25 William H. Goetzman, *Exploration and Empire: The Explorer and the Scientist in the Winning of the American West* (New York: W. W. Norton, 1966), 19–20.

26 John P. Foley, ed., *The Jefferson Cyclopedia: A Comprehensive Collection of the Views of Thomas Jefferson* (New York: Funk and Wagnells, 1900), entries 591, 592.

27 James P. Ronda, *Astoria and Empire* (Lincoln: University of Nebraska Press, 1990).

28 Ibid.

29 Susan Calafate Boyle, *Los Capitalistas: Hispano Merchants and the Santa Fe Trade* (Albuquerque: University of New Mexico Press, 1997) and Stephen G. Hyslop, *Bound for Santa Fe: The Road to New Mexico and the American Conquest, 1806–1848* (Norman: University of Oklahoma Press, 2002).

30 For more on this trade, see Brooks, *Captives and Cousins*.

31 David J. Weber, *The Californios versus Jedediah Smith, 1826–1827: A New Cache of Documents* (Spokane: Arthur H. Clark, 1990) and Dale T. Morgan, *Jedediah Smith and the Opening of the West* (Lincoln: University of Nebraska Press, 1964).

32 Taylor, *In Search of the Racial Frontier*, 48–52.

33 Nathaniel J. Wyeth to M. J. Sublette, July 1, 1834, in *The Correspondence and Journals of Captain Nathaniel J. Wyeth, 1831–6* (Eugene: Oregon University Press, 1899).

34 Michael J. Lansing, "Plains Indian Women and Interracial Marriage in

the Upper Missouri Trade, 1804–1868," *Western Historical Quarterly* 31:4 (Winter 2000): 413–33.

35 George Catlin, *Letters and Notes on the Manners, Customs, and Conditions of North American Indians* (1844; New York: Dover Publications, 1973), vol. 1, 2.

36 For more on this process around the globe, see Bruno Latour, *Science in Action: How to Follow Scientists and Engineers through Society* (Cambridge: Harvard University Press, 1987), 215–47.

37 Clyde D. Dollar, "The High Plains Smallpox Epidemic of 1837–38," *Western Historical Quarterly* 8:1 (January 1977): 15–38.

38 Annie Heloise Abel, ed., *Chardon's Journal at Fort Clark, 1834–1839* (1932; Lincoln: University of Nebraska Press, 1997), 127–33.

39 John Lauritz Larson, *Internal Improvement: National Public Works and the Promise of Popular Government in the Early United States* (Chapel Hill: University of North Carolina Press, 2001).

Chapter 3

Enforcing an American West

Our national birth was the beginning of a new history . . . in moral, political, and national life, we may confidently assume that our country is destined to be the great nation of the futurity.[1]

In 1839, John L. O'Sullivan, the New York editor who penned those words, wrote with the verve and good cheer that seemed quite natural to anyone with an eye to the developing West of the European Americans. What was there not be cheerful about? In less than 50 years, a handful of colonists had vanquished the most powerful nation in the world, not once but twice. Other European countries, with their own lustful schemes in North America, had to pause and reassess the potential of this new nation filled with political and economic upstarts. The country had muscled its way into world arenas and nurtured its thirst for expansion. While Native tribes in the Far West had negotiated places within the changing economics, managed exchanges with trappers, traders, and explorers, and positioned themselves for continuing relationships with Europeans and Americans, the outcomes of certain parallel events were going to have a direct impact on their lives. In the view of some, the future for the United States, as a national power and as an international participant, seemed bright. For others these thoughts were not reassuring.

In part, because of Thomas Jefferson – who never crossed the Mississippi River into the Far West but promoted it from the East – people of many stripes coveted that turf. But first they wanted to know more about it. An enthusiastic American press brought the descriptions of land and adventures of explorers to the stay-at-home easterners, allowing them to read about the flora and fauna, the people, land, and excitement of a seemingly endlessly exotic world. Eastern writers like James Fenimore Cooper, Washington Irving, and Francis Parkman brought literary authenticity to western images for people who would never travel to the actual towns and vistas. Their descriptions encouraged readers to imagine the West beyond as a pristine garden, one where salubrious climates, lush vegetation, exotic animals, and rich landscapes mixed together forming a near paradise for the taking. In poetry and song, the American West became more than the world beyond; it became the heart of many Americans. All that was needed was a powerful voice, such as O'Sullivan's, to articulate the impulses that had been energizing the imaginations of Americans for more than 25 years.

That western world in reality was taking on more complexity and facing more complications with each passing decade after 1800. Although the sentimental celebrated the wilderness aspects of western life, there was, especially in the Old Northwest, an urban dimension to the area that influenced economic structures, personal mobility, and cultural forms throughout the region. Commerce and transportation were key ingredients in the organizing of towns and those ingredients often accounted for the agricultural success or failure realized by farmers in the surrounding areas. Thus, early on these changing western spaces were a major influence in the construction of urban versus rural dynamics that came to dominate a considerable amount of American life.

There were other thorny issues. Economic depressions ravaged the country on a nearly seasonal basis, the Panic of 1837 only the most recent debacle. It had a bit of western flavor, closely linked as it was to poor lending practices associated with the highly competitive building of canals to reach the interior. The transportation network envisioned through canals had collapsed before the system of waterways had been completed, falling victim to the rising demand for railroad construction. At the same time, European immigrants flooded the nation, bringing new customs, odd tongues, unpopular religions, and a thirst for American jobs. The country strained against the broad range of demands the rapid changes made on its infrastructure. Housing, food production, education, and government were only some of the resources challenged by a swift growth in population. Especially at risk were those areas where the infra-structure itself was still in its infancy and they included the West.

On the political front, white southerners looked to the North with hardened eyes. White northerners looked on the South with growing contempt. Democrats and Whigs squared off against each other, the volume of their heated exchanges rising with each decade. The two parties seized any opportunity, as seen in the US Senate, to keep the political atmosphere hostile.[2]

All these conflicts rested in some fashion in the ugly matter of black slavery, too glibly described as a difference between the southern agricultural economy and the northern industrial complex. Most white Americans in all regions probably overlooked how the western commerce in Indian slaves contributed to the toleration of slavery for all persons of color. Regardless of what O'Sullivan had said about national confidence, underlying the country's very life was the paradox of an unmitigated system of human bondage in a nation constructed on the principles of freedom. Employers debated the benefits of paying wages versus maintaining a slave work force. Calls for free labor butted against racial coercion, leaving all the participants angered. The answers to many of these problems would be found in land, specifically the land of the American West.

Travelers bumping along the National Road, authorized by Thomas Jefferson in 1806, knew the answer was "land," even if other Americans did not. Here was more than 700 miles of roadway cutting a swath from Maryland to Indiana and Illinois, literally connecting the East and the West. Why have such a highway, if not to gain access to the American wilderness, to move beyond the turmoil of the East, with its increasingly nasty racial tones, explore new vistas, develop fresh markets of commerce, and extract the best from what appeared to be land for the taking? How better to sustain government expansionist and economic goals than to move its citizens into unsettled areas under the protection and sovereignty of the American flag? More than a national road had prepared the way for these travelers. The echo of voices from earlier events in Native and white communities proved to have a lingering impact and to bolster a sense of entitlement so often evident among those moving in on Indian lands at mid-century.

For example, the lessons about the value of the West had been learned from no less a personage than Andrew Jackson and they lasted well beyond his death in 1845. He gave Americans a "feel" for the back country, an image of what a "frontiersman" and, by extension, an American, should be like. He had defied the British in both the Revolution and the War of 1812 and in both cases did so away from the Atlantic Coast. He knew how to move through the hinterlands of North Carolina and Tennessee, at each phase of his life facing deeper toward the inner country, rather than turning to the East. He eschewed building a residence among the elite of Virginia, thus giving off the aura of man from the backwoods. So, Americans could overlook the fact that the Hermitage, Jackson's elegant home in Tennessee, was as much a slave plantation as any in Virginia or the Carolinas. When "Old Hickory" turned back to Washington to assume the presidency, he did so with the tight-lipped, angry-eyed visage that bespoke more of no-nonsense "frontiersman" and less of mannerly eastern gentleman. No matter, Jackson's rough edges were seen as admirable traits, to be expected of an ordinary person who lived in the hardscrabble world of the West.[3]

These characteristics gave legitimacy to Jackson's distaste for Native people. After all, no "true" "frontiersman" should be expected to tolerate either the presence or attitudes of Indian people. In this thinking, white Americans followed the poor lead of their government, which after the American Revolution had failed to organize and implement a clear and consistent policy concerning Native people living under the jurisdiction of the US Constitution, despite the best efforts of tribes to define their place and role. In 1824, bureaucratic efforts to reign in Indian relations had been placed with the Indian Department, under the authority of the War Department.[4] The placement of a civil agency within one devoted to military matters gave rise to confusion at both the federal and local level, compromised the nation's diplomatic integrity, and left Indian tribes scrambling to identify the best strategy for responding to American imperatives, whether of peace or war.

None felt this problem more than the Sauks and Mesquakies, led in the 1830s by Black Hawk. Burdened by a turbulent diplomatic history, the tribes, typically allied with the British, felt the crunch of advancing white settlement in the area of the Old Northwest. Black Hawk refused to yield, striving to retain fields in the Midwest and hunting areas further to the west. The goal was to hold some land for gardens in Illinois, while hunting for game west of the Mississippi River. In 1832, pillaging Americans wiped out the crops and agricultural stores. Black Hawk, fresh from his hunt in the West, retaliated, and settlers lashed back. After a first victory, Black Hawk was betrayed by his one-time friends the British, Native allies, and a political competitor in his own ranks. His American captors displayed him as a defeated foe, hoping, unsuccessfully, to convince other Indians of the futility of Native resistance. *superiority of whites*

This outcome for American settlers gave ballast to Jackson's refusal, as president, to implement the 1837 decision of the US Supreme Court that the Cherokees, members of the Five Civilized Tribes of the Southeast, could not be removed from their land by the states of Georgia and Alabama. The resulting diaspora saw more than 15,000 Indians forced off their land and removed to Indian Territory, in present-day Oklahoma.[5]

Anti-Indian types and residents living close to the desired land applauded the removal, as a way to rid the states of Natives who refused to "Americanize." In fact, these Southeast Indians had "Americanized" themselves quite successfully. Since the 1820s they had a written language and the production of their own newspaper pointed to the growing literacy. Cherokee political actions included acceptance of a new constitution, one that mirrored the tri-partite governing structure of the United States. Their entrepreneurial ventures included sawmills and local ferries. Wealthier families lived in substantial brick homes, owned black slaves, and used them in the tribal cotton fields. Those of lesser wealth, usually full-blood tribal members, lived on small farms where they raised cotton by their own labor. Overall, the agricultural productivity of the Cherokees generated envy in their white neighbors, whose land lust intensified after gold was discovered on Indian property.

Pro-Indian advocates and friends of the Cherokees were not of one mind on the question of forced Indian removal. Some religious reformers, however, accepted the program, arguing that it *how?* might be in the best interests of Native people. At least, William McLean (D–OH), chairman of the Committee of Indian Affairs in the US House of Representatives suggested as much to his colleagues, providing them with a letter from a government delegate to the Indians, who declared "the humane and enlightened missionaries of the South . . . are of the opinion that nothing but such a plan can save them from ultimate and final destruction."[6] According to their thinking, if Indians were isolated from the corrupting influences, especially alcohol and gambling, of white society, they would be able to make cultural adjustments more smoothly – a spurious

this didn't age well.

conclusion since these Natives had already engaged in several forms
of sophisticated acculturation.

Chief John Ross informed the US Senate that the 1836 Treaty of
New Echota that endorsed removal was opposed by the majority
of Cherokee voters and had not been approved by the Cherokee
legislature, but the federal body moved ahead with ratification. Ultimately, those who opposed the removal plan were rounded up and
banished from their homes. In March 1837, they had been told by
General John E. Wool, the officer overseeing removal, that "I have
not come among you to oppress you, but to protect you and to see
that justice is done you, as guaranteed by the treaty."[7] However,
as the cold of the 1838 winter approached, the Cherokees were
herded off on a devastating march from Georgia to Arkansas and
Oklahoma.

Despite General Wool's assurances, the troops assigned to protect
the refuges refused to do so, instead allowing a variety of violations
to occur. As a result, whites following the exodus assaulted Indian
families with impunity, stealing the few goods they carried in their
wagons. For that matter, the bystanders also confiscated the wagons
and the draft animals. Among Native people, this event, wherein
approximately 4,000 died, became known as the "Trail of Tears," a
march so brutal that years later survivors often refused to speak of
it to their children and grandchildren.

Most especially there had been no thought or care given to the
outcomes of depositing thousands of people into an alien environment without their permission or that of the existing community.
The Indians of the Southeast had no history of life in an eco-system
so dramatically different from their home. The aridity and lack of
timbered land proved a hardship for these inhabitants of the eastern
woodlands. In addition, no decent provision was made for a transition in their agricultural economy from the East to the West.

Of further difficulty were the resulting Indian–Indian tensions
that arose in Oklahoma. No one had negotiated with the indigenous Oklahoma Indians about cultural and economic changes that
could result from a sudden infusion of different tribes. The Osages,
Comanches, and Kiowas, who had not agreed to give space to the
newcomers, resented the arrival of the Southeast Indians. Without adequate social and cultural preparation, not to mention the
economic crisis, there was no way that the Oklahoma land could
absorb the increased populations with ease, and frictions continued

for some period of time. The forging of new economies and new relationships challenged all the Native groups involved and their successes were often tempered by yet another arbitrary move by the US government.

The results for or responses of indigenous people forced off their land were not central to the strategies of white politicians and the desires of white settlers. Events in Texas further highlighted that reality.

Ironically, in the 1820s, the ambitions of the government in Mexico City provided the framework for the migrations that brought white American settlers into a vast territory of Indians and Tejana/os. In 1821, the people of Mexico succeeded in casting off the ruling power of Spain and turned toward the complex task of governing a massive territory, hindered by a weak system of communications, rural versus urban tensions, unclear international relations with Natives and Americans, and disagreements about political goals. Seeking to stabilize the northern border between Mexico and the United States, Mexican authorities devised a plan for controlled settlement by white Americans. They foresaw that such a strategy would provide a buffer zone between the two countries, extend the arm of Mexican authority into the hard-to-protect northern territory, and deflect the hostility that Texas Indians, especially the Comanches, held for Mexico.[8]

The Mexicans agreed to offer land grants – as much as 200,000 acres – to American men to be called *empresarios* – the first and most famous being Moses Austin, who at his death passed the authority to his son, Stephen. It became the duty of the *empresario* to organize the administration of a colony, doling out parcels to settlers and artisans who would populate, cultivate, and develop the land. From the early 1820s, Americans showed a land-greedy spirit in Texas. To prevent the émigrés from schemes to infiltrate beyond their appointed lands and deeper into Mexican territory, the Mexico City government, by the Immigration Law of 1830, outlined provisions by which the American must abide. The Mexicans gamely hoped that three restrictions would impose order on their plan: settlers had to be Roman Catholic, no slavery was permitted within the granted lands, and only family units, no single men, were allowed in the area.

The plan reflected the legitimate concerns of those in Mexico City, who understood the growing expansionist dangers and deeply rooted racist attitudes when dealing with the Americans.[9] Certainly, the Mexicans, heavily burdened under the Spanish, had reasons to feel uneasy about the racial politics of the Anglos, but the "no slavery" dictate appeared almost naive when inviting cotton farmers into Texas. It also demonstrated their unrealistic expectations for their own ability to control lands hundreds of miles from their government agencies, particularly when these lacked a solid infrastructure. Further, they ignored the already relentless land absorption by American settlers, since they blasted past the unenforceable restrictions of the Proclamation of 1763, nearly 70 years earlier.

The conditions for settlement quickly evaporated among Americans, who tended to flow into Texas from southern states known for their Protestantism, cotton agriculture, and black slavery. The Mexican dictates were easily abused: Protestant settlers pretended to follow Catholicism, black slaves were "freed" upon arrival in Texas and immediately "agreed" to a lifetime of service, and bands of single male adventurers flowed unceasingly across the border. Mexico made some concessions concerning the immigration rules, but the Americans grumbled, nonetheless. Rules aside, the size of the *empresario* land grants only whetted the appetite for more acreage among the Americans, whose land-harsh crops of tobacco and cotton had stripped their home soil of much of its vitality.

Other tensions also swirled through the countryside. While Stephen Austin was temporarily under arrest in Mexico City, colonists in Texas, freed from the *empresario*'s accommodating personality, indulged themselves in unrestrained saber rattling. Not all Tejana/os around the Americans supported the cumbersome and corrupt government in Mexico City. Some could see possible advantages in helping the rebellion-minded Americans to overthrow the increasingly disliked military-minded Antonio López de Santa Ana, who had figured prominently in the Mexican ousting of Spain.

The international stage was set for a confrontation between the infuriated Mexican government and the bellicose American settlers. No doubt the Americans dismissed the Mexicans as an easy target, for in their short residence, Anglos had done little to check their sense of political and economic superiority, not to mention their certitude concerning their racial superiority. It did not take much to convince some settlers that is was their duty to "free" Texas, although from what was blurry. The Americans, however, had learned about revolution through their own country's break with Britain and they knew about the importance of creating legitimacy, when acting in an illegal manner. On March 2, 1836, 60 delegates signed a declaration of independence that with its language of "inestimable and inalienable rights," "the usual instruments of tyrants," and "abolish such government, and create another . . ." suggested a close bond with the sacred documents of the founding of the United States.[10]

The resulting clash that roiled over the Texas countryside, less than 20 years after Mexico had invited the Americans to establish limited settlements, introduced a new set of heroic icons for some Americans: Davy Crockett, William Travis, and Jim Bowie. Each was an American émigré, who decided to cast his lot with the organizers of the Texas Revolution. The three died inside an abandoned San Antonio mission, the Alamo, on March 6, 1836. Their deaths were by order of General Santa Ana, who spent a week bombarding the fort before sending almost 2,000 soldiers careening across the crumbling walls to deliver a gory end to the fewer than 200 rebels. Ignored in this tale, destined to epitomize, in romantic terminology, American heroism against all odds, were the Tejana/os, inside the Alamo, who stood shoulder to shoulder with the Anglos; those men represented and died for their neighbors and families opposed to the increasingly repressive governance of Santa Ana.[11]

With the collapse at San Antonio, the names of Travis, Crockett, and Bowie became synonymous with the concepts of bravery and defiance, freedom and independence. How those traits applied to a group that had in actuality betrayed its arrangements with the legitimate governors of Texas was of far less importance to Americans than the fiery mandate to "Remember the Alamo" that rose from the ashes of the corpses burned outside the old mission. Those words echoed through American history, often as the rallying cry of attacking warriors, but more accurately as an anthem to the folly of embedding ill-grounded myths in the nation's consciousness before examining the social, economic, and political realities that energized the West.

Little more than a month later, April 21, 1836, the Texas leader Sam Houston defeated Santa Ana at the San Jacinto River. The fighting lasted about 20 minutes, but in the next several hours the Texans exacted a bloody revenge on the Mexican army in return for the Alamo. The armies of the Texans and the Mexicans had inflicted as much brutality on each other as possible. The Texas soil was drenched in the blood of Mexicans and Anglos, leaving a permanent stain on their relations.

But the Texas landscape also paid a price with fighting units marching back and forth across the region – herding livestock, dragging cannons, intimidating peasants, stealing food and supplies. For the bystanders to the war, the painful legacy of the Texas uprising was seen in a broad path of death and destruction. The Texas Revolution ended and the Mexican army moved south of the Rio Grande River. In Mexico City, Santa Ana managed to resurrect his fortunes and continued as a force in the military and political life of his country, although he failed to convince Mexico to recognize the independence of Texas, as he had promised.

As a result, an uneasy truce rested between Texas and Mexico, which continued to regard the northern province to be in rebellion. To the north, the US Congress remained hostile to the admission of a new southern state for the Union; accordingly, Texans established an independent nation, headed by Sam Houston as president.

If the anti-Mexico City Tejana/os hoped they would share in the governance of Texas, they were to be disappointed. Not only were they closed out of governing decisions, but the start of mammoth land fraud, as property titles inexplicably shifted from Tejana/o to Anglo families, robbed the Spanish-speaking community of its political power and further derailed its future.[12] It was a bitter blow for those who continued to bear little affection for the government of Santa Ana and had hoped the Texas rebellion promised greater equity for all the residents of what became the Lone Star State. Less surprised by the results were the Comanche Indians, who did not care much for the Mexicans and always had looked on the Anglo influx with hostility. Highly proactive in protecting their territory and building tribal strength, the Comanches remained a prominent force on the Texas Plains.

In neighboring New Mexico, some, with a low opinion of Santa Ana and Mexico City, continued to cling to hopes for the new Texas regime. By 1844, traders in Santa Fe chaffed under Santa Ana's embargo on trade with the Americans and that province flirted with secession. The *St Louis Reporter* dismissed the notion that the governor of Santa Fe would seek the protection of Texas, for it noted, "the citizens of Texas and New Mexico speak different languages, and are very dissimilar in habits, manners, and feelings."[13] The observation, while brief, captured the fundamental areas of conflict that inhibited the development of intercultural relationships that might have redirected the future of the region.

No such alliance arose between Mexico and Texas and for 10 years, the latter enjoyed limited success as an independent nation with a clouded economic and diplomatic future. Despite those drawbacks, its Anglo population continued to increase dramatically. The open vistas of land, the soil greed of southern agricultural crops, and the ease with which Tejana/os were being pushed to the margins made Texas a magnet for white settlers. They poured into Texas, but never abandoned their sense of connection to the cultural and political custom of the United States. These nouveau-Texans stamped their US identity into Texas. They continued to sing the hymns of their Protestant homes, read newspapers from American cities, buy their fashions from US merchants, ship their children north to school, follow the political fortunes of Whigs and Democrats, and speculate on the odds for a civil war in the United States.

No matter how much Texans played the role of Americans in exile, however, the cotton industry's reliance on slavery made Texas unattractive to northern abolitionists, who were determined to block the admission of additional slave states to the Union. When a deal for statehood was finally hammered out, war with Mexico came with the bargain. The government in Mexico City continued to see Texas as a province in rebellion and moved to prevent its absorption into the United States. The US in turn adopted the questionable position that it was defending territory that "rightfully" belonged to the former Texas Republic. Despite the rush to war, not all Americans supported the military action. For example, a foe of the Polk administration, Truman Smith (W–CT) of the House of Representatives, in language destined to reverberate across the decades, declared "the war was unnecessarily and unconstitutionally begun by the president and . . . he is in every sense responsible for all the consequences."[14]

The Mexican War lasted only two years, but it was bloody and cruel in the extreme. Fired by its earlier revolution, Texas claimed rights to parts of Colorado and New Mexico. Texas did not prevail in that land grab, but the overall dominance of the United States in the Southwest was secured. In 1848, by the Treaty of Guadalupe-Hidalgo, Mexico ceded more than two-thirds of its territory to the expansionism that pulsated out of Washington, DC. Not only did the territorial conquest please Texas Anglos, but also in that same year, their long-time foes the Comanche Indians counted deadly losses in a smallpox epidemic, only to be followed in 1849 with the equally disastrous cholera, illnesses the tribe did not believe to have been accidental. Disease accomplished more than war, devastating this powerful Native group, altering its future on the Plains, and intensifying Comanche suspicions about the ethical conduct of their Texas adversaries.

As in all western disputes, control of land fueled the Texas story. Mexican officials had thought they could seal off the borders between themselves and the Indians by bringing the Americans into Texas. They realized their error, as Anglo adventurers, more organized, better armed enemies than the Natives, violated the agreed on conditions and borders. Later, adding insult to injury, Texas, after a brief flirtation with independence, negotiated favorable state benefits and moved under the mighty protection of the United States.

As a consequence, the United States looked across the hundreds of thousands of acres with satisfaction – the Mexicans had been repelled south of the Rio Grande and Texas had accepted a $10 million payment in "lost" land claims, as well as retained control of its public lands and wetlands. All the consternation that made up the history of early Texas had little or nothing to do with "democracy" and "freedom." It had everything to do with the acquisition of land to come under the authority of the United States government. By the 1840s, the Southwest, often described as desolate pioneer turf or the haven for highly aggressive Indian tribes, was firmly set within the authority of the government in Washington, DC.

In the face of these developments, came the inevitable question – with all this power and conquest in hand, with the ineffective and wounded leadership in Mexico City, and with the acres of open land available for crop development, why did the United States not charge forward and absorb all Mexican territory? Why did the United States halt its soldiers and pioneers at the Rio Grande River? Why not capitalize on that mandated spirit that the United States spread itself across the continent, ford the Rio Grande, and continue south to plant the American flag on the highest building in Mexico City? Many thought it would have been easy to do, but clearly the United States government hesitated.

Perhaps part of that hesitation stemmed from the original three settlement conditions demanded by the Mexican government. Those three conditions – the practice of the Catholic religion, the prohibition of slavery, and the demand for families – touched on powerful sentiments in American thinking.

Protestant Americans looked south to Mexico and saw a country of deeply entrenched Catholicism and were uneasy. The United States already had a long history of anti-Catholic and specifically anti-Mexican sentiment.[15] In the eastern United States, Roman Catholic European immigrants flooded cities of the Atlantic Coast. Native-born white Americans had seen foreign women dressed in the habits of the nun, heard the sounds of alien prayers, watched the introduction of Catholic services, and worried about changes to their neighborhoods. Nativist societies, set to protect the white American Protestant way of life sprang into vitriolic existence. In 1846, Edward Beecher, of the famed abolitionist family, sourly warned the Ladies' Society for the Promotion of Education in the West that Catholic female academies were springing up in western locations, a sign that Papists might overtake America through education.[16] These circumstances challenged Americans who wondered what it would mean to have another national front on which people murmured their religious petitions before statues, sang their hymns in Latin, and voiced allegiance to a foreign head of state, located in a mysterious place called "the Vatican." How could Protestant America manage two large geographic areas permeated by a worrisome, even frightening, faith?

Second, the presence of Anglo families in the Southwest spoke to the extension of the values of the Republic. It pointed to the customs and rituals of persons who based their lives and government on English law. How would the thousands of Spanish-speaking people of Mexico be integrated into the English mores? How could they, considered by white America to be a degraded, even mongrelized society, understand the "morals" and "values" of US society? More importantly, what would happen to a nation of English speakers and Spanish speakers, where the latter would dominate in size?

Third, the prohibition of slavery was perhaps the most critical in the cooling of America's zest for more territory. Anglo Americans saw in Mexico a nation of people of color. When they looked back inside their own country, it could not be disputed that they had mismanaged the interactions between themselves and those of African descent. Indeed, that relationship was so fouled by the 1840s that most informed Americans bemoaned the stain on democracy and

[margin handwritten note: → Attitude of superiority. American expansion completely relied/relies on the disregard for other peoples' way of life!]

recognized civil war would be the only way to erase that blot. How could Anglos, whose notion of expansionism was closely tied to the spreading of democracy, take on an entire country of color, extend the rights of a democracy to these adopted citizens, and continue to hold American-born blacks in bondage? Conversely, was it realistic to absorb Mexico and attempt to lay the mantle of slavery over its people – people who only a quarter of a century earlier had thrown off the yoke of Spanish oppression? How likely was it that such people, given their history of success against an oppressor, would bow again so quickly to overlords? The dilemmas were more than political; they were terrifying to those who thought about American constitutional issues.

In confronting these realities, Americans faced the essential contradictions in their quest to extend the reach of democracy. Acquisition of the land and the inflation of American prestige were attractive. However, the Catholic presence, the Spanish language, and the implementation of the principles associated with democracy and freedom within a territory inhabited by people of color, for whom most white Americans had only the lowest regard, appeared to be more than the country was prepared to undertake in the 1840s. For once, the US government stepped back from absorbing western land.

No less tumultuous were events in the Pacific Northwest, where yet another saga was fueled by the cravings for land. As already seen, British, American, Spanish, and Russian adventurers and fur trappers had tramped through the present-day territory of Washington and Oregon since the early 1800s. By the 1820s, Spain and Russia had withdrawn their diplomatic forays into the area, retreating from their military interests and abandoning the economic goals of their Native allies. This circumstance left Great Britain and the United States to compete for the lucrative resources and build alliances with local tribes loosed from their ties to the departing countries. The two nations jockeyed back and forth for position, but the British had the stronger claim and the stronger presence, especially in the person of John McLoughlin, the powerful overseer of the widely known Hudson's Bay Company.

Still, the Americans, remembering their Lewis and Clark legacy, were not to be denied. As Texas was catapulted into the American imagination by settlers drawn from the southern states, Oregon benefited from the long-time interest of New Englanders. Since the late 1700s, merchant vessels from New England had lazed along the Oregon coast, bartering for pelts from local Natives.

The topic of Oregon, as a land venture, was more or less kept before the people through the business interests of two Massachusetts entrepreneurs, Hall Jackson Kelley and Nathaniel Wyeth. Their Northwest business exploits of the 1830s fell short and they failed to establish permanent settlements. However, they demonstrated the potential to be realized if one employed direct merchandising strategies to link a hinterlands region to a stable commercial zone. Understanding there were benefits to be accrued from such an arrangement helped to give face and name to another group of Americans eager to head for the West.

Oregon was to get its pioneer zealots in the form of religious missionaries. In the American Board of Commissioners for the Foreign Missions, based in Massachusetts, came a group capable of organizing Oregon settlers, who were to be dedicated to proselytizing among Native people. Spurred on by a fanciful tale that the Indians in the area were pleading for whites to come and teach the ways of the Christian religion, idealistic church members lined up to carry the message. The Nez Perce, Wyandotte, Salish, Cayuse, and Spokane Indians already knew plenty about negotiating with white society and they were not unfamiliar with Christianity, given the way Natives had guided Roman Catholic missionaries through many areas for many years. The lives of the Northwest Indians, however, were about to be irrevocably changed.

In 1834, Jason Lee led a Methodist group into the Northwest. He consulted with John McLoughlin at Fort Vancouver and agreed with the British factor's pointed recommendation that he should drift south away from British turf and set up his mission in the Willamette Valley. In 1837, after a successful recruiting tour in the East, during which he paraded Indian children before enthralled church audiences, Lee returned to his settlement with a sizeable group of Oregon-inspired settlers. The company included more artisans than preachers and confronting the rich lands and agricultural opportunities, the mission lost the last of its flagging piety and assumed a secular direction.

But other missionaries in the East had not forgotten their dreams of taking Christianity to the Northwest Indians. As early as 1834, Marcus Whitman, a young physician from New York, expressed interest in the goals of the American Board of Commissioners for

Foreign Missions (ABCFM) and actually traveled with fur traders from St Louis to Fort Laramie on a sort of reconnaissance trip to assess the prospects for another mission among the Indians. Convinced that he had good things to bring to the locals, Whitman hurried back to New York to formalize his mission assignment. In keeping with the ABCFM rules that sponsored only married missionaries, Whitman wed a stranger, a woman whose matrimonial motives, like his, were driven by the Willamette Valley. In 1836, Marcus and his bride Narcissa arrived in the Oregon Territory to establish the Waiilatpu Mission, near the Walla Walla River, where they ultimately endured both personal and professional difficulties in their efforts to win over the Natives, especially the Cayuses.

If Narcissa Whitman thought she would enter a pristine wilderness environment where Native people frolicked in child-like simplicity awaiting word of the Bible, her first sighting of Fort Vancouver, under the director McLoughlin of the Hudson's Bay Company, must have startled her. While the stockade enclosure was not huge, it included more than sixty buildings to accommodate the work of millwrights, shopkeepers, and artisans. Its farmlands included abundant crops of fruits, fig trees, cucumbers, beans, peas, and beets, barley, wheat, potatoes, and turnips. The healthy dairy herds produced a regular supply of milk, butter, and cheese. The travel exhausted Whitman, who in a statement foreshadowing the rise of the urban West, declared, "Vancouver [is] the New York of the Pacific Ocean."[17]

In addition, there was plenty of politicking in the air. Nez Perces, trying to influence the placement of white missions and protective of their access to Anglo economic benefits warned Narcissa Whitman, during the stop at Fort Vancouver, that their tribe did not "have difficulty with the white men as the Cayouses [*sic*] do and [you] shall find it so."[18]

Whether the Nez Perces spoke only out of self-interest or not, from the outset, the Cayuses, caught in the shifting local scenario, objected to the construction of a mission station on their land. The small settlement was a daily visual reminder of white intrusion and yet another factor to destabilize their local place with other tribes. The Cayuses pondered their less than satisfactory possibilities with both their Native and Anglo neighbors.

As for the Whitmans, missionary work proceeded over a rocky road. The medical skills of Marcus and the maternal inclinations of Narcissa might have won them a place among the Indians. Yet, over the years, matters soured between the New England missionaries and the Cayuse people. The Whitmans, busy with a growing family, a steady traffic of settler wagons, and their missionary program seemed oblivious to the seriousness of the Cayuses' feelings.

The events surrounding the Whitman mission captured several patterns of social, economic, and political interactions between Native people and Anglos in many parts of the West. Social and diplomatic alliances among the region's Natives were in transition, so that the arrival of whites disrupted the emerging formulation of Indian–Indian relationships. The competition between and among trapping and trading companies, as well as nations, added more confusion to the mix. So, too, did the erratic interaction between Natives and whites, which fluctuated between cooperation and conflict. Finally, whites in the area did not always agree on common goals, whether economic or religious, resulting in almost constant backbiting and undermining of each other.

The arrival of Marcus and Narcissa Whitman showed a road ahead for a West where traditional Anglo family groups became the primary unit by which white society displaced indigenous peoples and occupied territory for the United States. The life of Narcissa Whitman in the West was not merely a western history footnote about an overly naive woman of little importance. Rather, Whitman personified the mid-nineteenth century notion of women as civilizers, society's vessels of purity, piety, and domesticity, guardians of the hearth, and protectors of the commonwealth. Even in this different environment, Narcissa Whitman actively promoted those values, conducting herself as if she still resided in a Massachusetts town. She was reputed to maintain eastern courtesies when addressing Indian women, using terminology that had no relevance in Oregon. Her insistence on this brand of femininity, so inappropriate to her circumstances, however, mirrored the cultural expectations of many Anglo women who followed her into the West.

The Whitmans, undaunted by the reality of their situation, determined to "win over" the Natives to Christianity, despite the fact that they butted awkwardly against the Indian culture around them and, after several years, could not count a single solid convert among their Native neighbors. At the same time, the little cluster of buildings drew other Anglos, some who stayed to help advance the mission, but most of the wagons headed for other parts of the

Figure 3.1   These German Jewish immigrants developed a multi-faceted business relationship with local Kiowa Indians, a complex interaction for two groups each struggling to preserve cultural and religious identity in New Mexico. *Source:* Courtesy, Palace of the Governors, Museum of New Mexico, 7890.

Northwest, using the settlement as a place to recover from the trail or sit out the winter before the final push to a destination promised to be rich in watered and fertile soil.

On the one hand, the Cayuses were further displeased by the seemingly endless stream of whites and, as a small tribe, they had no powerful political ally, either Native or European, to back their resistance. Still, it had to rankle as they looked around at the results of the wagon traffic, especially after 1843 when annual waves of pioneers journeyed the more than 2,000 miles of the Oregon Trail.

The migrants, after all, did not travel in tidy lines, as so often depicted in Western films. Rather, they spilled across the land, weaving and twisting, kicking all into mile-long trailers of dust. And they were not a quiet crowd. The animals were bawling and bleating, wagons groaning and creaking, whips cracking through the air, men yelling and swearing by day, singing and laughing at night. Here they left the remains of an untidy camp, there the livestock destroyed the grasses and pigs fouled the drinking water. Husbands and fathers, as unwitting environmental predators, peeled the bark from trees to make a resting place for the family. In sorrow, they scraped out rough graves and left their dead where they had fallen, the West becoming a free-form cemetery, a matter particularly distasteful to Native peoples. Everywhere these interlopers and their migrating culture left their various marks on Indian spaces and moved on, apparently unaware of the long-term ramifications of their presence.

On the other hand, faced with decreasing economic choices, as whites further encroached on their land, the Cayuses realized they had cornered the market in selling horses to passing travelers, desperate for fresh animals. The horse trade gave them access to a new business. They found other ways to press for a bit of profit, as one white woman recalled about crossing a dangerous falls, "me and my children . . . was taken over by two [I]ndians which cost a good many shirts . . . the [I]ndians are thick as hops here and not very friendly."[19] Few persons cared if matters of human civility were at stake. All persons felt the strain of cultural wrangling and responded in favor of one's own.

Realistically, the Cayuses had not settled on what would prove to be a long-term viable economic trajectory for the tribe. They would make some money here and there, but ultimately, the stream of alien wagons would stop – stop because the settlers had taken up the best of the available land, reducing even further Native chances to define their livelihood in the shifting economic structures.

At the same time, the Indians struggled against a Christianity that would eviscerate their own rituals and beliefs. Protestant missionaries, in general, demanded an all or nothing response to conversion, leaving small flexibility for weaving Native religion into Christian practice. Yet Narcissa Whitman did report she was making some little progress with Native language and that Indian women "appear anxious to converse with us and to be understood by us."[20] The confusion that marked the dialogue with the Indian community had to further obfuscate possible relationships, especially among people already stung by changing patterns of political and economic events.

Weakened in all the aspects of their lives, further stress for these

Indians, as for so many other tribes, came from various white-borne illnesses, against which the Indians had no natural biological protection. When yet another epidemic swept through the Cayuses – this time, measles – the Indians, with many grievances stockpiled, vented their anger on the mission personnel. When only sickened Indian youngsters died, after Whitman gave medical care to all the afflicted, some Indians insisted the doctor had deliberately allowed their children to expire. On November 29, 1847, Cayuse Indians swept into the mission. Marcus and Narcissa Whitman, along with 12 of their associates, were killed and more than 50 women and children temporarily taken into captivity.

Like many acts of Indian retaliation after years of violations, insults, and setbacks, the Cayuses' "victory" was brief. The hostages were ransomed, the Cayuses were harassed at every turn, the white government demanded the perpetrators be identified, and finally six of the tribe hanged for the mission deaths. The Cayuse people fell onto hard times, dying off or moving on to a reservation with Indian neighbors in the area in 1855. For the Whitmans, it was a long agonizing day of dying, far from the eastern homes they had left with such lofty visions. It was a pathetic end to a pathetic venture for everyone, except those who clamored for more Anglo presence, especially in the form of an organized territory of the federal government.

Those voices were not to be disappointed, especially since the British had been pulling back from their declining fur trade in the region. Still, there had been tension simmering between the two countries about what should be the boundary and armed conflict seemed a possibility more than once. In 1844, the Democrats had chanted the catchy slogan, "Fifty-Four Forty or Fight," a call for the United States to demand all territory as far as Alaska. Calmer negotiators suggested extending the existing boundary at the 49th parallel, west to the Pacific Ocean, but keeping Vancouver Island with Great Britain. In 1846, this dividing line between British Canada and the United States was established, creating the longest unguarded international boundary in the world.

What remained for the Americans was intense political debate over whether Oregon as a territory would permit slavery or not. In the US Senate, far from the banks of the Columbia River and the fields of the Willamette Valley, eastern politicians used the language of exaggerated politeness to quarrel with one another about Oregon. Phrases such as "denominated sophistry," "cowardly aspect," "gospel of freedom," "piracy," "arrogant presumption" flew from one side of the Senate aisle to the other, but the nexus of each argument concerned the issue of slavery in the Far West of Oregon.[21]

Once again, the conflict of the North and the South about whether US soil would be governed as a slave or free state centered on land in the West. In August 1848, Oregon officially became a territory of the United States; the acreage included present-day Oregon, Washington, Idaho, and parts of western Montana and Wyoming. The pesky problem of slave or free had been resolved to the satisfaction of white citizens by local law that banned blacks from being inside the borders of the Oregon Territory.

The tumultuous events in Oregon were not the only disturbances on the Pacific Coast. California, where Natives, Spanish, Mexicans, Africans, and Anglos mingled, represented yet another arena with a contentious history. California, with its great size and varied topography, was home to Natives who lived according to varied cultural and economic patterns. The bands, however, tended to be small and established themselves in villages. Some areas supported life in a stingy manner, making the search for food a constant. In well-watered and more verdant regions, small bands of Natives lived with some ease, little inclined to seek bounty through warfare.

After 1770, the Spanish were a permanent presence in California. As they did in Mexico, the soldiers came accompanied by friars creating a dual, and often competing, presence of both secular and religious interests. The outcomes for the indigenous populations followed the unhappy examples to the south; military presidios lacked sufficient funding and staffing; mission priests wanted to replace traditional economic and cultural practices with their own notions; Natives resented and resisted alien intruders and their forms of labor and religion.

These interactions did not take place in a vacuum, but in an environment charged with human sexuality. Again, there was a colonial community in which men dominated, but did not agree on what represented appropriate sexual conduct. In the absence of a significant number of Spanish women, the soldiers turned their sexual attention to Native women, often with violent results. The friars objected to liaisons outside of marriage and responded by quarreling with their military colleagues and inflicting harsh punishments on the Native women. Their notion that "separation of the sexes," whereby they locked Indian women in miserable box-like quarters, would preserve "virtue" proved deadly in a literal way. The smothering circumstances facilitated the rapid spread of disease, and Indian people died by the thousands. So widespread and pervasive were the impacts of these epidemics that the Native population of California faced a nearly complete physical fracture, from which it would never recover.[22]

These problems were compounded after the Mexican Revolution of 1821, when a defeated Spain withdrew from California. Officials of the new Mexican administration were left to govern a territory, already in cultural trauma, that included California, Nevada, and large segments of Arizona and Utah. Here again was a huge territory so far from a foreign political administrative center that settlement and expansion goals, even had they been formulated with thoughtful judgment, were destined to collapse in a morass of ill-will, confusion, and injustice. What occurred was a tendency to focus on coastal development, an economic move that again brought the lay government into conflict with the mission priests. In the end, by 1836 the secular powers had championed and land shifted from privileged church control to an elite class of Mexicans, whose cultural profile – a mix of Hispanic and Native – dominated in much of California. This was yet another turn in policy that brought slim benefits to Natives. They continued as agricultural laborers, their rigidly assigned economic status providing the basis for the highly stratified racial society California was destined to become.

By the beginning of the Mexican War in 1846, California looked like just one more piece of geographic destiny for the United States government. After the experiences of Texas and Oregon, who would really believe that California was not a natural acquisition, one that would make the United States an Atlantic to Pacific nation? Indeed, the obstacles of Mexico in Texas and England in Oregon had been successfully removed, thanks to "bold" Americans, who had not permitted a few international niceties to slow their advances. Certainly, members of the US Congress, far from the land in question and representing eastern and midwestern states, spoke with passion in favor of such an aggressive behavior. The 1846 abortive Bear Flag Revolt, an embarrassing attempt led by John C. Frémont to oust the Mexican government, stoked the convictions of the American Congress that California should be the next booty added to the Republic.

However, not all politicians agreed. Senator Thomas Corwin (W–OH), a vehement opponent of the Mexican War, also challenged the California land hunger of his colleagues, scoffing that one called such expansion reasonable because San Francisco was the best harbor on the Pacific. Corwin asked, "We want California. What for? 'Why,' says the Senator from Michigan, 'we will have it'; and the Senator from South Carolina says '. . . you can't keep our people from going there . . .' Sir, it is not meet that our old flag should throw its protecting folds over expeditions for lucre or for land."[23]

The 1848 Treaty of Guadalupe-Hidalgo settled the matter, as California was part of the massive acreage Mexico ceded to the United States. California had already endured ripples of invasion and clashes of culture for almost 300 years. Nothing that had gone before would equal the shock waves of upheaval and change wrought by the 1849 discovery of gold along the American River near the city of Sacramento. In the resulting Gold Rush it was as if a monster earthquake, generated by human activity, rattled not only California, but the world. When it was over, nothing in California was what it had been, nor would it ever be again.

In the first instance, a thundering herd of people from all points of the globe descended on California, where, of course, no preparation had been made, nor indeed would many have known how to set a stage for the thousands of '49ers who came for the gold. The mining era took on a decidedly bachelor characteristic, as the incoming population was overwhelmingly male. In the early days of mining, as husbands dashed from the East, the Midwest, South America, Canada, and Europe, wives and children remained at home, awaiting the happy word of a great gold strike.

Typically, the women who appeared in the first weeks of the hastily constructed mining towns were prostitutes, female workers excluded from the physical occupations associated with mining, but intent on earning their share of the booming profits. In general, these were young women, who worked in the saloons, brothels, and tents that quickly dotted the horizon of a mining town. Many were poor and illiterate and few found in prostitution a lucrative career. Rather, women worked in dank rooms and saloons, made little money, were subjected to various forms of violence, and died at a young age, often by their own hand. Their economic success as participants in the Gold Rush remained elusive.[24]

The nearly all-male populations largely working-class laborers – miners, freighters, blacksmiths, carpenters – with some discomfort, adjusted their domestic expectations to accommodate a world in which they could not rely on women to do the cooking and washing. Living together in small cabins the men learned to take on chores they once would have regarded as totally outside their gender behavior. The chance, however, that gender roles might become permanently reorganized disappeared quickly as a community took on a more diverse class structure.[25] Men of greater social status – engineers, company managers, reporters, church pastors, store owners – joined forces with the women they chose for marriage to cement class layering and gender expectations. The arrival of middle-class white woman often suggested as the reason for the demise of the roaring life of the camps did not alone explain how gender changes collapsed, the male working class was undone, and the female working class of prostitutes suppressed.

Middle-class men set up legal and social parameters that ensured their power as community leaders. They passed the laws and implemented the restrictions that guaranteed their local hegemony, but with droll witticism insisted they did so because of the pressure they felt from their wives. Such an explanation was self-serving and not reflective of the reality of the public and private power of middle-class women. At the same time, middle-class women certainly endorsed those regulations and cultural expectations that kept them in a preferred circumstance. To hold them solely responsible, however, for the rise and power of middle-class standards, was but one way for men to deflect their own public actions.[26]

In the scramble to find gold, few would have suspected that western mining would expand to include silver, copper and, to a lesser degree, lead and zinc. The search for riches saw frenzied hordes doing a pioneer settler about-face, now dashing past the once desirable agricultural lands, clamoring up mountain and trail to the jagged rocky ground, where ore waited for discovery.

In the process, huge areas of the West came under an environmental assault of unprecedented magnitude. Digging and blasting, hacking and cutting were the daily chores of miners, who attacked one locale with ferocity, only to leave it behind, as they rushed off to a new possibility. In so doing they invaded some of the most isolated enclaves of the California Natives, literally turning their living spaces upside down and destroying their environment. The results were disastrous for Indians who, forced out of their food supply areas, died by the scores. The rapacious nature of the industry was best encapsulated in the development of hydraulic mining, a process that shot highly pressurized water along areas of loose gravel, cutting away trees, plants, and soil to uncover the ore.[27]

In the nostalgic retelling of the Gold Rush, the images tilt toward those of the lonely prospector – he with his pan, pick axe, and mule, struggling through the mountainous areas of California or Nevada, in search of the "big strike" – but these were largely pictures drawn by fancy. In reality, the day of the lone prospector was short, for western mining was an industry that shifted from one stage to another with rapidity. Once the surface gold was panned out, it became clear that extracting the ore deep beneath the ground would require large amounts of capital, not something individual poor prospectors could produce.

Businessmen, living far from the West, became the backers, providing the resources for organizing companies, hiring personnel, purchasing heavy equipment, and overseeing the complex process of sinking deep underground shafts. Western mining turned on an international axis, drawing in the knowledge of mining engineers and owners from a number of European countries. In other words, the California Gold Rush rapidly and of necessity came under the control of a new class of businessmen who found in western mines one of the most promising venues for collaborative entrepreneurship across regional, national, and international borders. The Gold Rush of the American West might more properly be identified as an exercise in international financial cooperation.

Early in the mining era, the lonely prospector with his mule and panning tools morphed into the mine employee, a common laborer. He stood in line each morning hoping to be summoned by the foreman for a chance to descend into the bowels of the West for precious ore, shovel the find into small cars, or on the surface hurry across the mine yard to unload the rock and start the laborious sorting process. Miners competed each day for this work, but enjoyed little job stability, as profitable yields might evaporate almost as quickly as they had started.

It was not long until the mining industry became the locus for some of the most brutal clashes in American history. Many of these clashes concerned the quest for power between and among various national groups. A mining camp did not function as an

"American melting pot," despite the fact that the Gold Rush was a multi-cultural and multinational event that raised the economic expectations of people around the globe. Instead, the camps fell into parochial clusters wherein Anglo men used economic and legislative restrictions, buttressed by heavy doses of murder and mayhem carried out by hired goons, to dominate the industry.

For example, Chinese laborers, who came to California early in the mining era, encountered a nearly constant hatred in the West. Both as individuals and in their communities, the Chinese, almost all men without families, were subjected to ridicule and venomous attack. The early experience of the Chinese in the mines told of the future for these immigrants, who, by virtue of their race, were viewed as outside the debate about improved working conditions or fair wages for laborers. Western mining communities burdened Chinese miners with false accusations of theft, higher prices, and ad hoc taxes, until they pushed them as far out of the industry as possible.[28] The unmitigated hatred heaped on the Chinese immigrants increased over the several years they spread through the Rocky Mountain West, ultimately culminating in a chant, "The Chinese Must Go!" heard across western mountains and in the halls of Congress; finally East joined West in promoting discrimination.

Other clashes turned toward the inevitable conflict between the miners and the managers. As labor practices developed over several years across the mining districts it became usual that a mine frequently hired one national group – such as Irishmen in Coeur d'Alene, Italians in Arizona, or Greeks in Utah – the relationships between the workers and the managers often fell out along lines of national–religious discrimination. The opportunity for a better life in America that immigrants had hoped to find when they signed with a gang boss in the home country, failed to materialize in most mining communities.

Western mining boasted some of the most deplorable working conditions in American industry. The underground labor was hazardous, with floods, explosions, and cave-ins common occurrences. Wages were tightly controlled, and benefits non-existent. In addition, there were deadly health risks for the miners, who inhaled toxic materials, while they risked death and permanent crippling on a daily basis.

Although across its history, America witnessed little hard-core radical activism, the western mining industry contained some ele-

Figure 3.2 After the first disorganized and violent years of mining, some Chinese miners had an association with the Colorado School of Mines, possibly working in one of the experimental mines with Professor James Underhill. *Source:* Courtesy, Denver Public Library, Western History Collection, 23 X-21651.

ments of such political attitudes. As the decades passed and labor circumstances seemed only to worsen, western miners showed themselves willing to join to such organizations as the Western Federation of Miners and, after 1905, the Industrial Workers of the World (IWW). Their activities, which took place around the turn of the century, indicated that many western miners felt little had changed for them since the heady days of the 1850s and 1860s.

The events of the 1840s and 1850s stretched across reaches of western lands, touching many corners and many cultures, often in unexpected ways. For example, by the early 1800s, the Shoshones and Bannocks, as well as the Goshutes, Paiutes, and Utes – all Native tribes living in and around Utah in their migrations – had not been much bothered by white settlers hurrying to occupy what they considered a harsh environment. So it must have been something of a surprise in 1847 when men, women, and children not only stopped their carts and wagons near the Great Salt Lake, but also took up residence on a soil whites had studiously avoided and at that time claimed by Mexico. Thus began a project by Brigham Young, leader of the Church of Jesus Christ of Latter-day Saints (commonly known as Mormons) to organize and construct a home base for this American bred religion. Young, who replaced church founder Joseph Smith after his 1844 murder by an Illinois mob, believed that in Utah his faithful would be beyond the reach of those who violently opposed the church, especially for its controversial practice of plural marriage. Armed with practical plans for laying out towns, developing agriculture, building irrigation canals, and controlling the populace through church activities, group prayer, written directives, instructional lectures, police auxiliaries, and mutual aid societies, Young, by the sheer force of his administrative skills and formidable personality, brought Mormon Utah into existence.

While other white settlers avoided settling in the semi-arid climate, Young enthusiastically called church members from the East and Europe to join him in what became known as the Great Basin Kingdom. The converts to Mormonism, mostly of northern European stock, responded with equal zeal and the white population of Utah jumped to 6,000 by 1849 and within four years to 20,000, despite the limited rainfall, parched summers, and frigid winters.

Natives in the Great Basin entered into a relationship distinct from Indians near other white settlements. Because Mormons held that indigenous peoples were one of the lost tribes of Israel, the church considered Indians crucial to the theological origins of the LDS faith. Mormon proselytizing took on an exceptional fervor and marked some success. Despite this, and a church policy of "feed rather than fight," relationships were not entirely cordial, as Utah's Indians relinquished their lands and fields to a new community only grudgingly. In the 1853 war led by the Ute chief Walkara and the 1858 attack on Fort Lemhi that killed two Mormon missionaries, Natives indicated there were limits to what they would tolerate, whether religious conversion, land losses, or both.[29]

In addition to the internal management of Utah, external politics also demanded much of Brigham Young's attention. The relationship with the United States government was tenuous, given the general hostility to polygamy, which clashed with certain public notions of Victorian sexuality.[30] The Saints, who saw polygamy as a God-directive, albeit one only sanctioned for the elite of Mormon men, constantly feared the US army would be sent to suppress them.[31] Young successfully deflected this possibility at the end of the Mexican War, when Utah came under the jurisdiction of the United States and he was appointed governor of the territory.

By 1857, relations between Utah and the federal government had not improved and war hysteria gripped the territory. In this climate, Mormons attacked a wagon train of Missouri emigrants, killing more than 100 people. For many years, blame for the murders, known as the Mountain Meadows Massacre, was in one fashion or another unjustly placed on nearby Indians. Brigham Young did not allow such unfortunate events to deter him and continued his vision to make Utah a Mormon controlled paradise. Young, at his death in 1877, could count more than 100,000 Mormons toiling on farms, investing in cooperative mercantile ventures, and pursuing local manufacturing.[32]

As relations between Utah and the federal government had been influenced by the Mexican War – Brigham Young had sent 500 men, a "Mormon Battalion" as a good will gesture to the United States – other areas of the West were also affected by that conflict. Again, the issue before the nation was whether new western territories, so greatly expanded after 1848, would enter the Union as slave or free land.

In the US Congress, once again the West dominated the political arguments by Congressmen from the North and the South. In this case, the outcome was known as the Compromise of 1850, by which California with its mother lodes of gold, entered the Union as a free state. New Mexico and Utah territories were to vote in their legislatures on the question of local slavery. The troubling subject of human bondage and the West was not resolved by this decision.

Shortly, slavery and western lands were again before the members of Congress. In 1854, the Kansas-Nebraska Act, designed to organize government for those areas, gave the people of a new territory the right to decide on slavery by popular sovereignty, the vote of the people. This act nullified the earlier Compromise of 1820 that had divided free and slave states at the geographic measure of 36 degrees 30 minutes north latitude, now opening the new territories to all sorts of political maneuvering. It took no time for advocates on both sides to see the way to victory lay in filling a territory with their own voters. Pro-slavery forces from the South and free-soil voters from the North careened into Kansas, which shortly was ablaze with violence and murder. The abolitionist John Brown added to the tally in "Bleeding Kansas" with his attack on Potta-watomie Creek, where he murderously cut down five pro-slavery men. By the time Brown was apprehended and hanged in 1859 for his raid on Harper's Ferry in West Virginia, the South and the North were hardened in their commitment to war. The Civil War was not much fought on battlefields of the West, but it was most definitely fought about the West, its lands, and slavery.

In the historical narrative, geography surpassed humanity in importance because the concept and the rhetoric of "Manifest Destiny" – the idea that a deity who favored white people wanted them to spread democracy – referred largely to land and little to people. Had the place of people been paramount – among others, Mexicans in Texas, Cayuses in Oregon, Asians in California – perhaps a greater sense of common interests, shared values, and future goals could have been formulated and different regional trajectories experienced. Most especially, the rhetoric of conquest might have yielded to the issues of justice, democracy, and the right of the governed that were articulated and guaranteed in the founding documents of the United States.

In 1851, thousands of Indians from the tribes of the Great Plains, including Sioux, Cheyennes, Arapahos, Mandans, and Gros Ventres, converged on Fort Laramie in Wyoming for negotiations with the United States. The government commissioners asked the tribes to recognize the military's right to build roads and forts through Indian lands, agree to cease warring on whites and each other, and accept a division of the Great Plains that would delineate boundaries for each tribe. For its part, the government promised the assigned lands to the tribes in perpetuity, material goods, and protection from marauders. The treaty was a failure from the outset. What the Native representatives actually agreed to or thought they agreed to remained a point of conjecture for many years. In some ways, it mattered little. What did matter was that Indians of many tribes saw some of the ingredients confronting them but not the full combination of signals that might have convinced them to seek different and broader concessions from the government. Partial rather than total knowledge damaged them at the treaty table.

Had those Natives been able to hoist themselves far above the earth's surface and gaze down on the map of the continental United States, they would have seen that many transformations facilitated in new ways to advance Anglo America. They would have seen the

American flag flying in Texas, Oregon, and California. They would have noticed wagon trains forming up, each one with pioneer families and pioneer livestock. They would have observed Protestant missionaries, Mormon missionaries, and Catholic missionaries carving out new spheres of influence. They would have wondered about new farms being staked off with houses and barns and pastures. They would have counted more traders running along the Santa Fe Trail. They would have seen more ships slipping into San Francisco Bay. They might have seen the network of local railroads that each year chugged closer to the West. Above all, they might have noted the glint of gold in Colorado, Idaho, Utah, New Mexico, Nevada, Montana, and the Dakotas and thought about the stampeding whites who would come to claim it. Those Indian negotiators would have acted on the reality that the sovereignty of the United States government surrounded them. The Anglo changes in Texas, Oregon, and California had drawn a geographic noose around the Great Plains, one that would further strangle Native life ways.

But, of course, they could not suspend themselves above the land and see these things in their totality. Nor could they know that when the Civil War ended in 1865 white Americans and Europeans would look to the West, believing it a way to relieve the personal and national sadness left by the battles of Bull Run, Shiloh, Antietam, and Gettysburg. These were not places in the West, but their blood-soaked fields impelled people to turn away, to look for a new landscape, one that offered a way to forget the killing of brother by brother. Once again the West was important to the East. The American West was about to enter the most intense and disturbing phase of its passionate history.

NOTES

1 John L. O'Sullivan, "The Great Nation of Futurity," *United States Democratic Review* 6:23 (1839): 426. *The Making of America Series*, Cornell University, <www.mtholyoke.edu/acad/intrel/osulliva.htm>.

2 Anne M. Butler and Wendy Wolff, *United States Senate, Election, Expulsion, and Censure Cases, 1793–1990* (Washington: GPO, 1995), 51–3, 57–9, 62–4.

3 Robert V. Remini compiled the most comprehensive studies of Andrew Jackson. For example, see *Andrew Jackson and the Course of American*

Democracy, 1833–1845 (1984; Baltimore: Johns Hopkins University Press, 1998).

4   In 1849, the Indian Department was renamed the Bureau of Indian Affairs and transferred to the Department of the Interior.

5   Sean Michael O'Brien, *In Bitterness and In Tears: Andrew Jackson's Destruction of the Creeks and the Seminoles* (Westport, CT: Praeger, 2003).

6   US Congress, House of Representatives, *Register of Debates*, 20th Congress, 1st Session, p. 251, A Century of Lawmaking for a New Nation: US Congressional Documents and Debates, 1774–1875, Library of Congress, <www.lcweb2.loc.gov>.

7   "John E. Wool, Brig. Gen., "Address to Cherokees, March 22, 1837, Headquarters, New Echota, Georgia," Southwestern Native American Documents, 1730–1842, <http://dlg.galileo.usg.edu/nativeamerican/jpg/ch078a.jpg>.

8   Nugent, *Into the West*, 46–7.

9   Raymund A. Paredes, "The Origins of Anti-Mexican Sentiment in the United States," in Manuel G. Gonzales and Cynthia M. Gonzales, eds., *En Aquel Entonces: Readings in Mexican American History* (Bloomington: Indiana University Press, 2000), 45–52.

10 "The Unanimous Declaration of Independence Made by the Delegates of the People of Texas in General Convention at the Town of Washington on the 2nd day of March 1836," p. 1, Avalon Project, Yale Law School, <www.yale.edu/lawweb/avalon/texdec.htm>.

11 Paul D. Lack argued that during the Texas Revolution, Tejana/o loyalties were sharply divided, but regardless of which camp Mexican Americans supported, overall the behaviors of the two armies resulted in widespread death and destruction for civilians. See his "Occupied Texas: Bexar and Goliad, 1835–1836," in Emilio Zamora, Cynthia Orozco, and Rodolfo Rocha, eds., *Mexican Americans in Texas History* (Austin: Texas State Historical Association, 2000), 35–49.

12 Widespread challenges to land titles were especially prevalent after the Mexican War of 1846–8. Armando C. Alonzo, "Mexican-American Land Grant Adjudication," in Gonzales and Gonzales, eds., *En Aquel Entonces*, 64–71.

13 *St Louis Reporter* quoted in *Brooklyn Daily Eagle*, January 9, 1844, 2, <www.eagle.brooklynpubliclibrary.org/>.

14 US Congress, House of Representatives, *Appendix to the Congressional Globe*, 30th Congress, 1st Session, p. 383, A Century of Lawmaking for a New Nation: US Congressional Documents and Debates, 1774–1875, Library of Congress, <http://memory.loc.gov/ammem/amlaw/lwcglink.html#anchor30>.

15 Paredes, "The Origins of Anti-Mexican Sentiment in the United States," 46–51.

16 Edward Beecher to the Ladies' Society for the Promotion of Education at the West, quoted in Thomas Woody, *A History of Women's Education in the United States*, 2 vols. (1929; New York: Octagon Press, 1966), vol. 2, 456–7.

17 Narcissa Prentiss Whitman, *My Journal: 1836*, Lawrence Dodd, ed. (Fairfield, WA: Ye Galleon Press, 1982), 50–3, quote, 48.

18 Ibid., 57.

19 "The Diary of Elizabeth Dixon Smith," in Kenneth L. Holmes, ed. and comp., *Covered Wagon Women: Diaries and Letters from the Western Trails, 1840–1849* (1983; Lincoln: University of Nebraska Press, 1995), 139.

20 Whitman, *My Journal: 1836*, 17.

21 For an example of the Senate debate, see speeches of Samuel S. Phelps (W-Vermont) and Thomas Corwin (W-Ohio), US Congress, Senate, *Appendix to the Congressional Globe*, 30th Congress, 1st Session, pp. 1156–9, A Century of Lawmaking for a New Nation: US Congressional Documents and Debates, 1774–1875, Library of Congress, <http://memory.loc.gov/ammem/amlaw/lwcglink.html#anchor25>.

22 For a full discussion of this subject, see Albert L. Hurtado, *Intimate Frontiers: Sex, Gender, and Culture in Old California* (Albuquerque: University of New Mexico Press, 1999), 1–19, and Steven Hackel, *Children of Coyote, Missionaries of St Francis: Indian–Spanish Relations in Colonial California, 1769–1850* (Chapel Hill: University of North Carolina Press, 2005).

23 US Congress, Senate, *Appendix to the Congressional Globe*, 29th Congress, 2nd Session, p. 217, A Century of Lawmaking for a New Nation: US Congressional Documents and Debates, 1774–1875, Library of Congress, <http://memory.loc.gov/ammem/amlaw/lwcglink.html#anchor29>.

24 See Anne M. Butler, *Daughters of Joy, Sisters of Misery: Prostitutes in the American West, 1865–1890* (Urbana: University of Illinois Press, 1985), 50–1.

25 Susan Lee Johnson, *Roaring Camp: The Social World of the California Gold Rush* (New York: W.W. Norton, 2000), 183–5.

26 Butler, *Daughters of Joy, Sisters of Misery*, 63, 151–3.

27 Drew Isenberg, *Mining California: An Ecological History* (New York: Hill and Wang, 2005).

28 Johnson, *Roaring Camp*, 208–18.

29 Gregory E. Smoak, *Ghost Dances and Religious Identity: Prophetic Religion and American Indian Ethnogenesis in the Nineteenth Century* (Berkeley: University of California Press, 2006), 71–4, 77.

30 John D'Emilio and Estelle B. Freedman, *Intimate Matters: A History of Sexuality in America* (New York: Harper and Row, 1988), xiii, 117–18.

31 Precisely, the Mormons practiced polygyny, the taking of more than one wife. Polygamy correctly means having more than one spouse at a time and could refer to plural husbands or plural wives. In reference to Mormons, the word "polygamy" is commonly used.

32 An extensive literature covers all aspects of the Mormon experience. Leonard J. Arrington is widely regarded as the leading figure in Mormon scholarship.

Chapter 4

Imperial Wests

THE BUTCHERY
How General Custer and His Men were Slaughtered.
Latest Information Concerning the Horror in the Valley of the
Yellowstone.[1]

Americans could scarcely believe the news dispatches from Salt
Lake City. The word flashed from city to town to countryside. The
flamboyant, daring Lieutenant Colonel George Custer and his Seventh Cavalry lay dead, strewn across a Montana field, their naked
bodies hacked apart with gaping and grotesque wounds – American
soldiers left to bloat in the summer sun. The June 25–6, 1876,
shocking and gory demise of George Armstrong Custer and his
group of more than 250 soldiers and scouts, at the hands of Indians
along the Little Bighorn River, reverberated with disbelief through
the American nation.

Such devastating ignominy for one of America's best known
military figures only days before the celebration of the country's
centennial certainly dampened the coming patriotic festivities. Most
believed that the 100th anniversary of the United States of America
should be about victory against all odds, not defeat before "inferi-
ors." Journalists and politicians rushed to anguish for the "stripped
. . . and horribly mutilated" dead and denounced the living as "savages" who should be "whip[ped] . . . into subjection," for "their
incessant warfare and their numerous murders of white settlers and
their families or white men wherever found unarmed."[2]

The fires of anti-Indian sentiment, already glowing bright, burned higher yet as white Americans demanded swift and merciless retaliation. Some commented discreetly that Custer had been "rashly imprudent," if not stupid, when he knowingly, in hope of military or political acclaim, charged his outnumbered Seventh Cavalry into an Indian encampment of approximately 2,000 Natives. The Sioux, Cheyennes, and Arapahos gathered that day at the Little Bighorn must have thought the attack insane, but speedily took advantage of Custer's poor judgment.

Custer, a preening self-promoter, surely was surprised, as he heard the horrific screams and peered through the swirling dust, by the ferocity of the Indian forces – men and women – who responded to his troops that June morning. Yet in terms of his nation's destiny, the vain lieutenant colonel, startled and humiliated, did not die for naught. Literally, Custer died for his country – just not in the way that he would have expected.

Those safely beyond the West did not dismiss the events on the Little Bighorn or the foolish lieutenant colonel as sad but distant frontier happenings; rather, the grisly Custer defeat was celebrated as a national calamity throughout the Midwest, South, and East, in the press, along the streets, from the pulpit, and in the halls of Congress. As such, it resonated across the country and facilitated America's varied industrial interests in the Far West, adding exactly the sort of sensational story that played on racial emotions, excited boulevard sentiment, and advanced the agenda of powerful people far from the banks of the Little Bighorn River.

Custer, who had graduated last in his class at West Point, had plenty of detractors, and compiled a rather shoddy professional and personal biography, became yet another convenient symbol of the "bravery" and "courage" of the West. Above all, his death, written in melodramatic language, served to be the rationale for subduing all Indians – not just the Sioux, Cheyenne, and Arapaho warriors at the Little Bighorn – and "advancing" white "civilization," especially in the form of economic and political development, into all corners of the region.[3] Soon after June 26, 1876, some broadened the scope of the Montana fight and intoned, "A general Indian war seems to be necessitated by the result of the late disastrous campaign."[4] Few took the time to note the implications of a surprise attack on families going about their daily routines, or that the Lakota Chief Red Horse could have told them, "The soldiers charged so quickly we could not talk," or that self-defense of one's home and loved ones represented a cherished American value.[5]

The events at the Little Bighorn indicated that poor communication, contradictory goals, and conflicting policies within both white and Indian societies continued to hamper the formulation of a consistent western diplomacy across cultures. Who, in fact, was the deciding diplomatic voice for Natives and who for white society? Should political, military, or entrepreneurial sectors within each society have the final say about interactions between cultures? Was it the role of the US army to conduct armed actions against the Natives, or was the military to function as the federal peacemaker, keeping all western residents subdued? Should the military implement the same policies of enforcement for offending whites, as for Natives? Was there a difference between what eastern administrators expected to be the policy and what actually happened in the field? Was there a difference between what Native negotiators expected to be the policy and what actually happened in the field? With these questions largely unanswered, all parties found themselves moving along conflicting trajectories. Thus, when problems arose, haste, self-interest, and violence marked the events, many of which had occurred years before the drama at the Little Big Horn.

For example, in the mid-1860s, hundreds of Navajo Indians each day entered the inner grounds of Fort Fauntleroy in New Mexico. Entire Native families moved about freely around the public areas, and some Indian women lived at the fort with white officers. Considerable economic exchange went on, with fresh produce sought by the soldiers and durable goods by the Indians. In the ensuing social atmosphere, constructed in a remote area where all people enjoyed few distractions and recreations, Indians and whites regularly entertained themselves with high stakes horse races. The competitions were raucously intense and considerable money changed hands. When after some heavy betting, Natives disputed the honesty of one of the races, the soldiers drew weapons and fired into the crowd of angry Indians. Within moments, the scene turned from shared recreation to military massacre with men, women, and children sprawled dead about the grounds.

The surviving Navajos, their memories fresh with the bitterness of the "Long Walk," a deadly forced march from their Arizona home to New Mexico, fled the racing area. Enraged, they abandoned their daily visits to the fort, turning their attention to the countryside, setting fires, and killing army livestock.

The post officers faced the awkward task of explaining the peace-keeping mission collapse to superiors. Hoping to sooth injured feelings, the post commander sent the Indian women living with various officers as his amend-making emissaries to the offended Navajos. The women – whose residence at the fort had eased Native–army interactions, made the interior grounds accessible to Natives, and brought desired economic benefits to their Indian families and tribe through their sexual liaisons with the military – were beaten by their relatives and sent back to the fort.[6]

The New Mexico event pointed to the many ways, across the West, that Native people grappled with ever-changing ground rules in their negotiations with whites and inside their own tribes, as well as the ambivalence created by shifting gender expectations. The result was that Indian–white diplomacy unraveled even further and in the confusion additional violence flared between Indians and whites. During the Civil War, the problems escalated, as regular units left for eastern battle duty and Indians dealt with an assortment of local militias, made up of volunteers. These local units, though not trained and armed as were professional soldiers, could be wildly undisciplined and erratic in their military conduct.

For example, in 1864, Colorado volunteers, under the command of a regular army officer, John Chivington, who employed the well-known African American scout James Beckwourth, launched a dawn attack against a village of Cheyennes, who thought themselves under the protection of a nearby fort. The sleeping Indians had no chance to fight or flee and were cut down quickly. The bodies of the dead, mainly women and children, were mutilated and, soon after, grotesque souvenirs, including genitalia, waved in front of excited Denver crowds. Known as the Sand Creek Massacre, this event added to fury about the deaths of Shoshones at the Bear River Massacre in Idaho only one year earlier and fanned further Indian hatreds as word of these many murders spread among the tribes.

With the end of the Civil War, the regular army returned to the West and to its pre-war program to eliminate hostile encounters between settlers and Natives, specifically by overseeing the containment of Indians on reservation lands. The deployment of regular troops was expected to bring stability to the West, control aggressive actions of whites against Indians, and eliminate the Indians'

Figure 4.1 Indian burial teepees containing wrapped bodies were grim reminders of the Native American death toll, resulting from military engagements that totaled more than 1,000 between 1866 and 1891. *Source:* Courtesy, Denver Public Library, Western History Collection, B-417.

warfare capabilities. However, the army, charged to keep order, often found the fractious settlers, yearly increasing in number, more trouble than the Natives. When given the choice between controlling white farmers, miners, and laborers, or using its force against nearby Indians, the military, an agency of a white government, usually selected the latter group. Thus, the United States army, charged by the federal government to be the instrument for maintaining peace in the West, emerged as the institutional face of violence sanctioned by the federal government, earning the enmity of both white settlers and Native peoples.

Natives in many locations were outraged by the inconsistencies in their negotiations with officials that could lead to betrayals such as those at Fort Fauntleroy or Sand Creek, and retaliated whenever they could. The result was that explosions of violence dotted the western horizon. Between 1865 and 1868, Cheyennes, Arapahos, Kiowas, and Comanches on the Plains, and Snakes and Paiutes in the Northwest, all used war as a defensive strategy to stop further incursions into their territories. Typically, Indians enjoyed some local success and white settlers fell back, at least briefly. Natives, however, mainly fought along tribal lines, failing to establish firm pan-Indian alliances that would have given them a stronger position before whites could regroup, enlarging the force of their numbers and firing power.

This aspect of Indian political life undoubtedly hindered the outcomes for Natives when the United States government summoned them to an 1867 peace conference in Kansas. The result of the fall meeting was the Treaty of Medicine Creek Lodge, in which the tribes of the southern Plains ostensibly agreed to a division of Indian lands and accepted a permanent reservation in western Oklahoma. The treaty prohibited the Indians from moving beyond the established reservation boundaries or using their traditional hunting areas. Given those egregious restrictions it was doubtful that there was common agreement among the various tribes in attendance, delegates had the authority to make such a decision for absent tribal members, everyone among the Natives understood both the spirit and the letter of the law, or those who did had any intention of honoring such a sweeping transformation of their homeland.

The treaty was a first step in a new government program that, once President Ulysses S. Grant took office, came to be known as the peace policy. Its signature feature was that Indian agents were to be drawn from among religious ministers and the Society of Friends (Quakers), thought to be guided by humanitarian impulses. The Indians were to comply with reservation boundaries or be hunted down by the army. Still, there were other aspects to the peace policy, specifically funding to develop education and agriculture, the goal of which was to transform reservation Indians into white Americans.

Reservation schools were both day and boarding and many were run by Protestant or Catholic missionaries, between whom there was a fierce rivalry for Indian loyalties. After 1879, many tribes learned from having their children forced to attend the Carlisle Indian School in Pennsylvania that they could exercise greater parental oversight if their children remained on the reservation. An on-reservation boarding school was not always attractive, but at least in some cases permitted parents to check on the well-being of their children.

Despite the high hopes of some for the new directives, the peace policy never became the success envisioned by those seeking reform in Native affairs. Ministers and priests proved no more effective and no less corrupt than the agents before them. The Bureau of Indian Affairs remained mired in corruption. The melding of civil and military authority produced hostility and contradiction. The distances between administrators in the East and Native leaders in the West, the appointment of Ely S. Parker, a Seneca Indian, as commissioner of Indian affairs notwithstanding, doomed the project.

Accordingly, war between Natives and whites continued for more than 20 years. Indians were jaded from a long series of meaningless treaties and with a cynical eye saw that assignment to a reservation always meant a significant reduction in land controlled by tribes. Still, within Indian communities and between tribes, common political goals proved elusive. Thus, the diplomatic policy of Natives toward whites was often as uncertain as that of whites toward Indians. This diplomatic unevenness reflected more than simply a difference between older, more conservative Native leaders who encouraged compliance, and younger, more radical fire-brand tribal warriors who urged war. There was too much cultural, political, and economic transformation confronting Indians to describe their differences as simply generational.

In addition, at this time, Indians assessed and reorganized their relationships across tribal boundaries. As the years passed, Indian tribal groups were not only constantly adjusting to a different set of diplomatic and military circumstances, but also to changing internal tribal politics and cultural values. The alliances of the past did not always seem appropriate for the circumstances of the present.

The flow of European technology into Indian communities waxed and waned, contributing to indigenous economies that increasingly fluctuated between brief periods of prosperity and long stretches of poverty. On both sides, new persons came into power and they in turn did not share with one another the same interpretation of what had preceded or what should lay ahead.[7]

Whether for whites or Indians, attempts to maintain the peace through war extracted a high price for all concerned. Indian casualties would be impossible to tally, but by the end of the nineteenth century, the rapidly shrinking Native populations, decimated by war, disease, and low fertility rates revealed a picture of physical and emotional decline across all tribes. By the 1890 massacre of over 150 Lakota men, women, and children by US army forces at Wounded Knee, South Dakota, more than a thousand conflicts had taken place, with at least a thousand soldiers killed and another thousand wounded. One official estimated that for one 10-year period, 1872–82, the government spent almost 225 million dollars on the Indian Wars of the West.[8]

While the epic of Indian–white conflict warped the history of the West, it did not hold a monopoly on regional violence. In all corners of the West and between many different groups, violence remained a pervasive theme. Indeed, it might be argued that violence – in all its notions, behaviors, and impressions – acted as the adhesive, attaching and bonding all the parts of the western narrative. Violence simultaneously ripped apart and restructured social, ecological, and economic relationships during this era.

In the popular story, violence always assumed a distinctly masculine tone, one that has suggested men behaved in a physical vacuum, apart from the context of society. Even the violent history of Natives and the American government singled out images of war between Indian and white men. Women and children, faceless and nameless, apparently only appeared on the stage to act as the dead, whether from an Indian Sand Creek Massacre or a settler wagon train attack.

Yet the volatile nature of western violence did not draw race, class, or gender boundaries. It did not even discriminate between human society and the natural environment. Rather, violence in many forms and places shaped the West at all times, but especially in the second half of the nineteenth century.

Americans have chosen to remember some western violence as "valiant," "dashing," or "thrilling." Their memories, however, have been selective, allowing them to ignore the larger implications and the long shadow of violence, regardless of its genesis. The historian Richard Maxwell Brown reminded Americans that "violence has not been the action only of the roughnecks and racists among us, but has been the tactic of the most upright and respected people."[9]

Despite Brown's cautionary remark, the accounts of outlaws and vigilantes in the West have tilted toward the sensational and the fanciful. Somehow, the James brothers, Billy the Kid, John Wesley Hardin, Wyatt Earp, and the Younger brothers – killers all – achieved heroic stature. They were lionized in song and poetry, story and film, despite the fact their cumulative tally of no less than 50 murders included bank clerks, detectives, and innocent by-standers. Given that record, their murderous ways made them sound more like criminal neighbors to avoid, rather than champions for the ages. Additionally, even though it have been lumped together in the western narrative, one criminal definition did not necessarily fit them all in equal ways.

It was the historian Richard White who looked more deeply at the western outlaw and noted distinctions between a plain crimi-nal, a "social bandit," or the combination of the two. For example, Billy the Kid may have been part of the western regulator wars that took on a popular image of seeking justice, but that association did not eradicate his basic homicidal history. Indeed, Billy's pen-chant for killing people made him the perfect type to participate in regulator activities. Popular history has merged the homicidal behavior of Billy the Kid with every other "frontier" outlaw, also labeled as "noble." White saw that criminal actors could be moti-vated by more than one factor and influenced by prevailing social attitudes. Thus, these "social bandits," despite the clear illegality of their actions, held to values or convictions that transcended the written law, as well as the moral sensibilities of some segments of the population.

It was White who saw in lawlessness like that of the Jesse James–Cole Younger band, behaviors of former Confederate soldiers, acting on post-Civil War resentments against the victorious federal gov-ernment. Such gangs assaulted institutions directed by what they saw as vicious northern politicians and financiers, especially repre-sented in banks and railroads. Thus, these institutions became the targets of former Confederates who roamed about with few eco-nomic prospects in the emerging financial structure of the West.[10]

Perhaps no other western undertaking symbolized the place of the West in the national corporate structure than the building of the trans-continental railroad. A massive effort by laboring crews of immigrants, the railroad showered its wealth on a small coterie of businessmen. As an engineering feat, the railroad also showed the necessity of importing capital to the money-scarce West and represented the way profits flowed out of a rural resource rich area and into the coffers of coastal financial institutions. The railroad encapsulated some of the worst in labor relations, pitting Asian immigrants against Irish immigrants, as the Union Pacific and Central Pacific competed for obscenely generous federal dollars for the laying of the track. It gave new meaning to the concept of the "public domain," sucking up the best land along its thousands of miles right of way. It wedded itself to the banking industry, aiding the latter in the usury and deceit that broke the financial back of more than one farm family.

The first trans-continental railroad literally joined the East to the West, gave the US government better control of its western lands, connected families across the continent, assured better communication and mail delivery, threw another obstacle into the lives of nomadic Indians, encouraged greater farm settlement on the Plains, provided a way to move the resources of the West to industrial areas, transported the finished manufactured goods back into the West, opened the region for tourism, and solidified the financial power of industry over the West. It was small wonder that, on May 10, 1869, the day the tracks from the East joined with the West at Promontory Point, Utah, the bells rang from the tower of Trinity Church, located at the foot of Wall Street in New York City. Those bells, celebrating the triumph of eastern money and the potential of western riches did not echo through the South, where the vanquished former Confederacy knew it stood on the sidelines of the glowing and fresh national economic picture.

As a result, of such unvarnished corporate maneuvering, a community sharing the sentiments of James and Younger could see their actions as justified. Those outside the local community, supporting a different set of political and economic values, regarded the thieves as unmitigated criminals. But even these factors did not fully explain an ongoing affection for the western gunslinger.

Nor did it explain why only a handful of male perpetrators were singled out for "glory," while women outlaws were nearly totally ignored. A few names – Belle Starr, Calamity Jane – mingled with those of the male desperados and added a dash of feminine glamour and sexual allure in an otherwise decidedly masculine world of law-breakers. But the tabloid-like recounting of their lives, much of it invention, rarely dealt with the deeper issues of female criminality.

In the West, just as in the other regions of the country, society seemed confused by the female criminal. The nineteenth-century society of Anglo Europeans, whether in the American West or beyond relied on a narrowly defined set of precepts to explain the role of women.[11] That these notions of "gentility," "piety," and "passivity" applied, and then poorly, to only a small number of women did not dilute their power. Indeed, in general, society used a language of femininity as a way to explain *all* women and the standards of *all* womanhood, regardless of how inappropriate such designations were across cultures.

At the same time, nineteenth-century women faced added disadvantage as the scientific interest in criminal behavior took on an organized academic form. Most directly, based on several international scholarly or medical conferences, women who violated the social or legal codes dictating "respectability," found themselves with a new label, that of "social deviant." Thus, criminal behavior, misdemeanor, or felony loosened the link to womanhood, pushing a woman beyond the boundaries of "proper" society.

In the West, with its many male-dominated industries and its self-conscious lack of stability, women were held rigidly to the standard and definitions described above. Far from the free-wheeling, anything-goes "frontier" society popular in literature and film, western communities reacted harshly to women lawbreakers, whether they flaunted the legal or moral code. Clearly, power brokers, both in and out of the West, anxious to impose order on a rapidly changing but crucial American region, saw the importance of harnessing behaviors of several groups. If women, disadvantaged in various ways, could not be coerced into "acceptable" behavior, what hope was there for regional domination of other "miscreants?" The deep roots of political and economic discrimination twisted themselves around gender in western society, with significant results.

In all parts of the West, women criminals confronted a draconian judicial system. Typically, indigent women were poorly represented by attorneys, convicted on questionable evidence, and punished with longer and harsher sentences than their male counterparts.

While a masculine offender guilty of a misdemeanor might sit out his punishment in the county jail, a woman convicted of the same offense was often sent to the state or territorial penitentiary. It was often unclear whether a woman was incarcerated for breaking the law or for violating the "moral" standards of womanhood.

Prisons were built for male inmates and run by male administrators, so women entered into a gendered community that had few, if any, residential, work, health, or protective provisions for them. For women, decent living arrangements, reasonable diet, and careful supervision were all missing in western prisons. All forms of penal torture, including whipping, sexual assault, head shaving, beating, leather hoists, and seclusion in the black hole, were inflicted on women as commonly as on men. In addition, issues of race and class fueled local judicial decisions. In all jurisdictions, women of color were convicted in higher numbers, received lengthier prison terms, performed heavier prison labor, and served more of their time than white women.

As prisoners, women responded to their circumstances through a series of moves intended to disrupt penitentiary routines: they fought guards, they accommodated guards; they helped each other, they fought each other; they resisted work, they broke equipment; they sought release through parole petitions, pregnancy, and suicide. All in all, the saga of women criminals added another element to the power of violence in the West.[12]

In part, Americans have held to an inflated notion that the West was "masculine," a place where a "real" man righted his slights, even when it meant "taking the law into his own hands." Thus, it was only a step from honoring the violence of outlaws to according vigilantes an admired status. Somehow, mobs roaming the countryside and executing others by "lynch law" took on an aura of western righteousness. In the Far West, the history of vigilantism repeated the excesses of the eighteenth-century Regulators Wars of the Carolinas.

Rather than episodes where law-abiding citizens excised the outlaw, the bandit, and the horse thief from their communities, these events were part of the struggle for power in the emerging West. Many prominent and moneyed settlers – business owners, ranchers, and politicians – used their combined local status as the cachet by which they murdered at will and avoided censure for what were basically a series of orchestrated homicides. The economic outcomes of vigilantism always favored the well-to-do and further destabilized the attacked group – whether minorities, transient cattle rustlers, or poor sheep herders.

Further, vigilantism suffered from its own spontaneity. Vigilantes did not follow any set of articulated rules, nor formulated standards of conduct. Rather, action tended to erupt suddenly and was carried out by the momentum of emotion rather than a specific code of law. That some lynched persons were, in fact, criminals who could have been convicted justly in a court of law, obscured the more complicated issues at stake, most specifically that hundreds of people were murdered for who they were and not for what they had done. The underbelly of vigilantism in the United States revealed it for what it was and always had been – lawlessness which denied the right of due process to an accused and advanced the interests of a powerful few.

The impact of this dynamic on the shaping of western history led the historian Richard Maxwell Brown to label vigilantism as an element in the "Civil War of Incorporation," which had little to do with idealistic citizens addressing concerns about order and everything to do with the rise of business and capitalism as the defining forces in the modern American economy that would control the future of the nation. Thus, vigilantism, according to Brown, had less to do with a spirit of "frontier" independence and self-motivation than it did a rising conservative hegemony throughout the country.[13] In that scenario, the American West was not a region of wide open spaces and untamed cowboys. The West, with its resources and people, was a segment in America's march into industrialization. It was a critical ingredient in the rise of America's global economic power. As such, the West might be able to supply the imagery for national self-identity, but beyond those nostalgic songs about wide open spaces where the deer and the antelope played, the region was expected to take its place in the country's corporate complex.

The proof of that emerged in the developing labor unrest in the West. The push and pull of labor conflict that had emerged in the first years of the mining industry only gathered steam as the century progressed. Anti-Asian sentiment fueled much of the conflict, as more Chinese spread through western work areas. The intense violence against these new immigrants of the working, but not professional class, did not even slightly abate until passage of the Chinese Exclusion Act, passed by the United States Congress in

1882, whereby, for the first time in its history, the country closed its borders to an immigrant population based on their race and class.[14]

Although the worst of the anti-Chinese hatred slowed, it certainly did not disappear, and it laid the foundation for discrimination against other Asian groups who emigrated in later decades. Nonetheless, there was no shortage of ethnic hatred in the work fields of the American West. Typically, the more skilled and better paying jobs in the mine yards went to Anglo Americans and Anglo immigrants, while eastern Europeans or men of color took the lesser positions. Still, there were occasions when the various laborers temporarily dropped their racial divisiveness to present a united front against management, events that highlighted the extremely complex nature of western race relations.[15]

The West produced some of the names most associated with the American labor movement. The organizers Joe Hill and William "Big Bill" Haywood, as well as the famous American labor radical Mother Jones, were all connected to strikes at western mines. So, too were the Pinkertons, a private police agency that used a ruthless group of company enforcers to break the strikers' unity through intimidation, dynamite, fires, beatings, and murder.

There was no lack of violence. For example, in Idaho, through the 1890s, tensions and open violence marked the relationship between the Bunker Hill and Sullivan Mining Company and its union-prone workers. The Protestant mine manager showed little sympathy for his crews, writing to the absentee owner, "what a motley Irish crowd of old men and boys we . . . have" and indicated he hoped to replace these miners with "American workers."[16] State and national law enforcement agents were used against the strikers, the American Protective Association raised its nativist voice against the Irish immigrants, explosions occurred along the mine lines and an atmosphere of mutual distrust pervaded for more than 10 years. The "meet force with force" policy was less successful than when the company introduced employment and union regulations that hampered strikes, as well as some community amenities for the miners and their families.[17]

Closed out of labor negotiations in western industry were the prostitutes of western communities. Few looked on prostitutes as legitimate wage earners and their place in western history was often relegated to discussions about social life and entertainment. They were more correctly associated with western labor history.

Women who worked in prostitution flocked to those locations

where economic opportunity ballooned. Thus, prostitutes gathered around cattle towns, lumber centers, mining camps, military forts, and railroad depots, areas that depended on male laborers to work in out-of-doors occupations. Prostitutes did not seek employment in those jobs, but rather hoped to earn a living by skimming off some of the money held by men. In their jobs, they danced with men, "pushed" drinks for the bar, sang or played games of chance, and offered sexual relations. They performed this work in saloons, cabins, military "hog ranches," brothels, and small shacks, often known as "cribs."

Most women lived away from their place of employment and reported for work when the men appeared following their shifts. In general, the customers came from the same economic class – laborers and transients – so the opportunity to earn a substantial wage from such men was limited. Customers were little interested in paying prostitutes much for their services, while the women wanted to secure the highest possible fee. This led to an adversarial system of bargaining about the rate, an exchange that often took place between an intoxicated man and woman. The prostitute wanted the money in advance, while the customer hoped to delay payments and slip away without handing over his cash.

In addition, the women dealt with a long list of expenses. They lived in poor neighborhoods, but paid double the going rate for rent. Hack drivers or bartenders took a percentage for bringing customers to a woman's room. They paid inflated prices for the liquor they kept available for their customers. They faced repeated arrest for the violation of local ordinances and paid court fines and lawyer fees on a regular basis. To avoid arrest, some prostitutes delivered a weekly bribe or gifts to local law enforcement officers.

Generally drawn from poor families and with few employment opportunities, women entered prostitution at a young age – perhaps 12 or 14. Typically, they could not read or write. Like men, the women followed the booms and the rumor of same. Thus, their work made them migrant laborers, a group that historically has little community power and has been made unwelcome in local society. Given the overall intense sentiments concerning the "proper" role of "respectable" women, prostitutes did not find widespread social and economic acceptance in the West. In fact, local newspapers considered them a target for ridicule and reported the public happenings of prostitutes in lurid and mocking language.

This did not mean that prostitutes did not have a place inside the vice community, which operated along a clear hierarchy. In some cities entire families participated in various forms of vice and exercised control over the saloons and the activities associated with them. For example, in Denver, Jane Elizabeth Wallace Ryan, who with her children ran a number of prominent saloons and brothels, had a close association with the local authorities and did not hesitate to use those connections to act against other residents of the vice district.[18]

The Ryans ranked as one of the more prosperous of vice families. They owned more than one saloon in Denver, their establishments had solid furnishings, and the family dressed well, in the fashion of the day. Jane Ryan rented out cribs to poorer prostitutes. If they found upward mobility as a family, they were an exception among prostitutes, where very few women attained the status or ongoing financial stability of the Ryans.[19]

But even the Ryan family did not escape the frequent domestic violence that surrounded the women working in a vice profession; amidst an argument, daughter Annie Ryan shot and wounded her bartender. Like Annie Ryan, other prostitutes endured both intentional and accidental violence at the hands of their customers. Men in drunken rages attacked women beating them with weapons and fists; women died of gunshots and strangulation. Prostitutes also experienced violence from each other; they stole from each other, set fire to one another's possessions, and physically fought with one another. Violence was so common in prostitution that brothel life with a madam who would intervene when matters took a bad turn became the most desirable employment.

Prostitutes also were violent to themselves. They lived on the edge, moving frequently, working long hours, eating poorly, and residing in dingy quarters. With their overall weakened physical condition, venereal disease, pneumonia, tuberculosis easily overtook them but access to medical care was sporadic. Alcoholism and drug addiction were common and suicides were frequent. It is not surprising that prostitutes died at young ages.

Racial division buckled somewhat among prostitutes. It was not entirely uncommon for white and African American prostitutes to work in the same house. There was less mingling of Asian and Mexican women with Anglos, but it was not unknown. For example, in 1884, Jennie Conway made the burial arrangements for Adelle Sanchez, after the latter was shot and killed in Cheyenne.[20]

Conway and Sanchez represented much in the profile of western prostitutes. The unpredictability of their lives, the paucity of their income, and the overall societal indifference to their circumstances relegated these women to the edges of society. Carefully constructed friendships were not a hallmark of the profession. Although prostitutes adopted a series of strategies for managing the essentials of their lives, they did not often have the personal skills, educational background, monetary resources, or moral support that might have energized them to redirect their lives into other forms of employment. Given their low place among the working people of the West, prostitutes, assessed on moral rather than economic grounds, became a peripheral and poorly told part of the western narrative.

Regardless of what type of occupation they followed, male and female workers, like business owners and company managers, thought more of the lure of wealth than about the physical integrity of the land. That proved to be ironic, for it was the land – whether rich for farming or ready for resource extraction – that crazed western people. The West conveyed an aura of limitlessness – sweeping mountains, vast distances, crashing rivers, towering stands of trees and space, space, and more space. Newcomers allowed the land to inebriate them and prevent them from considering appropriate ways to use the West for human benefit without widespread destruction. That short-sightedness proved to be convenient as the national economy was shifting from rural-farm production to urban-industrial incorporation. Attitudes about the western environment exacerbated the reckless procedures that broadened the atmosphere of western violence.

The general stampede of huge populations into the West altered the landscape in every direction. The industries that came with the people needed the varieties of western land and hardly expected to leave the region as it once lay.

Mining practices showed some of the most obvious violence against the many elements that made up the environment. In the West, the huge copper pits at the Anaconda mine in Montana and at the Kennecott mine in Utah created environmental prototypes of what occurred when corporations launched large-scale extraction practices. The existing surface was permanently altered, not just at the digging site, but also at the dumping location. Local plants and animal life died, water sources were diverted or contaminated, machinery belched noxious fumes, and fires released toxins into the atmosphere. Furthermore, mining had such a mercurial quality – here today and gone tomorrow – that once a mine slowed, corporate interests, just like the miners themselves, scurried off to the next promising lode, leaving behind the scarred remains of their earlier efforts.

Lumbering followed much the same pattern. Indeed, the harvesting of forests in the Pacific Northwest replicated the cutting methods that had reduced the tree population in the East. Small rail lines provided transport through the dense woods and brought the cut trees to a sawmill built along the track. Not only was the natural environment assaulted, but the humans paid a price, as well. Lumber crews lived in crude camps, the houses raised on stilts, so that rotting wood and raw sewage could flow beneath.[21]

Less understood for its violence against the land was agricultural industry. The West had already been changed by the introduction of alien livestock, but in the spring of 1866 when the first herds thundered north out of Texas, the cattle industry wrought new environmental havoc. Cattle owners cared little for the damage or ill-will they caused as their herds moved across the lands of others, leaving behind the fatal Texas tick fever. The animals polluted rivers and land, but they and the herders proved to be a moving target – leaving their debris and passing on to the next resting place. Most especially, the cattlemen willingly took advantage of the vast public domain grasslands to rest and fatten the animals. With little or no regulation, the lands literally became the stomping grounds of the cattlemen.

The cattle industry, like mining, quickly slid into the hands of big business. During the nineteenth century, the American cattle industry became a highly sophisticated international business, with investors from Scotland, Wales, England, and South America. In the American West, the companies often belonged to absentee owners who left the daily operations in the hands of a competent manager.

The cattle laborers, common cowboys, among them a number of African Americans, were transients with slim political power. These migrant workers were left to deal with the physical and destructive work of moving cattle. Their jobs were highly dangerous, as they moved millions of cattle across and through the great acreage of the West. It was a brawling, smelly, dirty world – the stench-filled wrestling of cattle branding symbolized an industry driven by frenzy.

No less harmful to the western environment was the farmer himself. Farmers stared across a vast horizon and pondered how to demarcate their land for their homes, their barns, and their crops. In the West, they paced off the acres with barbed wire, changing the very face of the landscape. They uprooted the native grasses, scooped up the steel plow, introduced new crops, and bought into novel technologies – the tractor, reaper, thresher, and combine – all of which challenged the existing soil and grasses. With the natural surface altered, the great expanses of the American prairies could no longer absorb the usual ferocity of wind and rain.

But farmers often faced being their own worst enemies. Greater efficiency in the fields and larger yields typically encouraged farmers to overextend themselves. The erratic patterns of rainfall prompted farmers to dig deep for wells, develop huge irrigation systems, or explore the methods of dry farming. If these human alterations were not enough, drought, exhausted soil, hail, rain, and fires – all had the potential to plunge the farmer into economic depression. The cycles of prosperity and failure taxed land, water sources, and farm people.

Adding to difficulty for the farmers of the West was their dependence on the railroads that held the region in an iron grip. Railroads in many cases transported a total farm operation to the West. A rail car ground to a halt in flat, open country and a family with all its possessions and livestock were deposited on the ground, pointed in the direction of their homestead, and left as the train rolled on to another plot. Those who survived as farmers in these situations were those who knew soil and sun, climate and water. In other words, western farming was not for the rookie; success required farming experience and agricultural knowledge that could be applied to a totally new style of husbandry.

Even for the accomplished farm family, the unceremonious arrival foreshadowed the way in which the railroad changed from friend to foe. Farmers stood by the tracks and glumly watched cars hauling new farm equipment pass them by. The railroad companies charged exorbitant loading and unloading fees, finding ways to double the costs. They built grain elevators for storing farm crops, but only allowed a railroad spur to their facility, cutting off any possible competition. The companies controlled the best land along the route, encouraged farmers to put in improvements where they had purchased plots, and then, drawing on the farmers' new roads or wells, hiked the price on lesser sections that sold at a later date.

The railroads kept their cozy alliances with the banks, as well as with friendly judges, making sure that the farmers could not rise up against various mortgage and occupational discriminations.

The environmental and human price continued to pile up. The Order of the Patrons of Husbandry, founded by Oliver Hudson Kelley, of the Department of Agriculture in Washington, DC, and a former Minnesota farm owner, offered some social respite for isolated farmers, who lacked organization. However, meetings of the association, which came to be known as the Grange, almost immediately assumed a political tone – discrimination by the railroads, lack of redress before the courts. Banding together across the Midwest and West, farmers churned ahead demanding agrarian reforms. Their successes, known as Granger laws, included pricing limitations for freight and the establishment of commissions to supervise law enforcement. The railroads retaliated, eventually appealing to the US Supreme Court. The farmers prevailed in the 1876 Munn vs. Illinois decision, but the big companies quickly looked for ways to dilute the victory. In the long run, the history of western farming would parallel that of other extractive industries – it became one more major industry in the control of companies, eventually leading to the formation of American agribusiness at the expense of the individual farmer.

In the large picture of the West, industrial power brokers who triumphed and daily laborers who struggled left a less than gentle image about the processes of modern development in the West. There were, however, advances made and products introduced because of the resources of the West. For example, the dietary habits of the nation were overhauled because of the cattle industry, its partner, the refrigerated railroad car, and a clever advertising campaign that convinced American housewives beef should be a daily feature on the family dinner table.

The issue of improved standards of living did not hinge on the fact that western resources were used, but rather *how* they were used. Perhaps the matter concerned allocation of benefits and *which* people received or were denied the profits of the West. Wide-scale narrowly-managed industries privileged only some of the American population. Others, not only lost out in the immediate scenario, but their descendants for generations continued to feel the effects of political and economic marginalization. Had such questions and results been considered during the era of expansion and empire building, the outcome of western resource use – both natural and human – might have been a tale of better results. The West of the twenty-first century might not have been left to look back on the nineteenth century as an era of unprecedented abuse and destruction.

At the same time, despite the many unappealing forces that drove western history, there were important and positive aspects to the nineteenth-century narrative – aspects that influenced the entire nation and produced long-lasting impacts on American society. Granted, in concert with the other regions of the United States, the nineteenth-century West was marked by extreme volatility as people and governments acted in regretful and deadly ways. The West was, however, also a region where men, women, and children crafted communities, often against incredible odds. Accordingly, the nineteenth-century West left a legacy more complex than the residue of violence.

One area that added to that complexity concerned the expression of spirituality and religious organization in the West. Most peoples who inhabited the West appeared, in some fashion, to connect their humanity to the unique world around them. For example, the archaeological artifacts of pre-contact Anasazis suggest their ceremonies were closely associated with the southwestern climate, especially rain. The Pueblo people of the same region constructed a richly textured religious behavior, which assigned distinct importance to the rituals of men and women. Far into the Northwest, Native peoples took advantage of their deeply wooded environment to literally carve a system of elaborate totem poles and other religious objects, devising one of the most ceremonial of cultures among all Indians. Several Native communities displayed a strong reliance on spirit life and the importance of visions. Indians of the Great Plains were numbered among these and for them the buffalo had special spiritual significance. The rhythms of human life were closely associated with the power of the spirit world among many tribes. Accordingly, birth, sickness, death, or the onset of menses in a young girl were occasions that called for adherence to ritual and prayer.

The introduction of Christianity with the arrival of European nations altered but did not eradicate the religious systems of Native people. Part of their ongoing history in their western homelands always involved the efforts of individuals and groups to reclaim, retain, or reshape early practices. For example, the Ghost Dances practiced by Native peoples took place over several decades and became a process by which Indians reached deep into their cultural life and outlined their tribal identities within a reservation system that had systematically attempted to eviscerate tradition and ritual.

But the West also had an impact on the religions that invaded the region. After the first forays of the earliest missionaries, Catholicism made adjustments in the American West. Its first stories included many chapters of oppression at mission stations, especially in California and the Southwest. By the nineteenth century, there were, however, other elements emerging out of the Catholic presence. It had become obvious to church administrators that they would never convince a sufficient number of European priests to labor in the American West. Yet, the numbers of Catholic immigrants to the United States kept increasing through the nineteenth century. Thus the hierarchy faced a two-pronged dilemma: how could the church minister to the back country immigrants and how could it retool its mission efforts among Native Americans?

The Catholic church solved this problem, in large measure, by encouraging congregations of nuns to accept mission assignments in the West. After 1850, more and more religious women left their monasteries of Europe to trek to the unknown American West. Constraints of many kinds confronted the nuns – anti-Catholicism, gender bias, poverty – but, in the main, they pressed forward. With slim pocketbooks, they opened schools and hospitals, orphanages and boarding homes, introducing social services before local governments were able to do so. Over time, they showed themselves to be women often willing to learn from the people they served and the new environments they entered. Most importantly, their western lives had much to do with changing the style of women's religious life, as the European monastery evolved into the American convent.

The Catholic laity also responded to the church conditions around them. For example, those living in rural areas became accustomed to irregular visits from a priest. Families adapted the routines of religious life, sharing in community prayer and spiritual reading. On the reservations, some Native peoples continued to use their chapels during the long absence of the priest, holding prayer services with singing. As a result, the Catholic laity in the West developed a certain independence and a willingness to work as a community in religious affairs. Nowhere was this more evident than in the "Penitent Brothers" or "Los Hermanos" of New Mexico. The "Los Hermanos" followed an intense set of religious practices that included self-flagellation and a Way of the Cross service on Good Friday. Often dismissed to the borders of Catholicism because of these severe physical rituals, the brotherhood was overlooked for the way it served the local community as a mutual aid society, an activity congruent with notions of Catholic social activism.

Protestants also found challenges and benefits in the American West. The Congregationalists, Baptists, Presbyterians, Episcopalians, and the Methodists all had mixed results with western proselytizing. The Baptists,with revivals, and the Methodists, with circuit riders, each brought religious support that accommodated the realities of western life for isolated church members. There was, of course, an energetic interest in missionary work among Native Americans, as seen by the early attempts of the Whitmans in Oregon. The federal government was happy to assign various Protestant denominations to Indian reservations where, as agents and teachers, pastors carried both a religious and secular message about the benefits of conversion and acculturation.

After the Civil War, Protestant interest in western congregations dipped, as fewer young male pastors wanted to move to these locations, preferring church assignments in the East and the South. This void produced an unusual opportunity for women to be ordained and serve as pastors. A merged group of Universalists and Unitarians showed some interest in promoting this idea. By 1890, only about 70 women had taken on the role of a full-time pastor. Several served as co-pastors with their husbands and others were called to smaller congregations that had failed to attract a male minister. In general, female pastors reinforced the traditional roles of wives and mothers, calling for the promotion of the family. Although they were often quite successful at the local level, a movement to expand the place of female pastors in the West failed to materialize, with most eastern theologians insisting they did more harm than good. An early suggestion among the Mormons that women might be given the priesthood along with men also faltered, and fell into disrepute after the church relocated to Utah. Thus, the chances for women to ascend to priestly roles equal to those of men did not take hold in the West. Nonetheless, the presence of the women ministers, covering about 50 years, added a new dimension to the religious history of the American West.

Jewish immigration to the American West has been somewhat misplaced in the usual account of western change. Perhaps because the Jewish community did not set conversion of the Indians as a goal, it has seemed less of a religious presence in the region, a notion that is in error. Significant Jewish immigration to the West came with the first Gold Rush, where a number of young men sold various commodities in the mining towns. Certainly the most famous of these was Levi Strauss, who played an important role in the San Francisco Jewish community as a merchant and clothing supplier. Jewish men entered into all areas of commerce, as well as banking and politics.

Religious duties were carefully detailed for Jewish people and the West often challenged people living in remote places to meet those obligations. Jewish men and women, however, formed closely knit communities, where everybody shouldered a number of important religious responsibilities. Women struggled to keep a kosher kitchen and men formed associations for social support that eventually led them to organize local synagogues. Jewish families in such places as San Francisco and Denver were successful in convincing rabbis to move to their cities. As Jewish community life stabilized, especially in urban areas, leading families became some of the outstanding civic leaders and philanthropists of the West. Hospitals, theaters, museums, parks, and orphanages in several urban areas all came into existence because of the generosity of local Jewish families.

Clearly, some people used the West as an opportunity to advance and to change. While the West has often been portrayed as the playground of marauding cowboys, drunken miners, and lethal soldiers, it hosted a considerably more diverse population. Indigenous people and immigrants, even in the face of great discrimination, altered the contours of their lived experience. Most particularly, women of many backgrounds grew within themselves, for their families, their cultures, their communities in the West.

Pioneer wives and mothers, those women who packed up hearth and home, and climbed into Conestoga wagons to make the long journey across the plains and the prairies left an indelible imprint on the American mind. Typically, they were viewed as long-suffering pioneers or "gentle tamers," doggedly bringing "civilization" to the West. Of course, the West already had plenty of civilization and pioneer women did much more than adopt a posture of martyrdom and misery. One thing was certain – their travels into the Far West changed their lives in ways they had never anticipated.

Wives, along with their husbands, had hopes for the future as they turned their backs on the familiar and the known of the East. Their expectations, however, differed from the men, who saw the move westward as a chance for upward mobility and greater wealth. Women tended to perceive of the journey in overall family terms. Their concerns centered on the unknown dangers that lay ahead, ones that could threaten the safety and well-being of husband and children. They worried about how to manage shelter and sustenance, illness and accidents, poverty and death. They feared the distance from kith and kin, the contacts lost with relatives, not just for themselves, but their growing children as well. They harbored uncertainty about their own courage to live near Indians or undergo childbirth alone in the back of a wagon. They dreaded the fierce extremes of western weather that would descend on them with freezing blasts of cold or shimmering mirages of heat.[22]

Yet, in the face of these multi-faceted challenges, many women from the East and Europe proved themselves remarkably resilient and innovative as they transformed themselves into westerners. Perhaps in their letters, some women wanted to put the best face on their circumstances to alleviate the worries of aging parents in the East, but certainly some spoke with conviction, such as Mary M. Colby, a newcomer to the Oregon Territory, who wrote to her siblings about the success she and her husband had in establishing their farm and added, "I cannot say that I wish to go back to the states to live at present if ever."[23]

Less remembered are the many single women who tried homesteading by themselves or with siblings or cousins. South Dakota, Oklahoma, Montana, Colorado, and Wyoming land records all included the names of single women who took advantage of the Homestead Act of 1862 that gave 160 acres to citizens who wanted to work the land. Although women found it a challenge to break sod, plant crops, dig root cellars, and build small shacks, several felt the rewards to be worth the endeavor. In return, women could support themselves and other family members, make long-term financial investments, and enjoy the thrill of succeeding in the difficult world of western farming.[24]

Throughout the nineteenth century, women also relocated to

western urban areas, where they found unconventional work oppor-
tunities. Lola Montez danced her way across the theatrical stages of
San Francisco and Sacramento. Hannah S. Hutchinson worked in
Denver as a saleswoman of hygienic undergarments. In Wyoming,
Martha Maxwell had a thriving business as a taxidermist. Jane
Grey Swisshelm landed a position as the editor of the *St. Cloud Vis-
iter* newspaper in St Cloud, Minnesota. Each found a way to use or
bend gender expectations to secure employment.

African American women also looked to the West as a place that
might offer them opportunity or the freedom to raise their families, far from the unsavory reminders of slavery. With few tangible
improvements offered to them in the South, former slaves, many of
whom had ample agricultural experience, also looked to the promise offered by the 1862 Homestead Act. The chance to work 160
acres of family-owned land, build communities, and escape local
persecution resonated among African Americans after the Civil War.

Accordingly, by 1877, a small town named Nicodemus had formed
on the Kansas prairies. Soon, the numbers of migrants exploded,
giving rise to the term "Exodusters," to describe the mass migration
of black Americans to western lands. Encouraged by land adver-
tisements in handbills, speakers in churches, or black entrepreneurs
such as Benjamin "Pap" Singleton, African American families
became part of the agricultural movement into the West. The numbers of blacks seeking land in Kansas alone was probably in excess
of 25,000 persons. White southerners did not look on the exodus in
a kindly manner, fearing the loss of laborers needed for the tobacco
and cotton fields. Pushing off the threats and intimidation, African
American families left in numbers sufficient to support five rural
black towns in Kansas.

Black women took up their home-building in the popular sod-
houses – noted for their warmth in winter and coolness in summer
– and contributed to stabilizing the family income. African Americans always had greater difficulty securing store credit or bank
loans for farming expenses. The land they actually held was far
smaller than the expected 160 acres and not always located in the
most fertile areas. They owned fewer stock animals and struggled
to keep their animals healthy.

Thus, African American families often looked for secondary
sources of income to keep their farms going. The husbands and sons
took jobs in a nearby town – working in a hotel or blacksmith shop,

Figure 4.2 African Americans built community in the urban West through churches, clubs, and informal social gatherings, all of which frequently included group music. *Source:* Courtesy, Denver Public Library, Western History Collection, X-21525.

while the wives and daughters did the laundry of wealthier white families or took in boarders. Farming life on the Central Plains was remarkably harsh, but for some African American families, living in community, organizing local governments, establishing small businesses represented critical life opportunities for changing the direction of black life.[25]

Black women also found opportunity in urban centers of the West. There they took advantage of the more compact living areas to establish a network for themselves and for the black community. As a result, African American women became leaders in their church organizations and school districts, gaining important organizational experience that led them to be receptive to the women's club movement that arose at the end of the nineteenth and early twentieth centuries. Through the club movement, black women worked aggressively to promote benefits for all African Americans. They supported educational initiatives, child care programs, orphanages, neighborhood improvement programs, and anti-discrimination efforts. As they reached out to and aided their own black communities, they also raised their personal sense of self-esteem and accomplishment. Over the years, they further strengthened their clubs in California, Texas, Montana, Colorado, and Kansas, through associations with state-wide and national organizations for African American women. Attendance at annual conferences broadened the base of their knowledge about social service work and connected them to other women of color committed to enhancing western life for African Americans.[26]

Other immigrants to the West included Asian women, whose arrival dates were greatly influenced by the warp and woof of anti-Chinese sentiment. Fear of the Chinese, coupled with the desire of businesses to exploit cheap Chinese labor, along with desperate economic conditions in the mother country, kept Chinese women from joining the early ranks of immigrants. For approximately 25 years, the women who came were herded into prostitution, carefully controlled by Chinese businessmen. After 1875, the Chinese moved past an era when women immigrants were forced into prostitution and servitude, and the Chinese experience took on a strong family-centered tone. In part this resulted from American exclusion law that favored the merchants and professionals among the Chinese, and accordingly, gave a place to the wives of such men.[27] Women's numbers, however, remained somewhat low and, by virtue of language and widespread discrimination, they tended to stay inside the Chinese community. Because the larger society chose to have scant contact with Chinese communities, whites incorrectly assumed that women had little role and place. Such was not the case. Although their adaptation took place under the mantle of several different constraints, Chinese women learned to blend the role of homemaker and child bearer with wage earning work. As basket makers, seamstresses, laundry workers, storekeepers, and cooks, Chinese women made critical economic contributions to the well-being of their families.

Perhaps their most dramatic work was at the Chinese Telephone Exchange in San Francisco. There, at the turn of the century, young Chinese women stood on their feet all day, and with all pertinent telephone numbers memorized, connected the calls from Anglo businesses for day laborers to the few telephones inside Chinatown. Thus, these young women served as the critical link between the Anglo world and Chinese employment, building the base of the ethnic economy.

By 1900, the Japanese immigrant communities had stabilized, but lacked the women needed to build families. Among Japanese men of sufficient means there developed a social custom of the "picture brides," a system of arranged marriages across international waters. Although officials tried to enforce regulations that would prevent young women from falling prey to false promises or prostitution overlords, there were many flaws in the process and some questionable "marriages" resulted. Despite a tradition of non-wage, in-home domestic labor for Japanese women, most of the brides found their husbands expected them to enter the public work force. In both rural and urban environments, Japanese women labored in the fields or as domestic servants, all requiring heavy physical work and long hours, but returning little remuneration. Again, the barriers of language and rudimentary education, as well as a close monitoring system by the Japanese community, kept these first women immigrants part of a tightly controlled social network.[28]

Indigenous women watched these various events across the West with a curious eye. Within Native tribes everywhere in the West, women had seen their place and power, usually by force and aggression, shift across hundreds of years. With each flash of change, Native women had accommodated the new structures and demands. Their places as tribal administrators, agriculturists, political advisors, and religious leaders were repeatedly altered in Native–white diplomatic forays.

Frequently, the changes centered on sexual liaisons – coerced and chosen. In more than one tribe, women, as their traditional roles diminished, were pushed into white society to make a sexual link that could bring material gain to families. European American men, across all time periods, indulged themselves in these arrangements and provided some of the desired "bounty" for Native homes. Enhanced trade, diversity of food, better goods, including fabrics, beads, weaponry, and domestic tools were but some of the items that raised the standard of living for Indians. As tribal infrastructures buckled from war and disease, younger women had fewer opportunities to assume the roles of their mothers and grandmothers; thus, the door to using women as the conduits for alliances with whites opened wider.

Yet, there was an element of uncertainty and risk for the women. Men on either side of the cultural fence could turn against the others, which in turn left Native women caught between two groups of warring males. Inevitably, both sets of men verbally, physically, and emotionally abused the women, blaming them for sexual behaviors foisted upon them for political and economic reasons. Little attention was paid to the gender devastation that disrupted the patterns of women's traditional power in the ongoing conflicts between Native and white societies.

In addition, Native women increasingly considered the precipitous status of their mixed blood children. Among whites, such children might be derisively labeled "half-breeds," scorned and ostracized, but their fate inside Native society could be equally tumultuous. Indian mothers had to assess how to best position those children for a future that was increasingly dominated by white power. In other words, Native mothers watched their children negotiate an uneasy path in both Native and white societies. In the face of catastrophic cultural changes, decades of war, and divisiveness that solidified class structures within a tribe, mothers had to decide whether to guide their children to Native politics and plans or encourage them to latch onto whatever they could squeeze from an ungenerous Anglo world. By the beginning of the twentieth century, the balance of power shifted inside the tribes, as the mixed blood population ascended in number over the full blood tribal members. This further complicated the relationships between Indian and white worlds.

For some mothers, the choice was simplified through the appearance of the Indian reservation school. In a rapidly changing Native world, the school could offer important connections to white society. The reservations and missions offered work to Native men and women and the chance to make connections that would keep a family fed and clothed. Given that work future had severe limitations, the wages could be critical for a family. Here children could learn the English language, a growing expediency for those who wanted to draw something out of what was a crippling national policy toward Native life. Here all – Natives, whites, teachers, agents, pastors, nuns – were culture brokers, persons who came, often in ignorance, to the borders of their culture and looked across at another life way. Although reservation and mission schools compiled a notorious history for coercion and failure, there was a certain courage among all those participants in facing the differences of human experience. Additionally, the force of Indian families has been forgotten, for Native mothers and fathers could be adamant about what they would or would not tolerate in the classrooms and boarding halls. In 1900, a group of Navajo parents in Arizona vehemently rejected a suggestion that their children should be sent to a Catholic mission in New Mexico, protesting they would not break up their families, suggesting that school life was unhealthy, and questioning the benefits of an Anglo education.[29]

Overall, western history ignored the importance of Native women and how the ongoing interaction with European societies disrupted and displaced female roles. Perhaps one of the most demanding roles, however, was as the wife and mother who evaluated the possibilities of the future. Central to Native life, women were called on in a bombastic and chaotic world to make rapid life-directing choices – many of them unpleasant – about where Indian peoples would fit in a West that was increasingly white.

Mexican American women also witnessed permanent change in long-held gender practices. Those changes spanned class structures and many decades, encompassing broad territorial reaches in North America. As a result, the patterns of life for women varied greatly and depended much on where and how one lived. The expectations of a nineteenth-century sheep-herding girl in rural New Mexico may have differed markedly from those of a rancher's daughter in southern California. Nonetheless, the realities of a virulent anti-Mexican sentiment, much of it framed in salacious gender descriptions, provided the commonality of unmitigated discrimination. For Mexican American women, race and class collapsed into a unilateral prejudice that restricted their cultural identity and womanhood.[30]

Women of every community owned or developed an intense relationship with the American West. The values and goals of these women, however, frequently conflicted. They held to differing aspirations for themselves, their families, and their people. Their world views turned on opposing axes and they endorsed the male structures of their own society at the expense of promoting gender unity. Women who held public power, generally middle- and upper-class Anglos, acted in ways that solidified economic and political strength for white society. Women who did not have access to that kind of power watched and waited, as their sense of cultural identity further ignited and smoldered.

Accordingly, the combined narratives of these differing communities affirmed one of the unhappy truths of women's history. In a region where place and experience might have encouraged women to reach across divides and develop some framework for mutual understanding and human expression, the opposite occurred. Race and class might have been vehicles for dialogue, but became the standards for rigid division and hostility between and among groups of western women. There were exceptions, of course. Most promising was that western women of every race and class faced a twentieth-century West that would bring unprecedented change and empowerment through suffrage movements, labor protest, educational advances, and civil rights action.

As the nineteenth-century West closed, it left behind a collection of peoples both exhausted and energized from the dynamics of US empire building and the stresses of contested living. Some of those were the entrepreneurs and politicians who congratulated themselves for the anticipated prosperity they would reap from the human and natural resources of the West. Others were newcomers, who, though weary from all that had transpired, counted themselves and their families part of a better place than they had left, whether Asia, Europe, or the South and the East. They looked forward to what they could make for themselves and their families in the West, often doing so at great personal sacrifice. Others folded in despair, for they were not bettered by what happened in the West, only more pushed against the margins and not much able to respond. Their future was vague and their efforts wounded. Yet others surveyed their homeland, theirs before the counting of the years, and saw wave after wave of invaders – on prairies, beside rivers, by deserts, near oceans, at mountains. They calculated the hideous toll taken on their peoples and their families, breathed in the fires of pain, exhaled the rage of bitterness, and harnessed their energy into the voices of activism they would raise in the coming years. Despite these powerful forces, none could have anticipated how the American West, with its scars, the fury of its regions, and peoples would contribute to the dramatic events of the twentieth century.

NOTES

1 *Brooklyn Daily Eagle*, July 7, 1876, 3–4, <www.eagle.brooklynpublic library.org/>.

2 *Farmer's Cabinet*, July 11, 1876, 75:1, 2, Early American Newspapers, Series I, NewsBank and the American Antiquarian Society, and US Congress, Senate, US Congressional Serial Set, 44th Congress, 1st Session, Senate Executive Document 81, NewsBank, <www.infoweb. newsbank.com>.

3 The historian who has written most extensively on George Custer, always balancing the man's often contradictory and complicated inclinations, is Robert M. Utley. See his *Cavalier in Buckskin: George Armstrong Custer and the Western Military Frontier* (Norman: University of Oklahoma Press, 1988).

4 *Brooklyn Daily Eagle*, July 7, 1876, 3–4.

5 "The Battle of Little Bighorn: An Eyewitness Account by the Lakota Chief Red Horse, recorded in Pictographs and Text at the Cheyenne River Reservation, 1881," from Garrick Mallery, "Picture Writing of the American Indians," *10th Annual Report of the Bureau of American Ethnology*, 1893, <www.pbs.org/weta/thewest/resources/archives/six/ bighorn.htm>.

6 "Capt. Nicholas Nodt to Maj. Ben Cutler, September 7, 1865," printed in *Condition of the Indian Tribes*, pp. 313–14, Arrott Collection, New Mexico Highlands University, Las Vegas, New Mexico.

7 Loretta Fowler, *Shared Symbols, Contested Meanings: Gros Ventre Culture and History, 1778–1984* (Ithaca: Cornell University Press, 1987), 240–6.

8 Oliver H. Knight, "Indian Wars," in Lamar, ed., *The New Encyclopedia of the American West*, 545.

9 Richard Maxwell Brown, "Historical Patterns of Violence in America," in Hugh Davis Graham and Ted Robert Gurr, eds., *Violence in America: Historical and Comparative Perspectives*, vol. 1: *A Report to the National Commission on the Causes and Prevention of Violence* (Washington: GPO, 1969), 76.

10 Richard White, "Outlaw Gangs of the Middle Border: American Social Bandits," *Western Historical Quarterly* 12:4 (October 1981): 387–408.

11 Glenda Riley, *Inventing the American Woman: A Perspective on Women's History* (Arlington Heights, IL: Harlan Davidson, 1986), 6–7.

12 For additional information concerning women criminals, see Anne M. Butler, *Gendered Justice in the American West: Women Prisoners in Men's Penitentiaries* (Urbana: University of Illinois Press, 1997).

13 Richard Maxwell Brown, *No Duty to Retreat: Violence and Values in American History and Society* (New York: Oxford University Press, 1991), especially chapters 2 and 3, and "Western Violence: Structure, Values, Myth," *Western Historical Quarterly* 24:1 (February 1993): 5–20.

14 Erika Lee, *At America's Gates: Chinese Immigration during the Exclusion Era, 1882–1943* (Chapel Hill: University of North Carolina, 2003).

15 Gunther Peck, "Padrones and Protest: 'Old' Radicals and 'New' Immigrants in Bingham, Utah, 1905–1912," *Western Historical Quarterly* 24:2 (May 1993): 157–78.

16 Katherine G. Aiken, "'It May Be Too Soon to Crow': Bunker Hill and Sullivan Company Efforts to Defeat the Miners' Union, 1890–1900," *Western Historical Quarterly* 24:3 (August 1993): 308–31, quotes, 316, 317.

17 Ibid., 327–31.

18 Butler, *Gendered Justice in the American West*, 82–3.

19 Butler, *Daughters of Joy, Sisters of Misery*, opposite 130.

20 Ibid., 44.

21 David Buerge and Cecilia Murray, OP, *Evergreen Land: A History of the Dominican Sisters of Edmonds, Washington* (Seattle: Active Press, 1997), 84–5.

22 For a longer description that uses both narrative and fiction, see Anne M. Butler and Ona Siporin, *Uncommon Common Women: Ordinary Lives of the West* (Logan: Utah State University, 1996).

23 "Mary M. Colby to Dear Brother & Sister, February 1849," Bennett Family Papers, Haverhill Public Library, Cambridge, MA, quoted in Lillian Schissel, *Women's Diaries of the Westward Journey* (New York: Shocken Books, 1982), 157.

24 Glenda Riley, *A Place to Grow: Women in the American West* (Arlington Heights, IL: Harlan Davidson, 1992), 231–9.

25 For a full discussion of this movement, see Nell Irvin Painter, *Exodusters, Black Migration to Kansas after Reconstruction* (New York: Knopf, 1976); Quintard Taylor, *In Search of the Racial Frontier*, 136–9; Decoursey Clayton Lucas, "African American Homesteading on the Central Plains," *OAH Magazine of History* 19:6 (November 2005): 34–9.

26 Taylor, *In Search of the Racial Frontier*, 219–21; Lynda F. Dickson, "African-American Women's Clubs in Denver, 1890s–1920s," in Sucheng Chan, Douglas Henry Daniels, Mario T. García, and Terry P. Wilson, eds., *Peoples of Color in the American West* (Lexington: D. C. Heath, 1994), 224–34.

27 Judy Yung, *Unbound Feet: A Social History of Chinese Women in San Francisco* (Berkeley: University of California Press, 1995), 16–22, 26–41.

28 Yuji Ichioka, "The Japanese Immigrant Family, 1900s–1920s," in Chan et al., eds., *Peoples of Color in the American West*, 198–207; Evelyn Nakano Glenn, "The Dialectics of Wage Work: Japanese American Women and Domestic Service, 1905–1940," in DuBois and Ruiz, eds., *Unequal Sisters*, 345–72.

29 Anne M. Butler, "Mother Katharine Drexel: Spiritual Visionary for the West," in Glenda Riley and Richard W. Etulain, *By Grit and Grace: Eleven Women Who Shaped the American West* (Golden, CO: Fulcrum, 1997), 212–13.

30 Patricia Preciado Martin, *Songs My Mother Sang to Me: An Oral History of Mexican American Women* (Tucson: University of Arizona Press, 1992), Arnoldo de Leon, *They Called Them Greasers: Anglo Attitudes toward Mexicans in Texas, 1821–1900* (Austin: University of Texas Press, 1983).

Chapter 5

A Diverse, Urban, and Federal West

Up to our own day, American history has been in a large degree the history of the colonization of the Great West . . . And now, four centuries from the discovery of America, at the end of a hundred years of life under the constitution, the frontier is gone.[1]

On a warm day in Chicago in July 1893, members of the American Historical Association settled into their chairs at their annual conference to hear from a little-known young scholar. Frederick Jackson Turner, a 32-year-old historian from the University of Wisconsin, hoped to make his mark in a profession that did not reward many with fame. Such would not be so for the professor who stood before his audience and delivered a paper entitled, "The Significance of the Frontier in American History." Turner's fellow scholars listened closely to the first academic attempt to both characterize the history of the West and justify over a century of American colonialism in North America.

For Turner, the West was something already in the past. On that historic day, he argued that in demographic terms, there was no longer an American frontier. Citing the most recent census, Turner asserted that every square mile of the United States held enough Americans to be considered settled by the federal government. Holding to his belief that the frontier worked as an incubator for Americanness, Turner implied that, because white rural settlement had been successful, the West was no more. That this was so worried Turner, since without a frontier, the future of America might be in jeopardy.

Though they probably never heard of Turner or his scholarly ideas, those who lived in recently settled areas must have thought there was still plenty of "frontier." Furthermore, many westerners proved eager to contest any one idea of Americanness. Many bumped along on unpaved dirt roads, could not see to the next neighbor's house, drew water from a well, had no indoor plumbing, and read by the light of a kerosene lamp. Many lived in racially and ethnically diverse communities. Their daily experiences ran counter to the university professor's vision – especially his notion that the development of the West belonged to white society.

For instance, in 1899, only six years after Turner's presentation, officers of the Western Negro Press Association elected William Taylor, an African American newspaperman who published the *Utah Plain Dealer* in Salt Lake City, to the presidency of their organization. Their 1900 meeting in Salt Lake City drew black newspaper owners, editors, and reporters from across the West to the Wasatch Front. With two black newspapers in Salt Lake City, at least four others across the state of Utah, and tens of others in cities as far flung as Omaha, San Francisco, Oklahoma City, Helena, Portland, Topeka, Dallas, and Denver, the Western Negro Press Association meeting pointed to the crucial presence of non-whites in western settlement.

In 1896, the War Department ordered over 500 members of the all-black 24th Infantry Regiment to Fort Douglas, which overlooked the city. African American soldiers usually received less desirable, often bleak, rural postings, where they were assigned the task of subjugating indigenous communities. As the first urban stationing of black troops anywhere in a nation that adapted outright racial segregation by the 1890s, many locals feared violence. The city's African American newspapers reported that Utah's US senator even tried to dissuade the military from such a move, but to no avail.

Comporting themselves with dignity and professionalism, they produced a solid record of distinguished service. Slowly, the black soldiers won the grudging respect of many white residents of Salt Lake City. Additionally, the presence of the soldiers bolstered the local black literary clubs, lodges, and churches on which African American communities across the West depended in the face of rising segregation.

Still, life was not easy for blacks in Salt Lake City. Julius Taylor, the African American editor of a second black newspaper there, noted the segregation found all over the urban West. In mid-1898 he lambasted local white businessmen in the *Broad Ax*, for fostering a harsh racial hierarchy. The "color line" shaped black life in the city to "an alarming extent." The "hatred and intense prejudice against all negroes irrespective of their deportment or appearance" kept even "genteel Negroes" from being served in restaurants and shops.[2]

Salt Lake City offered other contradictions to Turner's statements. The largely Mormon white population that resided there had for decades remained on the margins of the nation. Their adherence to plural wifery alienated multiple generations of Americans who disagreed with the Church of Jesus Christ of Latter-day Saints' (LDS) religious practices. Outright war between the LDS church and the US government in the 1850s shifted to a law enforcement campaign in the 1880s that focused on imprisoning known polygamists and bankrupting the Mormon church. In fact, Utah's statehood was delayed by controversies over polygamy until 1896 – six years after the LDS church officially renounced the custom.[3]

The histories of African Americans and Mormons in Salt Lake City in the years immediately following the so-called end of western history suggest a more complicated experience than Turner imagined. Understanding the West solely as a frontier of American settlement, Turner missed other equally important dynamics. For example, envisioning the West's history exclusively in terms of rural settlement by whites overlooked the black men who met in Salt Lake City and other urban locations. It also presumed a western-derived Americanness that many Mormons adopted only unhappily and under immense pressure. Both stories pointed to dynamics that emerged in the nineteenth century and came to dominate the region in the first half of the twentieth century – urbanization, contests between diverse populations, and a powerful federal presence.

That most black newspapermen attending the 1900 Salt Lake City meeting came from cities went almost unnoticed. In fact, despite stereotypical visions of the West – including Frederick Jackson Turner's – as rural and open, by 1900 people who lived west of the Mississippi River were more likely to live in cities than any other Americans.[4] Equally important, not all those who settled on newly-wrested lands in the region were white. That African Americans, Chinese, Japanese, Filipina/os, and Mexicans lived alongside a smattering of native-born and immigrant whites in these cities and in rural areas meant that westerners rubbed elbows with a wide variety of people. The West proved more racially and culturally mixed than other parts of the country. That plurality, however, emerged in a context where racism directly shaped daily life. Social borders based on one's perceived racial and ethnic background permeated life in the West.

Finally, the War Department's decision to post black troops in Salt Lake City over local objections, alongside Washington DC's efforts to end plural marriage among the Latter-day Saints, presaged a broader presence for the federal government in the West. The United States, not private entities, remained the primary property holder west of the Mississippi River. In the years that followed, the national government amplified its power in the West. This combination of continued urbanization, demographic diversity, and the federal government defined the early twentieth-century West.

Western cities grew rapidly at the end of the nineteenth century. Urbanization, in fact, proved essential to American conquest. Cities served as centers of commerce and as transportation hubs for extractive materials. They fostered the movement of Americans into Native homelands. Through railroads, wagon roads, and mail routes, western cities spawned networks that speeded communication and eased the way for more settlement. Urban settlers still depended on capital and commerce from eastern cities. Ships from Boston and New York kept San Francisco and the Pacific Slope well supplied. East of the Rocky Mountains, Chicago took on the role of supplier for smaller western cities. The first extractive forces – unleashed by monies and technologies poured into the West by eastern and European capitalists – were funneled through growing western cities.[5]

By the 1900s, however, western cities, strengthened and stabilized, began flexing their muscle over their hinterlands. Flour milling interests in Minneapolis capitalized on the nearby railroad hub in St Paul, as well as the croplands of North Dakota, South Dakota, and eastern Montana. The Twin Cities dominated the economic, political, and daily life of its agricultural outback. Meat-packers in Kansas City, Omaha, and Fort Worth took their place as processing points for livestock and other rural products from across the Great Plains. Financiers and merchants in Denver extended their

reach over the whole Front Range. Seattle and Portland – rail termi-
nuses – became centers of capital and transport that reached north
to Alaska and east to the northern Rockies. Salt Lake City dominated the economics and culture of the Great Basin. Oklahoma City
benefited from the early twentieth-century oil boom in Oklahoma.
Merchants and investors in San Francisco controlled much of California's commerce and production, as well as that of Nevada and
Hawai'i.

In those places where local dominance promised to lead to
regional dominance, western cities jockeyed for the best position.
Spokane challenged Portland and Seattle, becoming the urban
magnet of greater Idaho and eastern Washington, which promoters
grandly dubbed "the Inland Empire." Boosters in early twentieth-
century Los Angeles bragged about that city's ability to trounce San
Francisco as the overseer of a vast economic network that might
reach west into the Pacific and south into Mexico.[6]

Establishing economic hegemony over nearby rural areas transformed local ecologies. Cities reworked the countryside through
extraction and industry. Railroads transported the rich solar and
geological wealth away from the rural West and into the urban
West. The nature found or created in rural landscapes became the
commodified products of industrial cities. Urban areas allowed
for the concentration, production, and reproduction of resources
that could not take place in agrarian or mountainous places. They
reshaped sunshine trapped in corn fed to livestock into pieces of
consumer-ready meat. They processed the fossil remains of ancient
life into refined oil for the kerosene lamps that lit people's homes.
They assigned abstract values to sun-kissed wheat that fueled futures
markets. They converted trees from rural forests into boards in
urban lumberyards. They turned raw copper ores into refined copper
wires as electricification swept across the United States.[7]

While the majority of these products stayed in their respective
city-hinterland regions, by the 1920s, growing numbers of western
resources found their way to national and international markets,
shuttled along the transportation and capital routes established in
the nineteenth century. Meanwhile, the scarred rural landscapes left
behind highlighted the environmental costs. Urban residents, awak-
ening to the decline of their surroundings, then began supporting
protection for much of the yet untouched lands, further asserting
control over rural lives and rural terrains.

Simultaneously, city dwellers often ignored how much they altered the land as their municipalities expanded. Less compact than eastern cities, western urban centers invested in wider streets, broader grids, and the latest electric streetcars. Growth, envisioned with nature in mind, also meant parks and city landscapes were planned – not haphazard afterthoughts. In some cases, planners took advantage of sprawling city designs, providing recreational spaces for urban dwellers. Sometimes they literally reconfigured the landscape, filling in wetlands and leveling hills to achieve the desired effect.

The creation of parks, parkways, and other green spaces too often came with social costs and societal tensions. Arranging city spaces also meant rearranging people. Frequently plans for urban renewal rested on the involuntary relocation of a city's poorest community. In cities such as Seattle, the material transformation of the urban landscape privileged the few and alienated the many. In Los Angeles, people of means enjoyed parks, while people of color faced barriers when trying to use recreational zones. Although there was a strong interest in beautification for westerners, the outcomes often revealed a failure to embrace schemes that would foster inclusivity in communities.[8]

Rapidly expanding twentieth-century western cities needed prodigious amounts of water. This matter highlighted the unevenness in the natural distribution of western resources. Typically located far from large water supplies, cities looked to rural areas for water, as well as raw materials for industry. Los Angeles, in particular, came up against water shortages almost immediately after the turn of the century. Led by William Mulholland, superintendent of the Los Angeles Department of Water and Power, city fathers cast their eyes to the snow-capped Sierra Nevadas. Targeting the Owens Valley, the municipality purchased land and water rights – in many cases, through deception or violence – and, by 1913, Los Angeles built an aqueduct that eventually drained the Owens Valley dry. Taking more water than needed, city administrators argued that they held the future in mind. More directly, for their own personal gain, they provided the water and electricity companies needed for the commercial expansion of Los Angeles real estate.[9]

That commercial expansion and its corresponding concentration of wealth led to western cities becoming centers of art and high society in their own right, giving rise to new cultural forms derived from western experiences. Besides the emergence of museums, opera companies, and orchestras that signaled cultural independence from eastern elites in the early 1900s, western cities fostered novel religious trajectories. The Pentecostal movement, a new form of Protestant Christianity that emphasized healing, speaking in tongues, and the imminent end of the world, emerged from the interracial Azusa Street Mission in Los Angeles in 1906. In an era when women rarely occupied the pulpit, itinerant minister Aimee Semple McPherson founded the Four Square Gospel Church in the same city in 1923. She flamboyantly flaunted makeup and expensive jewelry as she preached a popular evangelical message over the radio as well as in her church.[10]

Resource grabs, self-imagined cultural superiority, and challenges to religious tradition poisoned relationships between rural and urban westerners. More broadly, as rural landscapes became incorporated into urban outskirts and came under the heel of urban capital and culture, farmers, ranchers, laborers, and small town residents turned to legal and political resistance. Angered by outside control of their labor and resources, locals hoped to assert their own control over the spaces they inhabited. Lingering frictions from the late nineteenth century boiled over in the early twentieth century.

For instance, Hispana/os in New Mexico and Tejana/os in Texas struggled to retain their farms, ranches, and social place, as more white Americans moved into the area. Asserting Mexican or even Spanish understandings of property in the face of American claims to land, many Hispana/os and Tejana/os lost their lands in the courts at the turn of the century. Meantime, whites elevated New Mexico's colonial past in everything from architecture and food to state politics and literature. In Hispana/o communities, wage labor replaced family-centered work as the result of economic displacement even as the history of Spanish-speaking conquistadors, settlers, and priests was lionized to attract tourists and soothe social tensions. Forced to abandon ranching and farming, Hispana/os turned to jobs in the mining industry at the turn of the century. In Texas, Tejana/os found little recourse in a state bent on celebrating its own white revolutionary heroes. Too often, Tejana/os were driven from land ownership to sharecropping to survive.[11]

In other parts of the West, economic displacement led to labor organization. Miners – spreading out to lumberjacks and migrant agricultural labor –made up the bulk of the membership of the Industrial Workers of the World (IWW). Formed in Chicago in 1905, the IWW organized workers in extractive industries across the West. Calling for "one big union," these laborers took on large corporations and small businesses alike. While many of its members worked in rural jobs, the IWW also began organizing workers in western and eastern cities. Though membership never exceeded 150,000, the IWW offered stiff resistance in many labor disputes across the Rockies and Pacific Northwest, which earned it a reputation for violence and radicalism. IWW members found themselves in the middle of violent clashes as they organized farm workers in Wheatland, California, in 1913, lumber mill laborers in Everett, Washington, in 1916, copper miners in Butte, Montana, and in Bisbee, Arizona, in 1917, and lumberjacks in Centralia, Washington, in 1919. Big business called on government to break the IWW by legal means. State and federal authorities arrested IWW members by the hundreds, bringing down the union by the early 1920s.[12]

Splashed against the backdrop of broad economic and demographic shifts, conflict between rural and urban westerners took other forms. Urban sport fishermen along the Columbia River, as one example, used their economic and social status to wield political power by the 1920s. Arguing that they protected nature, these recreationists from the city challenged rural fishermen whose livelihood depended on daily salmon harvests. New fishing regulations that curtailed industrial net fishing were passed in Oregon in 1927. Such actions amplified an increasingly entrenched urban–rural conflict.[13]

Rural workers learned their lessons from urban activists and in turn utilized state politics to further their own agenda. In 1910, wheat farmers across North Dakota faced off against banking, railroad, and milling interests based in Minneapolis. Businessmen in the Twin Cities controlled the state's government until 1906, while Minnesota financiers continued to back and control small town banks across the prairie. In 1915, socialists organized immigrant farmers into the Nonpartisan League (NPL), a candidate-endorsing organization that argued for a state-controlled lending bank, a state-owned flour mill, a state-owned grain elevator, and state-sponsored crop insurance. Its support of suffrage also offered farm women the opportunity to organize and engage in public protest of their own. In a stunning victory in the 1916 elections, the organization took the governorship and a majority in the state legislature. Proclaiming "A New Day in North Dakota," the NPL geared up for the 1918 elections and established organizations in Minnesota,

Montana, South Dakota, Idaho, Colorado, Nebraska, and Washington. The movement frightened urban businessmen and bankers across the Plains and Northwest. Their counter-organizing snuffed the league out almost as quickly as it spread. Charges of communism and socialism landed NPL organizers in jails across the West, led to recall elections that ejected North Dakota's NPL governor and state legislators in 1921, and thoroughly neutralized the league by 1922.[14]

As urban–rural conflict grew in the early twentieth-century West, the federal government entered the fray. From the 1880s to the 1920s, politicians in Washington, DC, created a wide range of bureaucratic agencies that regulated economic activity across the rural West. Because the federal government owned over half of the land west of the Missouri River, these new agencies made for more change in the rural West. Furthermore, the infrastructure for urban growth – especially the need to supply burgeoning western cities with water – required large outlays of capital that most municipalities simply could not afford. Policy-makers hoped these nascent federal bureaucracies would regularize and balance the extraction of natural resources, crucial for long-term national economic growth.

Like urban–rural conflict, this latest assertion of federal power in the West grew from the late nineteenth century onward. Its roots lay in joint goals – the removal of Natives to reservations and the assignment of lands to become national parks. Both drew on idealized visions, one for Native peoples and their assimilation, the other for uninhabited wilderness that would refresh an American population alienated from nature by industrialization.

Federal troops first patrolled soon-to-be famous parks such as Yellowstone and Yosemite in the 1880s, disrupting the seasonal use patterns long established by local Indians. The intention was to keep Natives out of these bounded areas so that the territories might be truly uninhabited, fitting the American imagination of true wilderness. Soldiers also worked hard to keep local whites out of the parks. US army officers redefined hunting as poaching, and tried to apprehend those who harvested game on federal parkland.[15]

Other government agencies appeared to address questions surrounding use and extraction on public lands and waters in the West. Collectively understood as the bureaucratic result of the movement to conserve natural resources, these arms of government directly affected the West. As early as the 1880s, the US Fish Commission controlled fisheries in Oregon, Washington, and northern California. Their hatcheries applied science to the production of Pacific salmon to increase the harvests needed for a variety of competing economic interests. Pouring money into making fish, the federal government soon became a major presence in the Columbia River watershed. That salmon populations seemed in perpetual crisis further supported the government's ongoing role. The early 1900s saw even more reliance on supposed technical know-how that many believed only this federal fish commission could provide. Ironically, the inefficiencies and flawed assumptions of fish culture bureaucrats were mounting. By the 1920s, contention between local constituencies flared, ensnared in larger debates between scientists and bureaucrats. Nonetheless, the federal government continued to invest large sums in fish hatcheries.[16]

Other agencies tended to other resources. The General Land Office (GLO), a vestige of the nineteenth-century sale of public lands to private citizens and corporations, administered a vast public domain across the West. The Mining Act of 1872 (virtually unchanged today) allowed for unchecked private exploration and surface claims on approximately 260 million acres of federal land administered by the GLO. It vigorously promoted mining above other uses. Underground geological formations – harboring oil, natural gas, and sulfur – came under official regulation via the Mineral Leasing Act of 1920. The GLO assigned long-term leases on a competitive basis. Slowly, a loose form of regulation emerged from policy and court battles that encouraged oil and natural gas development on public lands in the West.[17]

Another federal bureaucracy devoted its attention to forests. Founded in 1905, the US Forest Service (USFS) took over lumber reserves across the West first formed by the federal government in 1891. By 1897, the government controlled almost 39,000,000 acres of forest. Industrial logging operations, which moved west from the forests of Maine, Michigan, Wisconsin, and Minnesota, wanted continued easy access to large stands of timber. Thus, local governments, timber companies, and rural ranchers who used the reserves as grazing lands fought hard against the reserve system.

An industrializing America depended on trees. Between 1879 and 1907, the amount of wood consumed in the United States doubled, from 6.84 to 13.38 billion cubic feet. Five hundred thousand acres of timber were felled every year just for railroad operations across the country. Furthermore, the lumber practices of the big timber corporations ensured large-scale fires in harvested forests. With increasing frequency in the late nineteenth century, fires seemingly ran rampant and out of control in many parts of the country.[18]

With Gifford Pinchot, a European-trained forester and scion to a New England fortune, at the helm, the USFS began an aggressive campaign of professionalization and regulation on lands across the West. In Pinchot's view, extraction to excess would leave the nation treeless, an astonishing prospect given the rich timber stands that had once blanketed North America. Thus, Pinchot aimed to rein in timber company harvests. He expected local ranchers to graze their livestock only in particular places and at particular times to avoid conflict with scheduled tree harvesting.

Whether natural or accidental, forest fires needed to be fought aggressively. Foresters saw unchecked flames as a waste of a crucial resource, not an ecologically necessary cycle that regenerated forests. They pointed to the large fires that swept the forests of the northern Rockies in 1910. Three million acres burned and over 50 firefighters died. The 1910 fires in the Rockies convinced many that all fire was destructive and that the USFS should use drastic, warlike tactics to suppress every fire. Despite the failures in combating the 1910 fires, the USFS prevailed in Congress, earning large monies for fires suppression and the further regulation of forest use.[19] Such a position ensured controversy – especially in the rural West, where the foresters' regulations changed day-to-day lives and exacerbated a feeling that "outsiders" interfered in western economic matters.

As a result, locals often resented USFS bureaucrats stationed in their small towns and on their lands. After a series of fires that swept through national forests in central Idaho in 1919, the *Lewiston Morning Tribune* (Idaho) noted the "losses under 'scientific' Federal control" that ran toward a "million acres." Indeed, the editor sarcastically suggested that "history reveals that the bureau has conserved to date 1,000,000 acres in fires." The bad fire year confirmed local suspicions of the "inefficiency of bureau policies." In contrast, "private holdings" of timber outside of national forest boundaries remained "untouched." The paper failed to mention that local businesses and stores benefited from the monies spent by the USFS every fire season.[20]

In a few instances, however, rural westerners periodically welcomed

Forest Service control. In 1907, locals successfully pleaded with the federal government to take on the razed forests and overgrazed meadows of the Bear River Range in northern Utah. They became part of the Cache National Forest.

Rural westerners sought out the federal government for help in using water as well. Settlers in regions with little annual rainfall often looked to irrigation as the answer to crop-withering drought. Making the desert bloom – pushing past the constraints of the land – became the goal of many. In so doing, they created a "hybrid landscape," a mixture of human artifice and natural dynamics.[21] Growing frustration about the inability of local investors and state governments to fund large-scale irrigation systems led to a push by westerners for federal control of such ventures. In 1902, Representative Francis G. Newlands (D–NV) successfully marshaled a bill through Congress that funded the creation of dams and irrigation projects across the region. Referring to such work as reclamation – reclaiming arid lands for productive agricultural use – the bill called for the sale of 160-acre parcels of land, with the money from such sales deposited into a fund for building the irrigation works necessary to sell more plots. After passage, the first projects included dam and irrigation ditch-building along the Strawberry River in Utah, Salt River in Arizona, North Platte River in Nebraska, Milk River in Montana, Yakima River in Washington, Truckee River in Nevada, Rio Grande River in New Mexico, Umatilla River in Oregon, and Uncompahgre River in Colorado.[22]

In the political struggle to pass the bill, small farmers pushing back the desert frontier became the rhetorical justification for passage. Yet, moneyed interests in the West stood to gain more. Many of the first projects poured federal dollars into private holdings – not the public domain. Those projects on public lands attracted some farmers, whose efforts to bring green life to brown deserts generally failed. In the meantime, Congress added Texas, with its hefty public lands, which had been left out of the original 1906 Reclamation Bill.

In 1907, the Reclamation Service sprang to life as a separate bureaucracy in the Department of the Interior. From 1910 to 1920, the agency struggled. Cost overruns, technical glitches, constant delays, and angry complaints from settlers who waited for the benefits hindered the young bureaucracy. In many cases, only construction companies and private firms profited from the government largess. Furthermore, as those small farmers who attempted to eke out a living on reclaimed lands left, larger agricultural businesses bought out their properties. In the years leading to 1930, the water projects – especially in California's Central Valley – did more to bring taxpayer money to corporatizing farms than to family farmers. As a result, coupled with technological advances such as the refrigerated train car and easily applied pesticides, California agriculture soared in the 1910s.[23]

Cities, as well as agribusiness, needed water. When the city of San Francisco looked east to the Hetch Hetchy Valley in Yosemite National Park, a leading advocate for nature preservation in that city – John Muir – embroiled himself and the still powerful Gifford Pinchot in a western controversy that attracted national attention. Anxious for a new water supply and busily rebuilding in the wake of the 1906 earthquake and fire that destroyed much of the city, San Francisco's politicians lobbied hard for a dam in the valley. They argued that the water provided by such a dam could cement the future prosperity of the West's largest city. In turn, through pamphlets, newspaper articles, and magazine pieces, Muir argued that the destruction of the beautiful valley tucked in the remote Sierras was unconscionable. Pinchot weighed in on the side of the city fathers, bringing his considerable political and technical prestige to the dam builders. Muir retorted that such "attacks" on the sanctity of Yosemite National Park "under the guise of development of natural resources" potentially "defraud[ed] ninety millions of people for the sake of saving San Francisco dollars."[24] After years of wrangling in Congress, the government moved ahead and approved the dam in 1913. Defeated, Muir and his adherents immediately began lobbying for the creation of an agency to administer and protect the national parks so that future development in the parks might be stifled. The US Congress approved plans for the National Park Service in 1916.

Given the importance of water, western states engaged in legal clashes over large water supplies crucial to urban growth and agribusiness. Resolving disputes over access to the waters of the Colorado River, for instance, required federal intervention. The Colorado River Compact, settled in 1922, broke up the ecological unity of the vast watershed that supplied the river into millions of acre-feet to be divided among seven states. In 1923, the Reclamation Service became the Bureau of Reclamation, which now had jurisdiction over both the compact and the river. Yearly, Congress appropriated more and more money to the Bureau, since demand from western constituents for water increased. Legal and political conflicts continued as cities and corporate interests and states vied for local control and federal dollars. These battles initially crippled the Bureau, but eventually made it a larger and more important power in western politics from the 1930s on.[25]

The transformative power of federally-supported agribusiness, federally-regulated resource extraction, and federally-sustained cities reached into the social arena. Because Natives and Mexicans called the West "home" before Americans arrived, the region always displayed diversity across race and class lines. But in the early twentieth century, even more peoples and cultures made the West their "home."

Economic and political machinations encouraged the creation of a West that itself fostered cultural and ethnic overlap with other parts of the world – notably, Latin America and the Pacific. Transient workers of every stripe made resource extraction, city building, and agribusiness possible. Indeed, those efforts exploited a large base of migrant laborers. Whether Greek, Korean, Swedish, Italian, Hungarian, Norwegian, or Filipina/o, such workers looked to employers for temporary stability as well as wages. Mobility, despite the romance of the road, brought little freedom for these men. A migratory lifestyle undercut their efforts to develop a local power base or to organize for fair wages and better working conditions. Ultimately, some only sojourned in the West, hoping to return to their homelands as soon as possible. Others laid deep roots in the region, establishing families, communities, churches, benevolent societies, and a network of newspapers.[26]

Corporations and business working in the West had long relied on foreign labor and that tendency did not decline in the twentieth century. Despite the Chinese Exclusion Act of 1882 and ongoing racism, Chinese and Chinese Americans continued to make lives for themselves. In cities and towns across the West, such as Butte, Denver, El Paso, Salt Lake City, Boise, Evanston, Virginia City, and Albuquerque, small enclaves of mostly Chinese men eked out a life despite constant harassment and hardship that had not abated since the days of the Gold Rush. Dependent on their connection with the large Chinese community in San Francisco, as well as with China itself, these communities slowly shrunk through the 1920s and 1930s.

In San Francisco, however, a large community of Chinese men and women emerged, and the early twentieth century saw it become the center of Chinese American life in the United States.

Chinese women built on the gains of the women's movements in China as well as the efforts of Protestant missionaries in San Francisco itself. The generation of Chinese American women that came of age in the 1920s found new opportunities in the city and encouraged transnational connections to their parents' homeland. The Chinese Telephone Exchange in San Francisco gave one group of Chinese women singular employment and showed the reliance of male workers on these telephone operators who managed the daily calls for employment in the Anglo community. Paid labor and transnational connections ensured a vitality in the Chinese community denied in similar enclaves elsewhere. More generally, Chinese families in America continued to shuttle back and forth across the Pacific, keeping China a vital part of their lives.[27]

Among Asian immigrants the Chinese were not alone. By 1909, 40,000 Japanese immigrants on the West Coast worked in agriculture, 10,000 worked for the railroads, and another 4,000 worked in canneries. As the Japanese population in America rapidly grew – especially in California and Hawai'i – so did Japanese urban enclaves. Facing the same racism and discrimination as the Chinese, but sometimes competing with the same, these Japanese immigrants organized themselves in relation to both challenges.

In 1907, the United States reached a "gentleman's agreement" with Japan in which the latter restricted travel to the former, effectively making Japanese immigration to the US difficult. In 1924, the United States banned all Japanese immigration. Cast as aliens by American law and Americans' daily practices, the Issei, first generation immigrants, were encouraged by Japanese diplomats through the 1930s to envision themselves as the easternmost extension of the Japanese Empire. Given these influences, Issei and their Nisei children forged their own vision of self and community under difficult circumstances. Community newspapers, such as the *Japanese American Courier* in Seattle, and *Kashu Mainichi* (*Japanese California Daily News*) in Los Angeles, proved especially crucial in shaping self-identity. Editors advocated that the immigrants imagine themselves as pioneers in a white America. In so doing, Japanese Americans simultaneously laid claim to a dual respectability. Their pioneer notions allowed them pride in the growing empire they left behind and cast them as central heroes in the Pacific-facing empire created by Americans in the late nineteenth and early twentieth centuries. This distinct transnational ideology helped them argue for their inclusion in western life and at the same time promoted a strong sense of themselves as bicultural through the 1930s.[28]

Like the Chinese and Japanese, Filipina/os made new lives in the United States. Unlike the Chinese and Japanese, Filipina/os were imperial subjects, residents of an American-administered colony. Acquired during the Spanish American War, the Philippines became a source of labor for expanding industries and agribusiness on the mainland. By the 1920s, the Filipina/o laborers joined Chinese and Japanese workers on the sugar plantations of Hawai'i, helping to build an Asian majority there. Embodying an expanded trans-Pacific economy sought by city leaders in Seattle, Los Angeles, San Francisco, and Honolulu, some Filipina/os sought higher-paying jobs found in the western United States. Already experienced in agricultural work, these workers traveled up and down the West Coast. Many settled in Seattle, which became a Filipina/o American center. In the 1920s and 1930s, some Filipino men and women took advantage of their colonial status – one which allowed for more freedom of movement than other Asian Americans enjoyed – to earn an education.[29]

Other Spanish-speaking Filipina/os found themselves working alongside recent Mexican immigrants in California farm fields. In the early 1900s, a new Mexican migration north to California, Arizona, New Mexico, and Texas occurred. It was facilitated by labor recruiters looking to outfit agribusiness, mining operations, and railroad connections that splayed deep into central Mexico. Women became the touchstone for their families as migrant networks extended across the Southwest. Catholic parishes provided another lode of continuity and community for recently arrived immigrants and long-time residents alike. From church picnics to service committees, Mexican Americans found sustenance in their religion in a Southwest that otherwise marginalized the new arrivals.

While El Paso and San Antonio served as the first labor markets – and thus the first urban centers for these migrants – Los Angeles became the eventual home of many who chose to live in cities after earning a stake as transient laborers. There, a rich and hybrid Mexican American culture emerged, distinct from the generations-old California/o community. With their newspaper *La Opinion* and a new musical genre that sparked an industry – the *corridos* – these immigrants claimed both Mexico and America and produced a unique culture all their own.[30]

Spurred by immigration, economic growth, and geographic proximity to an American Empire in the Pacific and Latin America, a fresh cultural and ethnic diversity made for an especially multicultural West. Yet, the original inhabitants of the land – Natives – also provided labor for rural extraction and agribusiness. In return, they earned higher wages than any found on reservations economically eviscerated by forced federal agricultural programs. Additionally, extractive industries found a place on reservations themselves. Shoshone-Bannock cattlemen, for example, survived and prospered in the 1920s and 1930s as surrounding whites' ranches failed. Adapted by Indians across the West, cattle ranching came to demonstrate firmly Native values and cultural meanings as communities made the industry their own. Such acclimatization was not limited to cattle. In the 1930s, Navajo miners successfully adjusted their family economies to new conditions when the federal government drastically reduced their sheep herds. A concurrent cultural adaptation – the national pow-wow circuit in which Natives from all over joined together in expressing cultural persistence and pan-Indian identity – flowered in the 1920s.[31]

That Native peoples persisted despite ongoing colonialism and that immigrants from nearly every direction entered the West demonstrated the seamless relationship between nineteenth- and twentieth-century Wests. Developing the American economy abroad followed directly from expansion across the continent. Soldiers, diplomats, businessmen, bureaucrats, geologists, and policy-makers who learned from their first western experiences traveled across the Pacific and south through Latin America, extending the reach of American economies and culture wherever they went. The completion of the Panama Canal in 1914 not only shortened the time and distance between East Coast and West Coast ports, but also accelerated these overseas initiatives.[32]

Given the continued federal interventions and transnational connections with both raw materials and people, maintaining the nation's borders became imperative. In fact, borders proved to be places where the United States defined itself as a nation that preferred white immigrants. Often forgotten, San Francisco Bay's Angel Island became the gatekeeping alter ego of Ellis Island for most immigrants from Asia. There, migrants from across the Pacific Rim were scrutinized and usually turned away. Guarding the nation from Asians included surveillance on the Canadian and Mexican borders. Both became passageways for Chinese and Japanese immigrants. In fact, immigration enforcement in Texas, New Mexico, Arizona, and California targeted illegal Chinese immigration – not illegal Mexican immigration – through the 1910s.

Only years after American railroads stretched deep into central Mexico, providing transport for workers, did the crossings of Mexican men, women, and children attract attention. In fact, labor recruiters often worked openly in border towns on both sides, even as the US Immigration Service began to limit this illegal activity. In 1917, new anti-immigration laws settled over the border, introducing head taxes, literacy tests, and mandatory showers for immigrants, all unevenly applied. In 1924, the federal government organized the US Border Patrol for the express purpose of guarding immigrant entry points along the US–Mexico border. This changed a long-accepted way of life along the border. Political differences rumbled between anti-immigration organizations and businesspeople whose industries relied on a continuous supply of low-cost Mexican labor. The federal government and businesses alike squabbled over Mexican immigration through the 1930s.[33]

The significance of internal and external borders ensured that ill-will permeated race relations through the West in the early twentieth century. Non-white migrants to the West – whether African American, Asian American, or Mexican American – lived inside boundaries set by the larger society. On the borders themselves, the crackdown on immigration that characterized the early 1900s made racial friction more heated. Violence flared on the Texas–Mexico border, as incoming Anglos clashed with the Tejana/o elite. With the Mexican Revolution roiling to the south, immigrants crossing the border daily, and the growing initiative to dispossess old-family Mexicans of their land and political freedom, armed revolt broke out in August 1915 in South Texas. As an uprising, the effort by angry Tejana/os failed – though the violence sparked the wrath of both the Texas Rangers and white vigilante groups, who brutally retaliated with more killing. Paradoxically, this violent episode, known as the Plan de San Diego uprising, pushed Tejana/os to reorganize and lobby for full American citizenship. Their activism challenged land owners who discriminated against local Mexican

Americans, at the same time that they encouraged more immigrant laborers to cross the border to work the newly-seized Anglo lands.[34]

Racism not only erupted, with heinous results, along boundaries – it often spilled over them. In 1921, a black man in Tulsa, Oklahoma, charged with the rape of a white woman, was held at the local jail. When a menacing white mob gathered outside the jail, black World War I veterans arrived to protect the accused. When gunfire erupted, blacks and whites entered into open combat on the city's streets. The fight continued all through the night. By dawn, white mobs invaded the African American neighborhood, burning and looting. As a response to white violence, city police and citizens rounded up 6,000 African Americans, interning them at the city's fairgrounds, baseball park, and convention hall. With few African Americans left to defend their neighborhood, the white mob was free to destroy black stores, black churches, and black homes. The black-owned and operated *Chicago Defender* reported that Tulsa police requisitioned private planes and dropped dynamite into black neighborhoods. The Tulsa riot counted over 100 victims and thousands of dollars worth of property destroyed, not to mention the long-term racial damage done to the entire city. Many years later, at least one embarrassed white resident excised stories about the riot from microfilmed copies of the city's major newspaper.[35]

The same year also saw declining commodity prices that sent most of the agricultural West into an economic depression long before the rest of the nation felt economic hardship from the 1929 Wall Street crash. As the Great Depression and natural disasters settled over the land, a federal government newly invigorated by the 1932 election of Franklin D. Roosevelt sprang into action. The effect on the West was incalculable. Legislation poured money into the financially-strapped region and strengthened the federal government's role as a major political and economic force there.

Drought, for example, transformed federal land management. The Taylor Grazing Act of 1934 introduced a permit system for the use of federal lands for livestock. Long-term and low-cost leases looked to prevent overgrazing and protect the cattle and sheep industries. Indeed, large operators gained control of local grazing boards and insured that the land served livestock owners. Debate over the future of other federal lands intensified, with some western politicians looking to turn government properties over to the states. Others argued that the states would only receive worthless, arid lands. In the end, the federal government retained control over the bulk of its public lands.

The federal government expanded its reach over agriculture as well, responding to the ecological disaster that struck the Great Plains in the early 1930s. Cast by contemporaries as capitalist conquerors, farmers plowed up marginal prairie sod with newly-invented disk plows pulled by gas-powered tractors through the late 1920s. Before the early 1930s, farmers were lulled by higher than normal rainfall amounts that disguised disastrous weather cycles, including little rain to the Plains. Newly-exposed soils dried out in the intense heat and kicked up into huge clouds of dust that blackened the sky. Entire counties in the Dakotas and in Kansas and Oklahoma seemed to blow away before the eyes of cash-strapped farmers.

Again, the federal government intervened. Bureaucrats and scientists attacked the problem with vigor, forming the Soil Conservation Service in 1935. Despite such government programs, farmers and small town residents – literally dispossessed by the wind and their own ecological overreach – packed their meager possessions and streamed out of the so-called "Dust Bowl" that centered on Kansas, Oklahoma, and Texas.[36]

Refugees of their own making, many of these migrants looked west to jobs as farm laborers in rural California. Industrially-organized agriculture there supplied innumerable fruits and vegetables to the rest of the nation. Growers, however, remained dependent on seasonal wage labor. Through the 1920s, they recruited Asian American and then Mexican laborers to do the work. Paid wages as low as the market would bear and often treated harshly, these workers made the industry successful. When refugees from the Great Plains arrived in California, they added to the mix of farm workers and faced similar forms of discrimination. Nonetheless, refugees – dubbed "Okies" (a reference to their former homes) – sometimes could find work. It became more difficult for Mexican workers to do so. Furthermore, in 1936, the federal government opened laborers' camps that offered community and stability for whites who fled the Dust Bowl.[37]

No such accommodations were ever considered for Asian and Mexican workers in similar straits. Indeed, Mexicans faced more than job competition from displaced poor whites by the mid-1930s.

Figure 5.1   Captured by Dorothea Lange, in her pictorial history of the Great Depression's social upheaval, this Tejana/o family, with a broken car and no other way to reach work in California, reflects the displacement, poverty, and uncertainty of the era. *Source:* Courtesy, Library of Congress, American Memory, Dorothea Lange Collection, 1735.

They also faced repatriation to Mexico. Policies formed by federal, state, and local governments defined recent Mexican immigrants and long-time US citizens of Mexican descent alike as aliens to be returned to their home country. In fact, many forcibly returned to Mexico were either in the United States legally, or were Native-born citizens.

Repatriation programs came first to Los Angeles, in 1931, as it seemed the economic downturn would persist for years. Employers, local charities, and the Immigration and Naturalization Service (INS) joined together by the mid-1930s to solve California's so-called "alien labor" problem. Between 1931 and 1934, Los Angeles officials put those categorized as "alien" in boxcars and shipped about one-third of the 150,000 Mexicans and Mexican Americans in the city south of the border. Official justifications for repatriation, as the programs came to be known, often cited the Depression and widespread unemployment. Not limited to southwestern cities, repatriation drastically changed the racial and ethnic composition of rural wage laborers across the West. By the late 1930s, the numbers of Mexicans and Mexican Americans repatriated to Mexico totaled around 500,000. At the same moment, white boosters of Los Angeles finished their decades-long efforts to sell the city to the world as a place with an ancient Spanish heritage. In architecture and in the schools, city administrators appropriated the myth of the Spanish missions even as they deported local Mexican residents.[38]

As the Great Plains withered in the dry heat, the Bureau of Reclamation redoubled its efforts to harness still-wild western rivers. Encouraged by the success of the Colorado River Compact – which finally settled long-standing disputes between western states about access to Colorado River water – as well as the infusion of federal monies available in the wake of Franklin D. Roosevelt's New Deal, the Bureau of Reclamation gained a new lease on life. In 1931, planners launched the work on an immense dam 30 miles outside Las Vegas. It was the project that would mark the previously weak agency's coming of age. Completed in 1935, Boulder Dam's millions of cubic yards of concrete glistened in the Nevada sun as an immense technological achievement. Equally crucial, the dam supplied the water and electricity necessary for continued urban growth in southern California. Renamed for President Herbert Hoover in the 1940s, the dam, as an engineering and popular success, infused new life – and fresh annual monies, effectively voiding the limited financial reach of the Newlands Act (1902) – into the Bureau and transformed it into an increasingly powerful arm of the mounting federal presence in the region.

The US Army Corps of Engineers began making over the Columbia River basin through similar large-scale dams. Dam-building, justified through its potential to supply cheap and sustainable electricity for the Pacific Northwest, as well as irrigation water for farms in eastern Washington and Idaho, began in earnest in the mid-1930s. Bonding regional industry with locally produced electricity, the federal government hoped to reengineer not only the river but also the communities on both sides of it. The two largest dams – Bonneville, finished in 1937, and Grand Coulee, finished in 1941 – employed thousands, including the out-of-work folksinger Woody Guthrie. Hired to promote the dams in a region that lacked enough people to take advantage of the inexpensive power, Guthrie penned 26 songs, including the classic "Roll On Columbia." Too often, however, the real rolling took place when aluminum came off the line in new regional factories attracted by what became a government subsidy for corporations.[39]

Celebrating both the workers who built the dam and the river they worked to harness, Guthrie's verses said little about the Native communities who lived aside the river's banks. Along with Indians across the West, these tribes seized on a change in the federal government's policy towards reservations. After years of cultural suppression and oppressive oversight for tribes, the Indian Reorganization Act of 1934 (IRA) offered limited self-government and federal monies for cultural rehabilitation. According to the Bureau of Indian Affairs (BIA), assimilation was to be abandoned in favor of fewer controls and greater tribal self-sufficiency. Instead, the Bureau, which administered tribal affairs throughout Indian country, relaxed controls and fostered self-sufficiency.

Controversies immediately broke out on many reservations. In the name of sponsoring self-sufficiency, for instance, the federal government sharply reduced sheep herds on the Navajo reservation because it feared silt from overgrazing would wash into the Colorado River and render the new Boulder Dam inoperable in just a few years.[40] In other parts of the West, questions of tribal identity and official membership bubbled to the surface. In Puget Sound, where innumerable Native groups possessed no land or tribal government, the IRA proved especially problematic. Nonetheless, many Native groups earned sovereign status, retained control over reservation lands previously vulnerable to allotment, and started reclaiming ceremonies crucial to cultural survival.[41]

By the time World War II began, Natives claimed a new prominence in western life. Twenty-five thousand Indians served in the armed forces, and in a show of patriotism that tapped into latent tribal cultures, many enlisted before they were drafted. Government officials, turning an eye away from the troublesome history of the past, proudly noted that over 30 percent of all eligible Indian men served – a percentage that far exceeded other ethnic and racial groups.

Nonetheless, there were exceptions. Leaders among the Zunis and Hopis, whose traditions validated only defensive warfare, tried to resist the draft, but failed. Yakimas interpreted the draft as a violation of tribal sovereignty guaranteed by an 1859 treaty. The federal courts ruled otherwise.

The outbreak of war offered fresh opportunities as well. Indians found jobs on and off tribal lands. Wartime industries in cities such as Minneapolis, Salt Lake City, Denver, and Los Angeles, attracted thousands of Natives from western reservations. In a wartime climate, extractive industries tapped into the rich resources of Indian country. Indians worked to integrate these new ways of sustaining life into their culture, making them their own, whether on tribal homelands or in far-off cities.[42]

Like Natives, rural whites, southern blacks, and Mexican immigrants flocked to fast-growing cities hosting brand new government-subsidized war industries. As part of fledgling industrial labor forces, these diverse communities brought even greater plurality to a much larger migration to the urban West. Cities such as Seattle, Tacoma, Portland, San Francisco, San Diego, Fort Worth, Dallas, Houston, Tulsa, Wichita, Denver, and Salt Lake City raked in the biggest number of migrants seeking work. In just one year, San Diego's population grew by 27 percent.

In some of those cities – most notably Los Angeles – enclaves founded in the early twentieth century fostered urban spaces that promoted multiethnic interpersonal relations. Class bound residents of these neighborhoods together and they mingled, along with wage laborers of every background, through the 1930s. While the war intensified a diverse migration to western cities, it also proffered new opportunities for residential segregation. City elites worked to exclude people of color at the same time that they planned urban growth to house the many new migrants to their metropolises.[43]

War jobs offered opportunities as well as new restrictions for white women and African American men and women. While some employers experimented with providing child care for working mothers, more often white women workers faced limits on the occupations they could fill. Even so, factory owners often hired white women before black women, many of whom were also newcomers to western cities.

In the earliest years of the war, production required so many laborers that even black women found more space to leave the home and engage in wage work in addition to their unpaid labor. Already transferring family and African American cultural institutions to their new homes, these women needed money to support those very things. Furthermore, these African American women remade western black communities in their own, more distinctively southern and activist, image in a few short years. War's end saw these women, white and black, summarily fired from defense industry jobs and replaced by returning servicemen. In the face of renewed discrimination based on gender and race, many African American women still chose to stay in the West and make their lives in western cities.[44]

The federal government's ever-growing presence in the West, spurred by wartime planning, accentuated the flow of government funds westward and also took pains to encourage the migration of rural Mexican citizens. After years of repatriation, the United States flip-flopped and formally agreed with Mexico to bring millions of Mexican citizens to jobs north of the Rio Grande. Farm and factory owners found the Mexicans to be a cheap labor force with few equals in a wartime economy where able-bodied white male workers were in short supply. While labor agreements promised wages equal to those earned by whites, appropriate housing, work contracts in Spanish, and medical care, few migrants enjoyed such basic guarantees. Known as *braceros*, these men and women found themselves exploited despite their immense contributions to the American war effort. The agreement lasted until 1964, when the federal government restricted immigration.

Mexican American youth, coming of age with a firmly rooted and distinctive identity, served in the armed forces alongside the white American soldier. Their counterparts outside the service fared less well. The so-called Zoot-Suit riots in Los Angeles resulted when white servicemen closed in on local Mexican American youth. Military training camps placed in mostly Mexican American neighborhoods created a cauldron that mixed defiant Mexican American youth culture with anti-Mexican sentiment. For over a week in the summer of 1943, whites assaulted and disrobed Mexican American men, while police responded by jailing the victims. The riots quickly tapped into deeper racial tensions. The *Los Angeles Examiner* noted that as "service men converged on downtown streets for the fourth night, they were joined – for the first time in large numbers – by civilians."[45]

Figure 5.2 Japanese American citizens, imprisoned in western camps during World War II, were encouraged to occupy their time with "mainstream American" projects, as this needlework from the adult education class in the Grenada Relocation Center in Colorado depicts. *Source:* Courtesy, Denver Public Library, Western History Collection, X-6581.

Racism fed other wartime hysterias. Almost 10,000 Italian Americans from California, deemed security risks, were relocated. A few thousand Italian nationals found themselves in internment camps for almost two years. In the wake of the Japanese attack on Pearl Harbor on December 7, 1941, Federal Bureau of Investigation (FBI) agents detained more than 2,000 members of the Japanese American community without trial. The majority spent the rest of the war in Justice Department camps in New Mexico, Montana, and North Dakota. Just two months later, without naming Japanese Americans or using the word internment, Franklin D. Roosevelt's Executive Order 9066 gave the military broad powers to forcibly deport immigrants and American citizens of Japanese descent just two months later. Popular sentiment, especially in California, pushed for such deportations. On February 27, 1942, the *San Francisco Examiner's* headline read: "Ouster of All Japs in California

Near!" As a result of this government action, over 120,000 Japanese Americans ended up in war relocation camps scattered across the rural West.

With racial sentiments intensifying and with some whites acting against Asian Americans indiscriminately, Chinese Americans noted that China had been fighting the Japanese for years. Major news organizations agreed. Staff writers in the December 22, 1941 issue of *Life Magazine* penned an article titled "How to Tell Japs from the Chinese" – an activity suddenly more important to white Americans who had seldom cared about the distinction.

Meanwhile, some Japanese internees tried desperately to prove their loyalty to the United States. At the camp near Heart Mountain, Wyoming, interned residents founded the *Heart Mountain Sentinel*, a regular newspaper for the camp. Its first issue included a notice that the editor had sent a copy to President Franklin D. Roosevelt with the "hope he will read it and find in its pages the loyalty and progress here at Heart Mountain." Others organized resistance to the draft. Since the government ignored their rights as US citizens by forcibly interning them in camps, these Japanese American men refused to serve. Some spent up to two years in jail before President Harry Truman apologetically pardoned them in 1947.[46]

Strained racial and ethnic relations pointed to the increasing diversity of the West, as well as its regional importance and its critical place in the war effort. Tied to the Pacific through commerce that pre-dated Lewis and Clark, the West made a natural staging ground for the battles that raged across the war zones of the 1940s. The West offered vast open spaces for military bases and proving grounds, ocean ports with easy access to battle fronts, nearby natural resources, and interior cities where industries could be located far from enemy forces. Indeed, the military openly worked for spreading industry and depots and stations around the country, avoiding a concentration of factories in the Northeast that might be eliminated in one military attack from Germany. For the federal government, military bases and airplane factories and shipyards in the West made for sense and security.

Even highly classified programs, such as the atomic-bomb Manhattan Project, worked best in remote locations that could be effectively hidden from the curious or the felonious. Far from the daily routines of Americans, Los Alamos, New Mexico, a research center, and Alamogordo, a desert test site, became the ground zero of their day. Remote locations were havens for scientists who planned and carried out the first nuclear designs and subsequent detonations.

Drawing on cheap electricity from dams built by the federal government, an expansive oil industry, and military spending, energy-intensive industries took root in the West.[46] The bulk of the subsidized industries manufactured arms and armaments. Military bases sprang up next to major cities, which themselves housed armament plants. By the war's end, the success of the atomic program insured that the armed forces envisioned the West as the best region in which to foster military research and development. Nearby raw materials, energy, and cheap labor, mixed with a military enlarged by wartime funding that persisted in the years after the war and a variety of research institutions hungry for the monies, made for a potent socio-economic brew. Labeled as the military-industrial complex by President Dwight D. Eisenhower's speechwriters in 1961, this commingling of arms, industry, workers, and thought defined a transformed region. The enlarged presence of the federal government in combination with more people living in cities than anywhere in the nation lay at the heart of the military-industrial complex that emerged from the West's past and dramatically shaped the West's future.

NOTES

1   Frederick Jackson Turner, "The Significance of the Frontier in American History," in John Mack Faragher, ed., *Rereading Frederick Jackson Turner* (New Haven: Yale University Press, 1999).

2   *Broad Ax* (Salt Lake City), June 18, 1898; Quintard Taylor, *In Search of the Racial Frontier*, 182–4, 210–11. See also Ronald Coleman, "A History of Blacks in Utah, 1825–1910," PhD dissertation (University of Utah, 1980).

3   Todd M. Kerstetter, *God's Country, Uncle Sam's Land: Faith and Conflict in the American West* (Urbana: University of Illinois Press, 2006).

4   Carl Abbott, *The Metropolitan Frontier: Cities in the Modern American West* (Tucson: University of Arizona Press, 1993), xvii.

5   Eugene P. Moehring, *Urbanism and Empire in the Far West, 1840–1890* (Reno: University of Nevada Press, 2004).

6   Katherine Morrissey, *Mental Territories: Mapping the Inland Empire* (Ithaca: Cornell University Press, 1997); Claire Strom, *Profiting From the Plains: James J. Hill, The Great Northern Railway, and Corporate*

Development of the American West (Seattle: University of Washington Press, 2003); Kathleen A. Brosnan, *Uniting Mountain and Plain: Cities, Law, and Environmental Change along the Front Range* (Albuquerque: University of New Mexico Press, 2002).

7   William Cronon, *Nature's Metropolis: Chicago and the Great West* (New York: W. W. Norton, 1991).

8   Matthew W. Klingle, "Changing Spaces: Nature, Property, and Power in Seattle, 1880–1945," *Journal of Urban History* 32:2 (January 2006): 197–230 and M. Lawrence Culver, "The Island, the Oasis, and the City: Santa Catalina, Palm Springs, Los Angeles, and Southern California's Shaping of American Life and Leisure," PhD dissertation (University of California, Los Angeles, 2004), 320–64.

9   Norris Hundley Jr, *The Great Thirst: Californians and Water, 1770s–1990s* (Berkeley: University of California Press, 1992).

10 Ferenc Morton Szasz, *Religion in the Modern American West* (Tucson: University of Arizona Press, 2000).

11 María E. Montoya, *Translating Property: The Maxwell Land Grant and the Conflict over Land in the American West* (Berkeley: University of California Press, 2002); Charles Montgomery, *The Spanish Redemption: Heritage, Power, and Loss on New Mexico's Upper Rio Grande* (Berkeley: University of California Press, 2002); Neil Foley, *The White Scourge: Mexicans, Blacks, and Poor Whites in Texas Cotton Culture* (Berkeley: University of California Press, 1997).

12 Melvyn Dubofsky, *We Shall Be All: A History of the Industrial Workers of the World* (1969; Urbana: University of Illinois Press, 1988).

13 Joseph E. Taylor III, *Making Salmon: An Environmental History of the Northwest Fisheries Crisis* (Seattle: University of Washington Press, 1999), 166–202.

14 Robert L. Morlan, *Political Prairie Fire: The Nonpartisan League, 1915–1922* (1955; St Paul: Minnesota Historical Society Press, 1983) and Kim E. Nielsen, "'We All Leaguers By Our House': Women, Suffrage, and Red-Baiting in the National Nonpartisan League," *Journal of Women's History* 6:1 (Spring 1994): 31–50.

15 Mark David Spence, *Dispossessing the Wilderness: Indian Removal and the Making of the National Parks* (New York: Oxford University Press, 1999) and Karl Jacoby, *Crimes against Nature: Squatters, Poachers, Thieves, and the Hidden History of American Conservationism* (Berkeley: University of California Press, 2001).

16 Taylor, *Making Salmon*, 99–165, 203–13.

17 Paul Sabin, *Crude Politics: The California Oil Market, 1900–1940* (Berkeley: University of California Press, 2004).

18 Alfred Runte, *Public Lands, Public Heritage: The National Forest Idea* (Niwot, CO: Roberts Rinehart Publishers, 1991), 47; Michael Williams,

"Industrial Impacts on the Forests of the United States, 1860–1920," *Journal of Forest History* 31:3 (July 1987): 108, 121; Stephen J. Pyne, *Fire in America: A Cultural History of Wildland and Rural Fire* (Princeton: Princeton University Press, 1982), 219–38.

19 Stephen J. Pyne, *Year of the Fires: The Story of the Great Fires of 1910* (New York: Viking, 2001).

20 *Lewiston Morning Tribune* (Idaho), August 30, 1919.

21 Mark Fiege, *Irrigated Eden: The Making of an Agricultural Landscape in the American West* (Seattle: University of Washington Press, 1999).

22 Donald Worster, *Rivers of Empire: Water, Aridity and the Growth of the American West* (New York: Oxford University Press, 1985), 156–70.

23 Ibid., 191–217. Steven Stoll, *The Fruits of Natural Advantage: Making the Industrial Countryside in California* (Berkeley: University of California Press, 1998).

24 John Muir, "Let Everyone Help to Save the Famous Hetch-Hetch Valley and Stop the Commercial Destruction which Threatens Our National Parks," (San Francisco, 1909), <www.sfmuseum.org/john/muir1.html>.

25 Donald J. Pisani, *Water and American Government: The Reclamation Bureau, National Water Policy, and the West, 1902–1935* (Berkeley: University of California Press, 2002).

26 Gunther Peck, *Reinventing Free Labor: Padrones and Immigrant Workers in the North American West, 1880–1930* (New York: Cambridge University Press, 2000).

27 Lee, *At America's Gates*; Yung, *Unbound Feet*.

28 Ronald Takaki, *Strangers From a Different Shore: A History of Asian Americans* (New York: Penguin Books, 1989), 182; Eiichiro Azuma, *Between Two Empires: Race, History, and Transnationalism in Japanese America* (New York: Oxford University Press, 2005); Brian Masaru Hayashi, *"For the Sake of Our Japanese Brethren": Assimilation, Nationalism, and Protestantism among the Japanese of Los Angeles, 1895–1942* (Stanford: Stanford University Press, 1995).

29 Dorothy B. Fujita-Rony, *American Workers, Colonial Power: Philippine Seattle and the Transpacific West, 1919–1941* (Berkeley: University of California Press, 2003).

30 Sarah Deutsch, *No Separate Refuge: Culture, Class, and Gender on the Anglo-Hispanic Frontier in the American Southwest, 1880–1940* (New York: Oxford University Press, 1987); George J. Sánchez, *Becoming Mexican American: Ethnicity, Culture, and Identity in Chicano Los Angeles, 1900–1945* (New York: Oxford University Press, 1993); Douglas Munroy, *Rebirth: Mexican Los Angeles from the Great Migration to the Great Depression* (Berkeley: University of California Press, 1999).

31 David Rich Lewis, *Neither Wolf Nor Dog: American Indians, Environment, and Agrarian Change* (New York: Oxford University Press, 1994); John W. Heaton, *The Shoshone-Bannocks: Culture and Commerce at Fort Hall, 1870–1940* (Lawrence: University Press of Kansas, 2005); Colleen O'Neill, *Working the Navajo Way: Labor and Culture in the Twentieth Century* (Lawrence: University Press of Kansas, 2005); Clyde Ellis, *A Dancing People: Powwow Culture on the Southern Plains* (Lawrence: University Press of Kansas, 2003).

32 Paul Sabin, "Home and Abroad: The Two 'Wests' of Twentieth-Century United States History," *Pacific Historical Review* 66:3 (August 1997): 305–35.

33 Lee, *At America's Gates*, 151–88; Shelia McManus, *The Line Which Separates: Race, Gender, and the Making of the Alberta–Montana Borderlands* (Lincoln: University of Nebraska Press, 2005); Sánchez, *Becoming Mexican American*, 38–62.

34 Benjamin Heber Johnson, *Revolution in Texas: How a Forgotten Rebellion and Its Blood Suppression Turned Mexicans into Americans* (New Haven: Yale University Press, 2003).

35 Scott Ellsworth, *Death in a Promised Land: The Tulsa Race Riot of 1921* (Baton Rouge: Louisiana State University Press, 1982).

36 Brad D. Lookingbill, *Dust Bowl, USA: Depression America and the Ecological Imagination* (Athens: University of Ohio Press, 2001) and Donald Worster, *Dust Bowl: The Southern Plains in the 1930s* (New York: Oxford University Press, 1979).

37 James N. Gregory, *American Exodus: The Dust Bowl Migration and Okie Culture in California* (New York: Oxford University Press, 1989) and Don Mitchell, *The Lie of the Land: Migrant Workers and the California Landscape* (Minneapolis: University of Minnesota Press, 1996).

38 Camile Guérin-Gonzales, *Mexican Workers and American Dreams: Immigrations, Repatriation, and California Farm Labor, 1900–1939* (New Brunswick: Rutgers University Press, 1994) and William Deverell, *Whitewashed Adobe: The Rise of Los Angeles and the Remaking of its Mexican Past* (Berkeley: University of California Press, 2004).

39 Richard White, *The Organic Machine: The Remaking of the Columbia River* (New York: Hill and Wang, 1995), 69–75.

40 Richard White, *The Roots of Dependency: Subsistence, Environment, and Social Change among the Choctaws, Pawnees, and Navajos* (Lincoln: University of Nebraska Press, 1983), 250–89.

41 Kenneth R. Philp, *Indian Self-Rule: First Hand Accounts of Indian–White Relations from Roosevelt to Reagan* (1986; Logan: Utah State University Press, 1995), 27–110 and Alexandra Harmon, *Indians in the Making: Ethnic Relations and Indian Identities around Puget Sound* (Berkeley: University of California Press, 1998), 190–217.

42 Kenneth William Townsend, *World War II and the American Indian* (Albuquerque: University of New Mexico Press, 2000), 61–102 and O'Neill, *Working the Navajo Way*.

43 Abbott, *The Metropolitan Frontier*, 8–12 and Mark Wild, *Street Meeting: Multiethnic Neighborhoods in Early Twentieth-Century Los Angeles* (Berkeley: University of California Press, 2005).

44 Gretchen Lemke-Santangelo, *Abiding Courage: African American Migrant Women and the East Bay Community* (Chapel Hill: University of North Carolina Press, 1996), 69–152 and Shirley Ann Wilson Moore, *To Place Our Deeds: The African American Community in Richmond California, 1910–1963* (Berkeley: University of California Press, 2000), 71–93.

45 "Crowds Downtown on Hunt for Zoot Suiters," *Los Angeles Examiner*, June 8, 1943. For the roots of those tensions and this especially violent manifestation, see Eduardo Obregón Pagán, *Murder at the Sleepy Lagoon: Zoot Suits, Race, and Riot in Wartime LA* (Chapel Hill: University of North Carolina Press, 2003).

46 Lawrence DiStassi, ed., *Una Storia Segreta: The Secret History of Italian American Evacuation and Internment During World War II* (Berkeley: Heyday, 2001); Bob Kumamoto, "The Search for Spies: American Counterintellegence and the Japanese American Community, 1931–1942," *Amerasia Journal* 6:2 (Fall 1979): 45–76; "Editor's Note," *Heart Mountain Sentinel*, October 24, 1942; Frank Chin, *Born in the USA: A Story of Japanese America, 1898–1947* (Lanham, MD: Rowman and Littlefield, 2002).

47 Neil Morgan, *Westward Tilt: The American West Today* (New York: Random House, 1961).

Chapter 6

Mythic West and Modern West

That's what I' m here to tell you about tonight. A Western . . . It's Honest, It's Adult, It's Realistic[1]

Across America on September 10, 1955, families settled in to watch the first airing of the new Western television show, "Gunsmoke." They knew it would be good because the Hollywood legend John Wayne stared out from the screen and told them so. In his sincere, no-nonsense, gravelly voice, Wayne recommended they enjoy the adventures of Marshal Matt Dillon, played by a young actor named James Arness. That fall evening, Marshal Dillon and his friends "Doc" Adams, Chester Goode, and Miss Kitty Russell brought viewers into what appeared to be an authentic Dodge City, Kansas, of 1873. Everything was there: the blacksmith shop, horse troughs, jail, wooden sidewalks, dry goods store, dusty street, old wagons, and the Atcheson, Topeka, and Santa Fe Railroad. Everything and everybody seemed so honest, so adult, so realistic, just as John Wayne had said. It was Matt Dillon himself who inspired the most devotion. Laconic and steady, the marshal, from his small office or astride his horse Buck, kept order in Dodge City. He knew who stepped from the stage, he dispatched the gunslingers, he protected the town, he was heroic, and he rode into American living rooms for almost 20 years. Americans avidly followed each episode of what became the longest running Western in television history, consistently earning number one ratings from an adoring public.

As the military-industrial complex grew to prominence in the post-World War II years, shaping the West's future, millions of tele-vision viewers across the United States welcomed into their homes these heroic images and stories set in the "Old West." By October 1958, six more westerns had joined "Gunsmoke" in the top 10 TV shows – "Wagon Train," "Have Gun Will Travel," "The Rifleman," "Maverick," "Tales of Wells Fargo," and "The Life and Legend of Wyatt Earp." From the early 1950s to the mid-1970s, television and movie Westerns dominated American entertainment.

The scripts for these small screen westerns depicted the late nineteenth-century West as a land in which one-dimensional heroes and "bad" men squared off weekly in violent, individualistic esca-pades that more often than not led to the triumph of good over evil. For citizens with deep-seated anxieties about the impending nuclear doom made possible by the Cold War, the programs portrayed America's previous triumphs to sooth those worried that the nation, even the world, might not survive the current struggle against the Soviet Union. To some commentators, television Westerns even pro-vided an ideological guide to victory in that struggle. The message was clear: the road to victory lay not ahead, but in a return to the ideals by which the West "had been won."

In their ideological context, however, television shows and major films captured little of the complex historical narrative of the American West. Their narrow focus on heroic gun battles between white men and the elimination of Indian resistance stressed the victories of indi-viduals and downplayed the importance of the federal government in the western past. They denied the injustice of the dispossession of Native communities. The programs also studiously ignored the impor-tance of women and people of color in western history.

In so doing, these westerns drew on familiar themes from the early twentieth-century forms of the genre found in literature, film, and radio. The Cold War context of the 1950s, however, influ-enced the American myth in an especially intense manner, tilting it toward this version of a fabled West. Even when this widely recog-nized mythic West faded from movie and television screens with the collapse of the Cold War, during the 1990s and 2000s it persisted in everything from Ralph Lauren ads and political campaign com-mercials to gangster rap. As a constant referent, the mythic West mingled with the military-industrial West to produce a modern region, influencing three interrelated arenas.[2]

First, collaborations between and among local businessmen and politicians, the military, and corporations turned the West into the primary venue for decentralized metropolitan growth, high-tech manufacturers, and new extraction industries that created a powerful regional economy by the late 1960s. As a result, in-migration to the region rivaled the population growth of the nineteenth century. The demographic shift resulted from an attraction to new economic and social opportunities in the West.

Second, new migrants joined with long-time residents to foster hotbeds of political dissent on both right and left. Whether through electoral politics or identity politics, westerners found themselves in the midst of the nation's most contentious political realignment of the century. Visions of individualism, innovation, and staunch nationalism – all tied to the region through the perpetuation of the mythic West in American television and movies during the 1950s and 1960s – stood at the center of these conflicts.

Third, petroleum-based agriculture and tourist service industries that used federally-managed public resources in the western countryside led to new and painful fissures across the region. Rural white westerners, especially, clung to self-images rooted in the mythic West to compensate for the continuing slide of their political and economic power in relation to urban westerners. Cultural images of a West that never existed or only briefly existed resonated in the claims of rural westerners who contested the region's future with insiders and outsiders alike.

Through the 1950s, prominent persons in the military-industrial complex re-centered defense installations from the crowded Northeast to the open Great Plains, Rocky Mountain, and Pacific Coast states. Building on the military shift to the West during World War II and the continued threat of Soviet world dominance, war planners thought the best place for staging America's next defensive program to be west of the Mississippi River. In 1948, the US Air Force Strategic Air Command relocated from Washington, DC, to the outskirts of Omaha, Nebraska. In 1951, the city officials and chamber of commerce of the small city of Colorado Springs convinced the US Air Defense Command, later known as the North American Air Defense Command (NORAD), to move its Long Island headquarters to Colorado. Flushed with success, Colorado Springs administrators only three years later celebrated that the first new service academy in more than a century – the US Air Force Academy – would be built in their town.

In California, politicians and naval officers, each coveting a choice spot for a new naval repair depot, concocted a competition among San Francisco, Los Angeles, and San Diego for the premier shipyard on the West Coast. All three were homes to major naval and other military bases, but the cities vied fiercely for the billions of dollars new or expanded military installations could pump into a local economy. San Diego's "Air Power Day," a municipal celebration started in 1953, illustrated the importance of the military to local economic well-being. It no doubt helped cement that city's bid for naval preeminence the next year, when the Pentagon, swayed by the promises of municipal, county, and state politicians, chose the Harbor of the Sun over its competitors for the repair shipyard.

Other western areas also aggressively sought military bases. Before a partial above-ground test ban treaty in 1963, Nevada's public lands were the preferred sites for US atomic testing. Minot, North Dakota, with its mid-continental location, offered the protection of large distances between its military installations and any roving enemy aircraft. As a result, in the 1960s, the United States government constructed a major base for Minuteman missiles near Minot.[3]

During these efforts to relocate strategic armed services to the West, research and development funds to private firms meant that more public money than ever before poured into military-allied companies. Fears about the inherent weakness of industries densely concentrated in the Northeast during a nuclear conflict meshed with western politicians' drive to boost local economies and the military branches attempts to preserve service supremacy. These made for a tightly-woven political-military phalanx of common interests.

Aircraft production, for instance, shifted from Buffalo, New York, and Dayton, Ohio, to Los Angeles, California, and Seattle, Washington, in the early 1950s. Small aircraft companies in Washington and California seized on innovative design and low production costs to entice the military, and with it, federal dollars. In Los Angeles, boosters emphasized open space, an agreeable climate, and an existing industry as suitable elements for extensive testing. The success of their campaigns was evident when small enterprises such as Douglas, Lockheed, and Northrop blossomed into huge corporations by the early 1950s. In Seattle, the Boeing corporation eventually dominated the municipal economy, with research centers, offices, and production plants scattered around the city as the

company rapidly expanded, benefiting from cheap electricity produced by the federally-built Columbia River dams. Building and
producing planes not just for defense contracts but also for commercial aviation, the company employed almost 150,000 people by
the mid-1960s. By the mid-1950s, Phoenix, Arizona, using similar
regional publicity campaigns, hosted such companies as Motorola,
Sperry Rand, and Kaiser Aircraft, all of which supplied western airplane producers with highly advanced small electronics.[4]

Cold War monies, military goals, and western scientists transformed the airplane industry into the aerospace industry. In the
West, rocket and electronics research meant that US Air Force generals seeking intercontinental ballistic missiles in the mid-1950s
could turn to nearby California institutions of higher learning.
The relocation of the airplane industry to the West benefited from
cutting-edge technological research at the California Institute of
Technology, the University of California at Berkeley, the University of California at Los Angeles, and Stanford University. All four
schools embraced the "multiversity" model, which focused an
institution's civic engagement on close collaboration between scientists and corporate capital. With the military funding corporations
that in turn looked to local research universities, these institutions
of higher learning only grew in stature – and in importance to the
nation's military – through the 1950s and 1960s. Over 3 percent
of all federal dollars spent between 1950 and 1955 went towards
research and development. Disproportionate shares of those monies
were directed to California's leading universities.

The development, however, was not confined to California. In
the 1960s, the observatories and laboratories of the University of
Arizona came to the attention of the United States military. Missile-
building Air Force scientists used them to pursue more knowledge
about the solar system, a potential arena for future Cold War conflict.
By the 1970s, other western universities promoted the multiversity
approach, so that they might reap the prestige as well as the cash.[5]

The cities that surrounded these intertwined networks of military bases, aerospace production, and research and development
became centers of post-industrial and high tech innovation. They
became home to spin-off companies, the first industrial parks, and
entirely new economic sectors. Stanford, especially, spawned technology giants such as Hewlett-Packard and laid the foundation for
what in the 1990s would become Silicon Valley.

The influx of federal dollars and the rise of the military-industrial complex also altered the physical spaces the university inhabited, as well as those of the communities around them. Stanford University reworked the rural countryside – the South Bay – into a decentralized, suburban, service-oriented landscape through the well-planned sale and development of its extensive land holdings in Palo Alto. New companies directly affiliated with research efforts at Stanford moved into low-slung industrial parks surrounded by manicured green spaces that replaced the grimy smokestacks of more typical urban skylines found in other parts of the country. The university tightly regulated the construction of both commercial and residential buildings and crafted an appealing, open, spread-out built landscape. Restaurants, shopping malls, and other services catered to an affluent intelligentsia that demanded culture in its latest forms.[6]

In other words, a new built form accompanied the rise of the military-industrial complex in the West. In a region where urban forms had already been sprawling and streetcar suburbs took hold early in the twentieth century, a new impetus for decentralized living appeared. From Los Angeles to San Diego, to San José and Seattle, defense industry employees and military families clamored for single family homes on privately-owned lots in wide-open housing developments. The proliferation of detached private spaces fit with development planning that intentionally removed shared public spaces found in older urban centers. Without downtowns, these new cities relied on multiple, horizontal, and loosely-knit centers. Spatially separated from industrial spaces and basic services, the new built form demanded more roads and at least one automobile per family. A new petroleum dependent car culture flourished in a land of western distances and was further subsidized by the 1956 passage of the National Interstate and Defense Highways Act.[7]

Suburban living contributed to a self-identification with innovation in the West that depended on a high quality of life, distance from older urban and intellectual centers, federal spending on both infrastructure and local corporations, and new built forms that fostered individualism and elbow room. It seemed to prove that the mythic West found on television and in movies had a twentieth-century counterpart – a contemporary land of open vistas, new beginnings, clean living, and economic prosperity. The West appeared to be the place where the best and brightest might go to make their mark and serve their nation in a geopolitical struggle against the forces of communism. California, in particular, seemed to embody the future of the United States. Though the mythic West proved mostly rural and the modern West mostly urban and suburban, both depended on conflation with the broader nation and a sense of general freedom. The journalist Neil Morgan claimed in 1961 that as a "fresh land, so serene and self-confident," the "West of today is very likely a close kin of the America of tomorrow," due to the "high threshold of abundance and energy," in the region. Eleven years later, the award-winning writer Wallace Stegner argued that this new western life had become "the national culture."[8]

Many Americans agreed. The potent combination of mythic and real Wests attracted white-collar workers from across the country. Between 1950 and 1970, over 20 million people moved west. Echoing a massive migration by whites 100 years before, these immigrants were generally young, married, and middle class, seeking or starting families. Through federally-funded post-World War II educational programs such as the GI Bill, a large white middle class developed, ready made for jobs that demanded scientists and engineers rather than the brute force and raw physical strength of heavy industry. Furthermore, many young men and women had seen the urban West for the first time during the war and they liked the open skies and sunny spaces. They responded favorably to the efforts of western boosters who highlighted amenable climates and good living – just like their nineteenth-century predecessors.

As a final factor, a variety of cultural messages suggested that creeping blight in inner cities was directly related to the presence of non-whites there. In fact, white flight to western suburbs displaced non-whites working in rural industries on the edges of existing cities. White flight itself proved an especially complicated dynamic, one predicated on fears of more diverse populations that led to deliberate housing discrimination subsidized by Federal Housing Administration and Veterans Administrations programs that envisioned non-white borrowers as mortgage risks.

By 1962, California had become the largest state in the nation, surpassing New York. This massive in-migration drew largely on the well-educated and burgeoning technocracy. The demographic shift west fostered further boom times, as new migrants propelled local economies forward. Affluence bred more affluence in the sprawling residential communities of a contemporary West, which bore little resemblance to the imagined West, except in the minds of many who inhabited it.[9]

The new military-industrial complex brewing in the West stood poised on the Pacific Basin. Economic opportunity and the pressing politics of the Cold War guaranteed the federal government and western businessmen would press forward. Projecting western capital even further west, Bechtel, the Bank of America, and Utah Construction and Mining turned to ventures in places as far flung as the Philippines, Shanghai, Tokyo, and Peru in the years immediately following World War II.

The nation physically firmed up its claims to Pacific Basin dominance through the admittance of Alaska and Hawai'i as states in 1959. Dubbed "the last frontier" for its remote and wild landscape, Alaska proved anything but to military planners. By the 1950s they used its proximity to the Soviet Union to construct the Distant Early Warning Line (DEW), a set of over 60 radar stations across Alaska and the Canadian Arctic designed to track incoming Soviet bombers. They also expanded World War II-era military bases across the territory. In the meantime, many newly arrived Alaskans ached for statehood. The anti-communist Cold War reactions of the early 1950s, embodied in the Congressional passage of the 1950 McCarran–Nixon Internal Security Act, angered Alaskans who now had to pass through immigration checkpoints whenever they returned to the continental United States. After years of partisan wrangling over questions such as Native land rights, the territory's penchant for the Democratic Party, and the large number of resident indigenous peoples, Alaska became a state.

Civil rights issues and the anti-communist backlash of the 1950s delayed Hawai'i's statehood as well. Hawai'i had long been a center for American military power in the Pacific and continued to be crucial during the Cold War. But politicians in Washington had other concerns. Accused of disloyalty, Hawai'i's dominant Democrats – like many across the country – purged themselves of labor-affiliated communists in the late 1940s and early 1950s. Nonetheless, given the large number of Asian Americans in the territory – mostly indigenous Hawai'ians and Japanese Americans – many southern politicians feared the specter of race mixing that they sought to prevent in their own states. Those who argued for statehood noted Japanese American loyalty in World War II as evidenced by their meritorious service in the armed forces. They also pointed to broader interracial relations in Hawai'i as an example of what many hoped would be a harmonious, multiracial American future. Such arguments won enough supporters to bring statehood in August 1959.

In these two initiatives for statehood, the "Aloha State" and the "Last Frontier" commingled the mythic and modern Wests, completed the country's final formal territorial expansion, and acknowledged the long history of Alaska and Hawai'i in the narrative of the American West. Territorial expansion on the movie screen suddenly found a real-life equivalent, one premised on national defense and racial politics. Individualistic freedom in open spaces that featured natural wonders awaited those adventurous enough to move to these western additions to the Union.[10]

Cold War concerns extended themselves into long-used spaces across the rural West. New extraction industries in the 1950s literally fueled the military-industrial complex. A fresh generation of prospectors sought uranium and petroleum to aid national security efforts. Crucial to the production of atomic munitions, uranium could be found throughout the Four Corners region, where Utah, Colorado, New Mexico, and Arizona meet.

In 1952, attracted by large reserves, artificially inflated prices for the precious metal, and a Vanadium Corporation of America processing plant in Durango, Colorado, miners flooded the region. Handheld geiger counters buzzed outside small so-called "yellow-cake" towns such as Moab, Utah, and Grants, New Mexico. Just 150 miles away, continued nuclear testing and downwind contamination of people and environment showed the lingering costs of the grey mineral so many rushed to find. New natural gas finds and calls for a pipeline connecting the Four Corners to western cities brought Shell Oil and Standard Oil to the region. Farmington, New Mexico, grew from 3,000 residents in 1951 to 25,000 in 1965, as people moved to get plentiful oil industry related jobs. These industries brought investments and people but also made the remote Four Corners region even more dependent on cities such as Salt Lake City, Utah, and Albuquerque, New Mexico.

In 1947, the literary critic, historian, and cultural commentator Bernard DeVoto, a Utahn, noted in *Harper's Magazine* that "at the very moment when the West is blueprinting an economy . . . based on . . . its natural resources, it is also conducting an assault on those resources with the simple objective of liquidating them . . .

The West is its own worst enemy." Even so, DeVoto failed to antici-
pate that the costs of post-war resource extraction would be borne
unevenly by westerners. The military-industrial complex locked
rural westerners into time-honored dependent relationships, this
time with urban westerners who took on fewer risks and collected
most of the benefits. Fulfilling DeVoto's prophecy, similar post-war
petroleum and coal finds in rural Texas, Oklahoma, Wyoming, and
Montana, tied the future of those hinterlands – and the people who
lived in them – to metropolitan regional centers such as Amarillo,
Texas; Oklahoma City, Oklahoma; Denver, Colorado; Cheyenne,
Wyoming; and Billings, Montana. All these cities profited. In the
meantime, rural people received short-term economic gains and
long-term eviscerated landscapes, especially once the Cold War
resource booms collapsed in the late 1960s and early 1970s.[11]

Holding together the urban and rural development sparked by
the military-industrial complex was the simultaneous and unprecedented manipulation of water by federal agencies in the post-war
West. Continued metropolitan growth and the new resource extraction it spawned hinged on bringing water to cities and farms from
the deep snow-covered Rocky Mountains and from underground
sources in the Great Plains. Politicians looking to justify the massive government expenditures that made the new military industrial
center of the West possible looked no further than the threat of
international communism. In Washington, DC, pointed claims were
made about the need to carefully manage water resources to foster
western growth and national security.[12]

Agribusiness interests and farmers on the southern and central
Plains quickly moved to tap the massive underground Ogallala
aquifer after World War II, with little regulatory oversight. The precious water worked its power on the region, changing them into a
vast green belt. Any sense that the aquifer might some day run dry
dissipated as the fresh water made the Dust Bowl a distant memory.

Meanwhile, on the northern Plains, the US Army Corps of Engineers and the US Bureau of Reclamation drew plans to conquer
the flood-prone Missouri River. The Corps claimed it could do
two things: make the Missouri River navigable and produce electricity. The Bureau countered that the few hundred barges that
traveled the river hardly required five massive dams in the Dakotas alone and that it should be given the authority to build dams
for irrigation. In 1944, a compromise between the agencies – the

Pick-Sloan Plan – resulted in approval for both visions. Completed in early 1953, Garrison Dam, the largest of the projects, inundated thousands of acres of reservation land long owned by the Mandans, Hidatsas, and Arikaras at Fort Berthold, North Dakota. As for the federal lake that replaced their homes? It was named "Sakakawea" in honor of the young Native woman Lewis and Clark met in 1804 at the Hidatsa villages.

The Bureau often won out where water infused post-war western politics through these conflicts over water. Led by the flamboyant Floyd Dominy, a Nebraska-born bureaucrat who symbolized the ways westerners reached positions of power in the federal agencies that most affected them, the agency grew in size and stature after World War II. The Colorado River Compact of 1948 divvied up the waters of that great river among Colorado, Utah, Wyoming, New Mexico, and Arizona and the Bureau of Reclamation made plans for a series of massive dams. The first would be built at Echo Park, where the Green and Yampa rivers met before the former flowed south to the Colorado. Building a dam at Echo Park, preserved and administered by the National Park Service as a part of Dinosaur National Monument, sparked an intense national debate. Advocacy groups such as the Sierra Club and the Wilderness Society squared off against local politicians and federal bureaucrats. After taking their appeal to the American public, the anti-dam forces triumphed in 1956. Nonetheless, the Bureau got the go-ahead from anti-dam forces to build Glen Canyon Dam on the Colorado in southeastern Utah, a project completed in 1966.[13]

A replay of the Echo Park fight erupted in the mid-1960s when the Bureau identified both ends of the Grand Canyon as locations for dams that would inundate portions of the national park there. Again, anti-dam forces – mostly metropolitan westerners – prevailed. The Bureau of Reclamation's efforts continued, however. The agency's final large-scale water program, the Central Arizona Project, was approved in 1968. A massive, 336–mile-long aqueduct to bring Colorado River water to Phoenix, Tucson, and the farmers of the southern Arizona desert, it cost four billion dollars. By the time the project neared completion in the 1990s, the Colorado River was little more than a trickle by the time it reached the US–Mexico border.

Exorbitant expenditures, unclear returns, proven ecological damage, and the failure to deliver water to small farmers chipped away at the prestige of the Bureau of Reclamation. But it took the dramatic failure of a brand new earthen dam on the Idaho backside of the Tetons in 1976, at a price of one billion dollars and 11 lives, to end the Bureau's lock on federal monies, as well as massive water projects. Institutional hubris, engineering mistakes, porous bedrock, and intense local pressure coalesced to bring about the building of the Teton Dam, despite many warning signs that it was a questionable dam location. As the dam melted away on a June morning, so too did the era of big dam building.

The redistribution of water from the Rocky Mountains to the burgeoning cities of California and the Southwest, subsidized by the federal government, made the Bureau of Reclamation second only to the military in its power to shape the post-war West. Its constant appeals for the nation to aid desert farmers – who in reality were rapidly organizing agribusiness corporations and sprawling municipalities – made it one of the largest spenders among federal agencies and the creator of the infrastructure of the newly prosperous cities in arid western climes.[14]

The federal intervention into rural rivers and aquifers watered the greatly expanded urban and suburban West. At the same time, the ideologies embedded in the American imagination about the rural West took root in these new affluent communities. Single-family homes on lots, often purchased with mortgage aid from the federal government, pushed more lower-income white families into the middle class and away from New Deal politics. The memories of the Great Depression slid away and were replaced by a post-World War II consensus built on consumer consumption.

Materialism and the lack of public spaces in turn led to a new search for community in the atomized suburbs. As newcomers mingled with rural westerners, preoccupied with the chance to sell off farms, ranches, and orchards for housing developments, a particular politics surfaced that offered community to new and old alike. It centered on notions of self-reliance, small government, libertarianism, and anti-communism. No region's past – especially in its idealized, television form – better fitted this civic philosophy than the West's. By the 1950s, dependence on federal dollars bred rural and suburban resentment towards the federal government.

Prime time television Westerns affirmed the feelings of these ranchers, businessmen, homeowners, and farmers. Real westerners took care of matters on their own. The character Paladin from the television show "Have Gun, Will Travel," righted wrongs in an evil world all by himself and at great personal sacrifice. So did Lucas McCain in "The Rifleman." In just a half an hour, with time out for commercials, these fictionalized male westerners kept women at a distance as they delineated good from bad in simple, straight-forward ways. Their actions made them manly and true Americans. This rehashed version of intertwined manhood and region resonated across the nation, which generally overlooked the large quantities of federal monies westerners continued to absorb. In fact, government-funded defense industries made the atomistic and individualized suburban life, as well as the subsidized rural life, possible.

As the hues of the Cold War tinted the production of television Westerns, it also colored the political outlook of modern west-erners. Support for reduced government and libertarianism flourished in the newly-developed western suburbs where view-ers endorsed supposedly western self-reliance portrayed week after week on television. These suburbanites added a healthy dose of anti-communism, thanks to their employment within a military-industrial complex constantly justified by politicians pointing to the threatening communist powers of China and the Soviet Union.[15]

By the late 1950s, writers consistently connected the American West they enjoyed on television and at movie theaters with anti-communist and self-reliant ideals they believed important for the nation. In 1958, one policy-maker, writing in *American Mercury*, famously asked, "Would a Wyatt Earp stop at the 38th Parallel, Korea, when the rustlers were escaping with the herd? Ridiculous! Would Marshal Dillon refuse to allow his deputies to use shotguns for their own defense because of the terrible nature of the weapon itself? Ha!"

The self-reliance and anti-communism of television Westerns appealed to the emerging New Right political movement, which depended on the modern West for image and leadership. In 1962, one conservative commentator writing in the *National Review*, knowing that approximately 60 million Americans followed tele-vision Westerns, posited that if "Wyatt Earp or somebody from Arizona or Texas with the glint of the western mountains in his eye – offers himself as a candidate on a platform of running the rascals out of town, 60 million of us westerners will put him into office." For this writer, the modern suburban West and television Westerns together encapsulated "the American Dream."[16]

Despite this ideology's dependence on masculine ideals, white suburban housewives, newly freed from wage work through class mobility, became the backbone of what came to be called the New Right. By the early 1960s, women who took the cultural message that stressed housework over wage work to heart nonetheless logged long hours articulating strategies and organizing neighbors in New Right causes. Contributing as much, if not more, to the New Right as eastern thinkers such as William F. Buckley, these western women led study groups and clubs dedicated to rooting out the collectivism that they believed led inevitably to communism. Housewives provided a ready audience for New Right messages, especially as they found new community in suburban non-denominational or evangelical churches that mixed traditional Christianity with modern technologies. Religion – long a source of women's activism, especially in the West – served as a ready antidote to the atheism of communism. Connecting religious belief to nationhood made sense. In so doing, they sparked an innovative grassroots movement that most outsiders failed to see. These women focused their efforts on the traditional domains of American womanhood: schools, child raising, and shaping citizenship. Along those lines they challenged school curriculums and what they defined as morally permissive trends in society.[17]

No wonder, then, that the two most prominent politicians in the New Right hailed from Arizona and California. In 1964, the New Right challenged moderate establishment Republicans from the Northeast and seized control of the Republican Party convention in San Francisco. They nominated the second-term senator Barry Goldwater as their presidential candidate. Born and raised in Phoenix, Arizona, Goldwater took his deeply-felt western persona with him to Washington, DC, when he became a United States senator in 1952. As the scion of a profitable department store family, he always looked to enhance his state's economy, embracing the expansion of federal spending in defense-related industries. He despised big government and its many bureaucracies. Goldwater's anti-communism stance, combined with his rigid dedication to outright libertarianism, drove his rise to prominence with the New Right.

With his strong views and rugged handsome features, he seemed the embodiment of both the mythic and modern West. Goldwater's bestselling 1960 ghost written memoir, *The Conscience of a Conservative*, made him the darling of middle-class, right-wing advocates. As a fiercely independent and outspoken politician – he famously uttered the phrase, "Extremism in the defense of liberty is no vice" in his acceptance speech at the 1964 Republican convention – Goldwater repelled as many voters as he drew; a truly polarizing figure, he was crushed at the polls in the 1964 presidential election. Ousted from Congress in the presidential defeat, Goldwater again played up his western lifestyle in 1968, as he campaigned for and won Arizona's other US Senate seat, which he filled until 1986. His failed presidential campaign marked the arrival of the New Right on the national scene and spoke of what was to come.[18]

The final days of Barry Goldwater's 1964 presidential campaign also introduced the voting public to Ronald Reagan. Broadcast to millions living in the Los Angeles area, Reagan's October 1964 speech in support of Goldwater electrified the New Right with its smoothly-handled message. It also returned Ronald Reagan to the celebrity spotlight, a place where he felt at ease.

Born in Illinois, Reagan had moved to southern California in 1937, after a brief stint as a radio broadcaster in Iowa, where he was known to locals as "Dutch." After starring in a number of B-movies, Reagan broke into the big time with two major roles in 1940: "Knute Rockne–All American," and "Santa Fe Trail." When his movie career flagged in the late 1940s, he jumped at the chance to lead the Screen Actors Guild. To the staunch New Dealer and Democrat, guiding a labor union in its fight to preserve acting's integrity in opposition to Hollywood studio power tactics made sense. Additionally, Reagan had always been interested in politics. After taking the reins of the Screen Actors Guild in 1947, he engaged the anti-communism concerns with which most labor unions grappled in 1948 and 1949. These experiences reshaped his personal politics, leading him away from the Democrats and into the Republican Party by the mid-1950s.

Despite growing political involvements, Reagan continued with his acting career. In the 1950s, he starred in three Westerns: "The Last Outpost" (1951), "Law and Order" (1953), and "Cattle Queen of Montana" (1954). The lure of television drew him, as it did other actors, and he soon jumped to the small screen. As a pitchman for General Electric from 1954 to 1962, Reagan honed an inspiring speech that he delivered to company employees across the country. His motivational talk focused on private property, the evils of the welfare state, and the importance of a strong national defense. Elements of that presentation became the basis for the Goldwater campaign speech that catapulted Ronald Reagan into the hearts of the New Right in 1964.

Reagan's most visceral connection to the mythic West came later, between 1962 and 1966 as an actor, host, and salesman on the television show "Death Valley Days." Outfitted in the appropriate cowboy attire, Reagan's manliness and sincerity won him devotion from television audiences, especially women. The fading movie star, still an imposing physical presence, had reinvented himself using television, a more intimate means of communication than the silver screen.

To many of Reagan's fellow midwestern migrants to California, his story was their story. The past had been left behind for a bountiful West that promised – and seemed to deliver – the good life. Reagan's rhetoric and example powerfully compared the mythic western frontier to the opportunities found in the modern West. With all these associations, the genial Reagan succeeded where the dour Goldwater failed. The Californian wrapped New Right ideologies into what the journalist Lou Cannon termed "sentimental populism." It swept him to victory in the 1966 California gubernatorial contest. Reagan used the same charms when he turned to the national stage, running for the Republican presidential nomination in 1976 and capturing the White House in 1980.[19]

Neither Barry Goldwater nor Ronald Reagan were accidents of history. Theirs was the western contribution to a national, right-wing, conservative movement. This thrust gained special power because its two stated enemies – moderate Republicans and liberal Democrats – also claimed leaders from the West. Richard M. Nixon, from Whittier, California, rose quickly through Republican ranks in the 1940s to become Dwight D. Eisenhower's Vice President in 1952. Nixon's meteoric rise stemmed from his ability to exploit anti-communism sentiments and to bring western Republicans into the establishment northeastern wing of the party. As those possibilities collapsed in the early 1960s, Nixon switched gears and shaped a message that appealed to the New Right and swept him into the presidency in 1968.

As for liberal Democrats, Texan Sam Rayburn, the legendary speaker of the US House of Representatives for most of the years after World War II, looked to protect the legacy of New Deal largess for the rural West. His protégé, Lyndon Baines Johnson, touted western toughness at nearly every opportunity. Through the 1950s and 1960s, the Stetson-wearing and ranch-owning Johnson accumulated political savvy as the US Senate majority leader, Vice President, and President of the United States. Johnson excelled at bringing federal dollars to the West, skills he used as president for his Great Society program, an updated renewal of Franklin D. Roosevelt's New Deal from the Great Depression. Rayburn and Johnson represented western constituencies thankful for big government and federal monies that developed infrastructure and industry. Yet both men, with their strong-arm tactics and mixed responses to racial justice, left complicated legacies in Texas. Regardless of their political affiliations, contradictory stances, and bitter opposition to each other, all these politicians – in varying degrees – cultivated a stylized masculinity grounded in connecting the mythic West to the modern West.[20]

National political upheaval – especially African American battles for civil and human rights – also gave shape to a New Left that equaled the New Right in both numbers and vitality in the West. It too rejected the social trappings of the military-industrial complex and the liberal Democratic consensus that held sway in many parts of the region, as well as in Washington, DC. Instead of standing for anti-communist and libertarian ideals, however, New Left groups rallied around anti-establishment and liberational values.

In 1961, the journalist Neil Morgan argued that in a "young and eager, cocky and eternally hopeful West . . . racial conflicts are milder than in other regions." Thinking, no doubt, of civil rights battles in the urban North and South, Morgan claimed that the freedom offered by the modern West made it a more peaceful part of the country. Individualism and an equal chance at prosperity could be had in the West – if one was white, educated, and middle class. The irony of this was not lost on blacks and some western white liberals, who emphatically supported civil rights for African Americans. As the Black Freedom Movement gained nationwide momentum in the mid-1950s, African Americans in the West spurred it forward with bold stands, innovative tactics, and some successes. One year before the landmark United States Supreme Court case of *Brown vs Topeka, Kansas Board of Education*, a local court in Phoenix, Arizona, ruled school segregation illegal. Two years before the 1960 Greensboro, North Carolina, and Nashville, Tennessee, sit-ins, African American students, with the support of local National Association for the Advancement of Colored People chapters, integrated restaurants in Wichita, Kansas, and Oklahoma City, Oklahoma. In the spring of 1964, an integrated group picketed San Francisco's Sheraton Palace Hotel for job discrimination. Within days and after hundreds of arrests, the city's mayor desegregated the workforce at all of San Francisco's hotels.[21]

Across the Bay, students at the University of California at Berkeley reacted to school rules dating from the 1930s that banned political activities or gatherings on campus. Introduced to activism through participation in civil rights demonstrations, a few students faced discipline for setting up a table, passing out leaflets on race conditions in the South, and asking for donations. When administrators called the students communists and reiterated support for the ban, protest exploded. Over the next three months, the Free Speech Movement, a loosely-knit but well-organized student coalition, orchestrated a series of large sit-ins. In December 1964 their actions culminated in a student strike and the largest mass arrest in California history. Berkeley, to that point a quiet Bay-area suburb, became the first flashpoint in a decade that saw much turmoil on university campuses. By 1965, the flexibility and innovativeness of Berkeley's New Left also made the city home of some of the first and the most famous anti-Vietnam War protests. As the women's movement of the late 1960s grew out of the sexism inherent in the Black Freedom and anti-war groups, Berkeley also became a center of feminist activism.[22]

In 1966, poverty-stricken black neighborhoods in adjacent Oakland bore one of the more famous elements of the Black Freedom Movement. Inspired by anti-colonial Marxist thinkers and growing discontent in the black community – signaled by riots in the mostly African American neighborhood of Watts in Los Angeles in 1965 – members of the Black Panthers wore all black clothing and openly carried firearms for self defense. Publicly brandishing weapons won them lots of attention; many overlooked the fact that California law permitted the public display of unloaded guns. The Black Panthers juggled the tropes of mythic western violence, flipping them about to make a point about federally-subsidized inequities in the modern urban West. Resolute in their collective effort to better their mostly African American community through social services and schools – including a free breakfast program for poverty-stricken children overlooked by Lyndon Johnson's Great Society programs – chapters of the Black Panther Party sprung up in black inner-city neighborhoods across the country. After a number of highly publicized and deadly gun battles with the Oakland police and elsewhere, the Panthers encountered intense pressure from local and federal law enforcement and lost most of their momentum by the early 1970s.[23]

One result of this cultural discontent was a broader youth culture centered on the Bay area, one that defied conventions in appearance, dress, literature, music, food, and world view. Like the anti-war movement, their so-called hippie lifestyle spread across the country quickly. As part of their performed defiance of capitalism and consumption, many adherents appropriated stylized cowboy and Indian images from the mythic West of movies and television. Folk music, cowboy hats, and rodeo imagery on one hand, and long hair, beads, and headbands on the other signaled their disapproval of modernity, but did not lead to a corresponding interest in actual cowboys or Native Americans.[24]

In fact, few realized that in the previous decade, the federal government had dramatically shifted its official Indian policy. In 1953, the government determined that Natives would be better off without reservations or any special relationship with the state. As racial integration gradually became a national ideal, this new termination policy was supposed to help bring Indians into the mainstream of American life. Dissolving reservations and relocating Natives to cities would be the vehicle for doing exactly that. These laws targeted specific Indian communities, including the Klamaths in Oregon, the Salishs and Kootenais in Montana, and mixed heritage Utes in Utah. A few nations agreed that the United States should terminate its official recognition and support of their communities, but most Indian groups fought this policy reversal that would renege on the federal government's treaty obligations.

This abrogation of long-standing treaties, sold to Indians with a promise of a paid-for relocation to western cities, ended in further disenfranchisement for some Natives. Reservation land no longer under the protection of the federal government immediately became liable to state and county taxes. Tribes did not have the funds to meet these obligations and white investors swooped down, pressuring Indians as individuals and groups to sell the now-private land, which often was their sole source of economic support. Meantime, the agreed-on urban support for Indians arriving in San Francisco,

Denver, Minneapolis, Salt Lake City, or Los Angeles rarely materialized. Buses dropped off whole Native families in large cities and left them to their own devices. The chaos wrought by termination and relocation programs across Indian Country actually strengthened Native civil rights organizations, such as the National Congress of American Indians. New Indian groups also formed, such as the National Indian Youth Council (NIYC). Various tribes working together managed to end the termination program in 1958.

A growing sense of Indian rights, deepening poverty, and white sportsmen over-fishing beds prompted the rebirth of Indian activism. In the early 1960s, NIYC activists and Puget Sound Indian communities turned to the courts for the restoration of indigenous salmon fishing practices in the Pacific Northwest. Local and state conservation agencies regulating fish harvests often ignored fishing rights retained by Natives according to nineteenth-century treaties with the United States government. Protesters, including the actor Marlon Brando and black activist Dick Gregory, gathered around Muckleshoots, Puyallups, Tulalips, Nisquallys, and others for "fish-ins" that argued for Native sovereignty to supersede state ordinances. In 1974, a federal judge finally ruled in the Indians' favor. The winds of protest swept north as Alaskan Natives organized a land claims movement of their own. These clear assertions of Native sovereignty laid the foundation for a groundswell of Indian action in the late 1960s.[25]

Combined with relocations that brought Indians together in western cities, where they could identify common Native issues regardless of tribal background, a new "Red Power" movement took shape. Urban Indian students in the San Francisco Bay area occupied the former federal prison of Alcatraz Island in November 1969 where, for 19 months, they protested against government Indian policy. Founded in 1968, the Minneapolis-based American Indian Movement, a response to police abuse and the absence of social services for Natives by Natives, involved itself in the Alcatraz occupation and other seizures of government property. The efforts of this group climaxed in a 1972 takeover of the Bureau of Indian Affairs building in Washington, DC, and a bloody standoff with FBI agents on the Pine Ridge Reservation at Wounded Knee in 1973.[26]

Claiming pride in an indigenous heritage also fueled a new movement among Mexican American youth. A walkout of over 10,000 high school students protesting underfunded programs and a rigid, Anglo-oriented curriculum in East Los Angeles in 1968

Figure 6.1   In 1969, Indian activists seized the abandoned federal prison on Alcatraz Island in San Francisco Bay, staging an 18-month protest for civil rights that brought world attention to their call for an end to discrimination and the return of Native lands. *Source:* Courtesy, Michelle Vignes.

ignited Chicana/o activism. Hoping that the previously pejorative term Chicana/o could unite a diverse Spanish-speaking community with rather different historical backgrounds – Tejana/os in Texas, Hispana/os in New Mexico, California/os in California, first- and second-generation Mexican Americans, and recent Mexican immigrants – these activists also looked to bring together rural and urban people of Mexican descent.

Tensions between long-time Mexican Americans and recent immigrants had long defined the broader community. Yet Rodolfo "Corky" Gonzalez organized a student conference in Denver in 1969 that defined Aztlán and its relation to Mexican-origin Americans, as well as Mexicans. Emphasizing a shared *mestizo* or indigenous background, they proposed the celebration of and a political fight for the restoration of Aztlán, the Aztec word for "homeland." Promoting ethnic solidarity around the Aztlán concept, the movement spawned a wide range of new organizations, as well as Chicano-oriented art, music, theater, and writing.

Much of the movement's energy came from Chicanas, motivated

by a desire to reorganize not only American society and Mexican American culture, but also gender roles and expectations. Some worked within the Catholic Church. Los Hermanas, a group of women religious and laywomen from Texas, founded a national movement that looked to transform both American society and the church. Adopting the motto "*Unidas en Accion y Oracion*" ("United in Action and Prayer"), these Chicanas connected feminist-oriented spirituality to social justice movements in order claim space for women in American Catholicism, American society, and the Chicana/o movement. Other Chicanas proved crucial to the founding of the Brown Berets in Los Angeles, who modeled themselves on the Black Panthers. In Los Angeles, the Centro de Acción Social Autónoma (Center for Socially Autonomous Action), devoted itself to convincing middle-class Mexican Americans that they needed to challenge federal immigration law and help new arrivals from Mexico. Despite FBI harassment, an organized political party, La Raza Unida, formed in Texas to represent the common interest of Tejana/os and Mexican immigrants in electoral politics.[27]

As Chicana/o activists looked to recent immigrants from Mexico as brothers and sisters in a broader Aztlán, they drew on a working-class Chicana/o movement already afoot in California's Central Valley. The Arizona native César Chávez moved to California in 1963, hoping to organize Spanish-speaking migrant and residential farm workers. Chávez anticipated the impact of the 1965 end to the federal government's Bracero program, which encouraged the legal immigration of Mexican migrants to work in western agribusiness. Seizing this as an opportunity to stand up against corporate farmers and the ease with which they broke strikes by having extra labor at the ready, Chávez partnered with Dolores Huerta to create the Farm Workers Association in 1965. Later known as the United Farm Workers (UFW), this labor group not only struck in the fields with non-violent tactics, but it also took its fight to American consumers, asking for and getting a grape boycott. Spreading into Texas, the UFW cooperated with Mexican unions across the border and marched on the Texas State Capital in Austin in 1966 in a push for new minimum wage laws. 1970 saw the UFW force farm owners into negotiation that resulted in UFW contracts for impoverished migrant workers. While neither César Chávez nor many of his supporters imagined themselves to be marching towards Aztlán, urban Chicano activists appropriated Chávez's victories as well as his largely migrant union to promote ethnic solidarity across class lines.[28]

In the 1950s, 1960s, 1970s, and 1980s, refugees from US interventions in the Pacific Basin and the attractions of American consumer culture brought a new wave of immigrants from Taiwan, China, the Philippines, Vietnam, India, Pakistan, Laos, Cambodia, and Korea. Whether middle-class professionals or war refugees, these newcomers concentrated in western cities. Nineteenth-century dynamics, such as racist fears that Asian immigrants would take jobs from white residents, surfaced immediately. These attitudes saddled war refugees with life on the bottom rungs of society and professionals with occupations that failed to match their training and education. Nonetheless, community groups and cultural centers sprouted up to assist these communities.

By the 1970s, the all-white casts of the television Westerns seemed a poor representation of a modern West in which many racial and ethnic groups laid simultaneous claim to their own culture and their right to fair and equal treatment as Americans. These ethnic clusters challenged what it meant to be western by rejecting the racial straitjacket of the mythic West and redefining the region in their own terms.[29]

Clashes over the interrelation of identity, society, and economic standing continued into the 1970 and 1980s. Across the West, they broke down along urban and rural lines as often as along racial fissures. Oil and gas extraction fostered the former. The rise of an energy economy, based on petroleum, had its grounding in pre-World War II Texas, Oklahoma, and California. Because the metropolitan spread of the military-industrial complex relied heavily on cars, oil extraction for local, regional, and even global markets proved more important than ever. In 1968, a massive oil find at Prudhoe Bay seemed to justify those who had argued for Alaska's statehood. As Middle Eastern and South American oil supplies became less dependable owing to political disruptions, Alaska became the nation's gas tank overnight. The concentration of corporate headquarters for energy companies in Houston signaled the maturity of the western oil industry, now owned by locally-based corporations.[30]

Oil extracted in large quantities also supplied western agribusiness with the means of chemical control over their land and the crops grown on it. Short-term fertility and profitability skyrocketed as pesticides and fertilizers became a cheap and integral aspect of modern farming in the West. These chemicals provided nutrients for the soil more profitably than chemical-free cultivation. Constructed climates and landscapes made for the year round availability of fruits and vegetables, which helped make the good life in the West possible. The massive technologies devised to make planting and harvesting crops more efficient ran on gas. Federal agricultural policies supported this dependence. Oil and gas companies even retained underground rights as they sold rural land holdings to farm companies. Clearly, petroleum underlay nearly every aspect of agribusiness. In turn, as family farms collapsed, corporate-owned ventures in monoculture fed the cities of the West, the nation, and in some cases, the world.

In combination with federally-subsidized water and the use of Mexico's migrant workers for cheap labor, agribusiness extended its already large reach across the interior West. In fact, agribusiness crossed regional boundaries as small corporations became large, multi-dimensional multi-nationals. Western dreams of harvesting for empire came true, at least in economic terms, as capital and agricultural commodities flowed in and out of the rural West. A nascent organic farming movement looked to reform petroleum-dependent agribusiness in the 1970s but, by the late 1990s, it had taken on many characteristics of what it critiqued, which proved problematic for the land, for workers, and for consumers.[31]

On top of economic hard times, the displacement of small-scale and family farmers by these post-war innovations, coupled with environmental costs and the continuing influx of non-white workers, fed rural discontent in the 1970s and 1980s. Repeated exposures to petrochemicals poisoned farmers and farm workers alike. The rush to make land more amenable to agriculture led to the devastation of wetlands and other ecosystems as well. Petroleum extraction also sharpened environmental degradation. Large oil spills off of Santa Barbara, California, in 1969, and Seward, Alaska, in 1989, destroyed both ecologies and local economies. As rural people tended to see fewer benefits and greater costs from oil development, the urban–rural split in the West was exacerbated.

Other extraction industries in the West also contributed to unrest among white westerners across the countryside. Mines tapped out minerals or closed in the face of dropping demand from America's heavy industry, itself going through hard times. When mining operations closed in Butte, Montana, in the 1970s, the city nearly took on a ghost town appearance. Logging companies in California and the Pacific Northwest faced competition from abroad and dwindling supplies at home. They also squared off against urban westerners with environmental sensibilities. City dwellers tended to prefer aesthetically intact landscapes to clear cut forests, even if that meant the loss of rural jobs. With these high stakes, battles over whether or not logging companies should increase their leases on national forest lands consumed westerners of every stripe.[32]

Gradually, providing wilderness tourist experiences in the midst of natural beauty replaced older forms of extraction economies in the rural West, however unevenly. Older tourist spots, such as Santa Fe, New Mexico, and Sun Valley, Idaho, continued to draw crowds. But the expansion of the ski industry, in particular, led to rural economies that locals hoped would never collapse. In the 1970s, depressed mining towns such as Park City, Utah, Aspen, Colorado, and Red Lodge, Montana, recast themselves as skiing destinations. Bisbee, Arizona, once the scene of intense labor and racial conflict, crammed its streets with antique stores and restaurants, reinventing itself as a weekend getaway from Phoenix and Tucson. In a similar vein, Moab, Utah, nestled amidst the newly established national parks of Canyonlands and Arches, became the mountain bicycling capital of the world in the 1980s, offering visitors recreational tours into the stark and beautiful slickrock country. Tourists who imagined they biked through an untouched wilderness were often stunned to stumble across old mine shafts and uranium tailings left from the 1950s and 1960s.

All these communities used elements of the mythic West to bring people who would spend their money and keep local businesses afloat. As the towns profited from tourism, they also suffered from the development of service economies. These created a different form of the same dynamic, that of dependency on outsiders. Furthermore, as the stakes for tourists rose, those rural communities that marketed themselves the best succeeded the best.

Virginia City, Montana, for instance, ultimately failed in its efforts to promote year-round heritage tourism centered on its connection to the mythic nineteenth-century West of miners and gamblers. Virginia City, Nevada, played on the same elements and succeeded in luring tourists in the Carson City casinos to make the trek up to the old mining town. Taking advantage of legal loopholes, American Indian communities across the West rushed to construct casinos in the 1980s and 1990s that might attract off-reservation gamblers and off-reservation monies. Rural westerners of all kinds entered into bitter debates about developing private and federal lands for old-fashioned extraction or preserving them to extract tourist dollars from urban westerners.[33]

Caught between serving urbanites in swanky resorts and fashionable bistros or wrestling with the same over whether or not the vast acreage of federal lands should be developed for industry or saved for recreation, some rural westerners struck back in the late 1970s and 1980s. In what came to be known as the Sagebrush Rebellion, rural westerners effectively defied the federal government and trumpeted the sovereignty of local law, institutions, and interests when it came to public land use. They garnered national attention. Splashed on the cover of *Newsweek* magazine in 1979, a stereotypical cowboy gazed out at the reader. The headline read: "The Angry West: Get Off Our Backs Uncle Sam."

Decades of resentment against environmental regulation swelled up and found expression in protest or even violence directed at government agents and officials. The movement looked for aid in the New Right; the new president, Ronald Reagan, telegrammed a prominent Sagebrush conference on public lands in Salt Lake City in 1980 with a clear message: "I renew my pledge to work toward a Sagebrush solution." Efforts to develop and privatize public lands by either sympathetic politicians or local agitators, however, ran smack into urban environmentalists from across the West, who opposed them at every turn. By the late 1980s, an uneasy truce settled over the public lands of the rural West. Strategically reborn as the "Wise Use" movement in the 1990s, the Sagebrush rebels used the language of conservation to again resist the metropolitan West and the values it seemed to foist on the federal government.[34]

The tumult caused by the influx of immigrant laborers, the demise of traditional extractive industries, conflicts with the federal government over land use, and the rise of service related tourism made many rural whites cling even more tightly to the mythic West. In memoirs and reminiscences published through the 1990s, western essayists such as May Clearman Blew noted that rural white male westerners, in particular, desperately hung on to cowboy lifestyles in the face of intense change. Others, such as William Kittredge, counted the costs paid by rural families and western landscapes for that clinging. Urban westerners, as well as those outside the region who wanted to see something of what they imagined to be an authentic western lifestyle, proved a ready reading audience receptive to both messages. They loved the idea of a persistent mythic West, but were less enamored with the economic assumptions and ecological results that emanated from such a vision of the region.[35]

In stark contrast, the rise of Silicon Valley, the internet, and the concurrent dot-com boom in the 1990s seemed to validate the post-World War II investment in the military-industrial complex and the metropolitan growth that went with it. In the shadow of Stanford University, a technological revolution flooded consumer markets with gadgets ranging from personal computers to cell phones, bringing vast amounts of money to the South Bay. That prosperity excluded local Mexican American residents whose labor propelled the technology boom forward. In fact, good economic times in the 1990s in Silicon Valley belied an ongoing migration from California. By the mid-1980s, the rising cost of living in California convinced many middle-class professionals of a decline in the state's quality of life. Racial tensions and growing inner city poverty – dramatized by the 1992 riots in Los Angeles – seemed to confirm those notions. A new wave of impoverished immigrants from Central America, where US interventions of the 1980s fostered civil wars and dislocation, heightened the concerns of well-to-do whites. No longer a land of milk and honey, California became a place to escape from rather than move to.

Most who moved, and these included second- and third-generation Mexican Americans as well as middle-class whites, sought homes in other western cities. By the late 1980s, a moneyed migration flowed from the Golden State to the Pacific Northwest and then shifted to the interior West. While bumper stickers in Oregon and Washington warned against the "Californication" of Portland and Seattle, thousands migrated north on Interstate 5. Long-time residents of the Northwest resented the rising property values and cultural demands that Californians brought with them.[36] A second wave of Californians moved out of the state in the mid-1990s, choosing cities such as Boise, Phoenix, Las Vegas, and Salt Lake City. Others cast their eye to beautiful parts of the western countryside, where they might buy a ranchette (a tract home with small acreage) and a pleasant view. This added gentrification to the list of rural westerners' concerns.

To many, these changes seemed to mark off a "New West," but much about them tended toward continuity rather than novelty. If

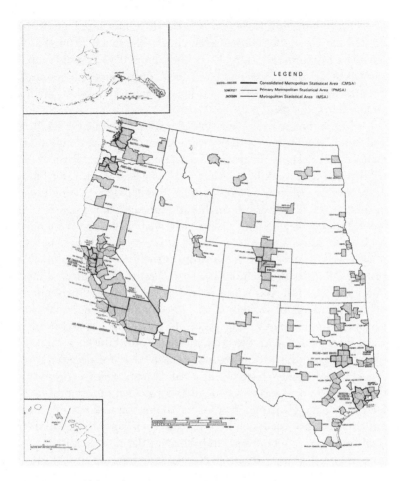

Figure 6.2 Although vast open spaces remain in the West, the increasing urban and suburban sprawl shows that cities with opportunities, diversity, and amenities will continue to challenge a regional identity long linked to rural landscapes. *Source:* Courtesy, US Census Bureau, Public Information Office.

anything, the rise of the military industrial complex, the flowering of a wide range of activism and dissent, and ongoing conflicts over landscapes all reinforced connections to the western past, instead of severing them. How else could President Ronald Reagan use cutting brush outside his suburban ranch above Santa Barbara, California, as a political statement that deeply implicated the interpenetration of region, myth, and reality in Americans' understandings of the West? That George W. Bush did the same at the ranch he purchased outside Crawford, Texas, as he readied himself for a presidential run nearly 20 years later suggested deep consistencies and connections in western history. The ever-present tension between mythic and modern persists today.[37]

Understanding today's West depends on training one eye on these and others continuities with the western past – both real and imagined – while keeping the other focused on new trends. Parts of the rural West face economic decisions that may lead to the same kinds of profitable, short-term booms and disempowering, long-range busts that residents lived through 100 years ago. Some denizens of nineteenth-century mining towns that went belly-up when mine shafts offered no more minerals look at service-based tourist economies with a jaundiced eye and turn instead to more sustainable ventures. Politics in much of the urban West revolves around race, in-migration, and class – just as it has for decades. Increasingly diverse, residents of western cities are reshaping the national conversation about what it means to be an American. The relationship westerners shared with the land still delineates how they think of themselves and the West. Opposed to each other for decades, rural ranchers and farmers have recently joined with urban environmentalists to form new and powerful alliances against suburban sprawl. Despite constant attempts by the federal government to force Indians to relinquish their rich heritage and their right to define their own future on reservations established in the nineteenth century, ever-resourceful and resilient Native communities transformed them into sanctuaries of cultural identity during the twentieth. Fighting persistent racism, Indians across the continent continue to tell their own stories not only in "Indian Country" but also at a new National Museum of the American Indian (authorized by Congress in 1989 and completed in 2004) that sits in the heart of Washington, DC. In all these examples, one constant remains. The presence of the past in the present – however contested – continues to drive change and define the West of tomorrow.

NOTES

1 John Wayne, introducing the first "Gunsmoke," September 10, 1955, <www.tv.com/gunsmoke/matt-gets-it/episode/13511/summary.html>.

2 Tim Brooks and Earle Marsh, *The Complete Directory to Prime Time Network and Cable TV Shows, 1946–Present* (New York: Ballantine Books, 1995), 1261; Gary A. Yoggy, "When Television Wore Six-Guns: Cowboy Heroes on TV," in Archie P. McDonald, ed., *Shooting Stars: Heroes and Heroines of Western Film* (Bloomington: Indiana University Press, 1987), 218–61; John H. Lenihan, *Showdown: Confronting Modern America in the Western Film* (Urbana: University of Illinois Press, 1980); Robert G. Athearn, *The Mythic West in Twentieth Century America* (Lawrence: University Press of Kansas, 1986); Michael L. Johnson, *New Westers: The West in Contemporary American Culture* (Lawrence: University Press of Kansas, 1996).

3 Ann Markusen, Peter Hal, Scott Campbell, and Sabrina Deitrick, *The Rise of the Gunbelt: The Military Revamping of Industrial America* (New York: Oxford University Press, 1991), 8–25, 174–210 and Roger W. Lotchin, *Fortress California, 1910–1961* (New York: Oxford University Press, 1992), 297–318.

4 Markusen et al., *The Rise of the Gunbelt*, 51–117, 148–73; Lotchin, *Fortress California*, 64–130, 173–205; Abbott, *The Metropolitan Frontier*, 64.

5 Markusen et al., *The Rise of the Gunbelt*, 90–100; George E. Webb, *Science in the American Southwest: A Topical History* (Tucson: University of Arizona Press, 2002), 151–218; Margaret Pugh O'Mara, *Cities of Knowledge: Cold War Science and the Search for the Next Silicon Valley* (Princeton: Princeton University Press, 2005), 36–96; Abbott, *The Metropolitan Frontier*, 65.

6 John M. Findlay, *Magic Lands: Western Cityscapes and American Culture after 1940* (Berkeley: University of California Press, 1992), 117–19 and O'Mara, *Cities of Knowledge*, 97–141.

7 Abbott, *The Metropolitan Frontier*, 123–8.

8 Morgan, *Westward Tilt*, 7, 26; Wallace Stegner quoted in Neal R. Peirce, *The Pacific States of America: People, Politics, and Power in the Five Pacific Basin States* (New York: W. W. Norton, 1992), 24.

9 Findlay, *Magic Lands*, 14–51; Gene Burd, "The Selling of the Sunbelt: Civic Boosterism in the Media," in David C. Perry and Alfred J. Watkins, eds., *The Rise of the Sunbelt Cities* (Beverly Hills: Sage Publications, 1977), 129–50; O'Mara, *Cities of Knowledge*, 58–94; Eric Avila, *Popular Culture in the Age of White Flight: Fear and Fantasy in Suburban Los Angeles* (Berkeley: University of California

Press, 2004); Matt Garcia, *A World of Its Own: Race, Labor, and Citrus in the Making of Greater Los Angeles, 1900–1970* (Chapel Hill: University of North Carolina Press, 2001); Morgan, *Westward Tilt*, 3–12, 27–41; Robert O. Self, *American Babylon: Race and the Struggle for Postwar Oakland* (Princeton: Princeton University Press, 2003).

10 Peter Wiley and Robert Gottlieb, *Empires in the Sun: The Rise of the New American West* (Tucson: University of Arizona Press, 1985), 34–6; Claus-M. Naske, *An Interpretative History of Alaskan Statehood* (Anchorage: Alaska Northwest Publishing, 1973), 47–74; John S. Whitehead, *Completing the Union: Alaska, Hawai'i, and the Battle for Statehood* (Albuquerque: University of New Mexico Press, 2004); Tom Coffman, *The Island Edge of America: A Political History of Hawai'i* (Honolulu: University of Hawai'i Press, 2003).

11 Raye C. Ringholz, *Uranium Frenzy: Saga of the Nuclear West* (Logan: Utah State University, 2002), 57–95; Arthur R. Gomez, *Quest for the Golden Circle: The Four Corners and the Metropolitan West, 1945–1970* (Albuquerque: University of New Mexico Press, 1994), 17–96; Michael A. Amundson, *Yellowcake Towns: Uranium Mining Communities in the American West* (Boulder: University Press of Colorado, 2002). Quote from Bernard DeVoto, *The Western Paradox: A Conservation Reader*, Douglas Brinkley and Patricia Nelson Limerick, eds. (New Haven: Yale University Press, 2000), 62.

12 Worster, *Rivers of Empire*, 262–5.

13 Mark W. T. Harvey, *A Symbol of Wilderness: Echo Park and the American Conservation Movement* (Albuquerque: University of New Mexico Press, 1994).

14 Marc Reisner, *Cadillac Desert: The American West and its Disappearing Water* (1986; New York: Penguin, 1993), 169–306, 435–40 and Stephen C. Sturgeon, *The Politics of Western Water: The Congressional Career of Wayne Aspinall* (Tucson: University of Arizona Press, 2002).

15 Becky M. Nicolaides, *My Blue Heaven: Life and Politics in the Working-Class Suburbs of Los Angeles, 1920–1965* (Chicago: University of Chicago Press, 2002) and Lisa McGirr, *Suburban Warriors: The Origins of the New American Right* (Princeton: Princeton University Press, 2001), 20–53.

16 David Shea Teeple, quoted in Yoggy, "When Television Wore Six-Guns," 230 and William F. Rickenbacker, quoted in Kurt Schuparra, *Triumph of the Right: The Rise of the California Conservative Movement, 1945–1966* (Armonk, NY: M. E. Sharpe, 1998), 83.

17 Michelle Nickerson, "Women, Domesticity, and Postwar Conservatism," *OAH Magazine of History* 17:2 (January 2003): 17–21.

18 Peter Iverson, *Barry Goldwater: Native Arizonan* (Norman: University

of Oklahoma Press, 1997) and Robert Allen Goldberg, *Barry Goldwater* (New Haven: Yale University Press, 1995).

19 Michael E. Welsh, "Western Film, Ronald Reagan, and the Western Metaphor," in McDonald, ed., *Shooting Stars*, 147–64; Lou Cannon, *Governor Reagan: His Rise to Power* (New York: Public Affairs, 2003), 3–126; Bill Boyarsky, *The Rise of Reagan* (New York: Random House Books, 1968), 104; Jonathan M. Schoenwald, *A Time for Choosing: The Rise of Modern American Conservativism* (New York: Oxford University Press, 2001), 190–220.

20 Robert Mason, *Richard Nixon and the Quest for a New Majority* (Chapel Hill: University of North Carolina Press, 2005); Jordan A. Schwarz, *The New Dealers: Power Politics in the Age of Roosevelt* (New York: Knopf, 1993); Robert A. Caro, *The Years of Lyndon Johnson: Master of the Senate* (New York: Knopf, 2002).

21 Quote from Morgan, *Westward Tilt*, 8; Matthew C. Whittaker, *Race Work: The Rise of Civil Rights in the Urban West* (Lincoln: University of Nebraska Press, 2005), 89–172; Quintard Taylor, *In Search of the Racial Frontier*, 278–91; Gretchen Cassel Eick, *Dissent in Wichita: The Civil Rights Movement in the Midwest, 1954–72* (Urbana: University of Illinois Press, 2002), 1–52.

22 W. J. Rorabaugh, *Berkeley at War: The 1960s* (New York: Oxford University Press, 1989), 8–47, 87–123 and Ruth Rosen, *The World Split Open: How the Modern Women's Movement Changed America* (New York: Viking, 2000), 94–142.

23 Rorabaugh, *Berkeley at War*, 48–86 and Philip S. Foner, ed., *The Black Panthers Speak* (1970; Cambridge: DeCapo, 1995).

24 Michael Allen, "'I Just Want to be a Cosmic Cowboy': Hippies, Cowboy Code, and the Culture of a Counterculture," *Western Historical Quarterly* 36:3 (Fall 2005): 275–99 and Philip J. Deloria, *Playing Indian* (New Haven: Yale University Press, 1998), 154–80.

25 Donald Fixico, *Termination and Relocation: Federal Indian Policy, 1945–1960* (Albuquerque: University of New Mexico Press, 1986); Kenneth R. Philp, *Termination Revisited: American Indians on the Trail to Self-Determination, 1933–1953* (Lincoln: University of Nebraska Press, 1999); Harmon, *Indians in the Making*, 218–44; Charles Wilkerson, *Messages from Frank's Landing: A Story of Salmon, Treaties, and the Indian Way* (Seattle: University of Washington Press, 2000); Richard E. Neunherz, "The Struggle for Fishing Resources in the Pacific Northwest of the Late Twentieth Century," *OAH Magazine of History* 19:6 (November 2005): 48–55.

26 Troy R. Johnson, *The Occupation of Alcatraz Island: Indian Self-Determination and the Rise of Indian Activism* (Urbana: University of Illinois Press, 1996) and Joane Nagel, *American Indian Ethnic*

Renewal: Red Power and the Resurgence of Identity and Culture (New York: Oxford University Press, 1996).

27 Richard Griswold del Castillo and Arnoldo DeLeon, *North to Aztlán: A History of Mexican Americans in the United States* (New York: Twayne, 1996), 125–47; Ernesto Chávez, *"¡Mi Raza Primero!"* *(My People First!): Nationalism, Identity, and Insurgency in the Chicano Movement in Los Angeles, 1966–1978* (Berkeley: University of California Press, 2002); Lara Medina, *Las Hermanas: Chicana/Latina Religious-Political Activism in the US Catholic Church* (Philadelphia: Temple University Press, 2004); Dionne Espinoza, "'Revolutionary Sisters': Women's Solidarity and Collective Identification among Chicana Brown Berets in East Los Angeles, 1967–1970," *Aztlán* 26 (Spring 2001): 17–58.

28 Richard Griswold Del Castillo and Richard A. Garcia, *César Chávez: A Triumph of Spirit* (Norman: University of Oklahoma Press, 1997).

29 Ronald Takaki, *Strangers from a Different Shore: A History of Asian Americans* (1989; Boston: Back Bay Books, 1998), 406–71 and Min Zhou and James V. Gatewood, *Contemporary Asian America: A Multidisciplinary Reader* (New York: New York University Press, 2000).

30 Anthony Sampson, *The Seven Sisters: The Great Oil Companies and the World They Shaped* (New York: Bantam Books, 1981).

31 R. Douglas Hurt, ed., *The Rural West Since World War II* (Lawrence: University Press of Kansas, 1998); Deborah Fitzgerald, *Every Farm a Factory: The Industrial Ideal in American Agriculture* (New Haven: Yale University Press, 2003); Julie Guthman, *Agrarian Dreams: The Paradox of Organic Farming in California* (Berkeley: University of California Press, 2004).

32 David B. Danbom, *Born in the Country: A History of Rural America* (Baltimore: Johns Hopkins University Press, 1995), 253–70; Nancy Langston, *Where Land and Water Meet: A Western Landscape Transformed* (Seattle: University of Washington Press, 2003); Richard White, "'Are You an Environmentalist or Do You Work for a Living?': Work and Nature" in William Cronon, ed., *Uncommon Ground: Rethinking the Human Place in Nature* (New York: W. W. Norton, 1995): 171–85.

33 Annie Gilbert Coleman, *Ski Style: Sport and Culture in the Rockies* (Lawrence: University Press of Kansas, 2004); Gomez, *Quest for the Golden Circle*, 149–91; Bonnie Christensen, *Red Lodge and the Mythic West: Coal Miners to Cowboys* (Lawrence: University Press of Kansas, 2002); Hal K. Rothman, *Devil's Bargains: Tourism in the Twentieth-Century American West* (Lawrence: University Press of Kansas, 1998).

34 Quoted in R. McGreggor Cawley, *Federal Land, Western Anger: The Sagebrush Rebellion and Environmental Politics* (Lawrence: Uni-

versity Press of Kansas, 1993), 71, 93; Richard White, "The Current Weirdness in the West," *Western Historical Quarterly* 28:1 (Spring 1997): 5–6; James McCarthy, "Environmentalism, Wise Use, and the Nature of Accumulation in the Rural West," in Bruce Braun and Noel Castree, eds., *Remaking Reality: Nature at the Millennium* (New York: Routledge, 1998), 126–9.

35 Mary Clearman Blew, *All but the Waltz: A Memoir of Five Generations in the Life of a Montana Family* (New York: Viking, 1991); William Kittredge, *Hole in the Sky: A Memoir* (New York: Vintage, 1993).

36 Stephen J. Pitti, *The Devil in Silicon Valley: Northern California, Race, and Mexican Americans* (Princeton: Princeton University Press, 2004), 128–47.

37 Joseph E. Taylor III, "The Many Lives of the New West," *Western Historical Quarterly* 35:2 (Summer 2004): 141–5.

Suggested Readings

By its nature, a concise history points readers down many roads, some of which remain less-traveled. Brevity, however, should not suggest that the field of western history lays dormant. The last 20 years have seen an explosion of worthwhile work. This admittedly partial guide to that scholarship will nonetheless steer more interested students of western and American history through the current literature.

Introduction

A number of significant overviews of US western history appeared in the 1990s and early 2000s, responding to new scholarship. Richard White's *It's Your Misfortune and None of My Own: A New History of the American West* (Norman: University of Oklahoma Press, 1991) and Clyde A. Milner II, Carol A. O'Connor, and Martha A. Sandweiss, eds., *The Oxford History of the American West* (New York: Oxford University Press, 1994) have been supplemented by the more recent appearance of Robert V. Hine and John Mack Faragher, *The American West: A New Interpretive History* (New Haven: Yale University Press, 2000) and Walter Nugent, *Into the West: The Story of Its People* (New York: Vintage, 2001).

Individual lives illuminate broader dynamics in Richard W. Etulain, ed., *Western Lives: A Biographical History of the American West* (Albuquerque: University of New Mexico Press, 2004), while the essays in William Deverell, ed., *A Companion to the American*

West (Malden, MA: Blackwell, 2004) also prove useful. Howard R. Lamar, ed., *The New Encyclopedia of the American West* (New Haven: Yale University Press, 1998) remains an invaluable reference work for students of western history.

Newer anthologies on western women and gender history serve as a counterweight to more typical narratives. See Matthew Basso, Laura McCall, and Dee Garceau, eds., *Across the Great Divide: Cultures of Manhood in the American West* (New York: Routledge, 2001); Sandra K. Schackel, ed., *Western Women's Lives: Continuity and Change in the Twentieth Century* (Albuquerque: University of New Mexico Press, 2003); Mary Ann Irwin and James F. Brooks, eds., *Women and Gender in the American West* (Albuquerque: University of New Mexico Press, 2004); and Dee Garceau-Hagen, ed., *Portraits of Women in the American West* (New York: Routledge, 2005).

Chapter 1

The vast recent scholarship on pre-contact Native America has been skillfully synthesized in Charles C. Mann, *1491: New Revelations of the Americas before Columbus* (New York: Knopf, 2005). For more detailed insights, turn to Shepard Krech III, *The Ecological Indian: Myth and History* (New York: W. W. Norton, 2000) and Alfred W. Crosby, *The Columbian Exchange: Biological and Cultural Consequences of 1492* (Westport, CT: Greenwood, 1972). A continental vision of early American history that integrates the insights of western history is offered by Alan Taylor, *American Colonies: The Settling of North America* (Penguin: New York, 2001).

David J. Weber, *The Spanish Frontier in North America* (New Haven: Yale University Press, 1992) remains the best single-volume treatment on the subject. For more on the Pueblo Revolt, see Andrew L. Knaut, *The Pueblo Revolt of 1680: Conquest and Resistance in Seventeenth-Century New Mexico* (Norman: University of Oklahoma Press, 1995). The intertwined relations of colonists and Natives in the Southwest are closely examined by Ramón A. Gutiérrez, *When Jesus Came, The Corn Mothers Went Away: Marriage, Sexuality, and Power in New Mexico, 1500–1846* (Stanford: Stanford University Press, 1991); Ross Frank, *From Settler to Citizen: New Mexican Economic Development and the Creation of Vecino Society, 1750–1820* (Berkeley: University of California Press, 2000);

and James F. Brooks, *Captives and Cousins: Slavery, Kinship, and Community in the Southwest Borderlands* (Chapel Hill: University of North Carolina Press, 2002). Ned Blackhawk, *Violence Over the Land: Indians and Empires in the Early American West* (Cambridge: Harvard University Press, 2006) skillfully examines the oft-neglected Great Basin.

Since the publication of Richard White's *The Middle Ground: Indians, Empires, and Republics in The Great Lakes Region, 1650–1815* (New York: Cambridge University Press, 1991), a number of scholars have focused their studies of French–Indian and British–Indian relations on intercultural collusion as well as conflict. The finest of these studies include Daniel H. Usner Jr, *Indians, Settlers, and Slaves in a Frontier Exchange Economy: The Lower Mississippi Valley before 1783* (Chapel Hill: University of North Carolina Press, 1992); James H. Merrell, *Into the American Woods: Negotiators on the Pennsylvania Frontier* (New York: W. W. Norton, 1999); Alan Gallay, *The Indian Slave Trade: The Rise of the English Empire in the American South* (New Haven: Yale University Press, 2002); Jane T. Merritt, *At the Crossroads: Indians and Empires on a Mid-Atlantic Frontier, 1700–1763* (Chapel Hill: University of North Carolina Press, 2003); and Kathleen DuVal, *The Native Ground: Indians and Colonists in the Heart of the Continent* (Philadelphia: University of Pennsylavania, 2006).

For more on the effects of the Proclamation of 1763 and the American Revolution on Native communities, see Colin G. Calloway, *The Scratch of a Pen: 1763 and the Transformation of North America* (New York: Oxford University Press, 2006); Daniel K. Richter, *Facing East from Indian Country: A Native History of Early America* (Cambridge, MA: Harvard University Press, 2001); Colin G. Calloway, *The American Revolution in Indian Country: Crisis and Diversity in Native American Communities* (New York: Cambridge University Press, 1995); and Alan Taylor, *The Divided Ground: Indians, Settlers, and the Northern Borderland of the American Revolution* (New York: Knopf, 2006).

Gregory H. Nobles, *American Frontiers: Cultural Encounters and Continental Conquest* (New York: Hill and Wang, 1998) puts old American frontier stories in intercultural contexts and historian Stephen Aron shares new insights about American forms of settler colonialism in trans-Appalachia in his *How the West Was Lost: The Transformation of Kentucky from Daniel Boone to Henry Clay*

(Baltimore: Johns Hopkins University Press, 1996) and *American Confluence: The Missouri Frontier from Borderland to Border State* (Bloomington: Indiana University Press, 2006). The essays in Andrew R. L. Cayton and Fredrika J. Teute, *Contact Points: American Frontiers from the Mohawk Valley to the Mississippi, 1750–1830* (Chapel Hill: University of North Carolina Press, 1998) also offer useful snapshots of settler colonialism and Indian–white contact in its varied forms. Finally, Peter S. Onuf, *Statehood and Union: A History of the Northwest Ordinance* (Bloomington: Indiana University Press, 1987) clarifies the far-reaching significance of the Northwest Ordinance.

Chapter 2

Any understanding of the trans-Mississippi West that Lewis and Clark entered must begin with Colin G. Calloway, *One Vast Winter Count: The Native American West before Lewis and Clark* (University of Nebraska Press, 2003). James P. Ronda, *Lewis and Clark among the Indians* (Lincoln: University of Nebraska Press, 1984) and James P. Ronda, *Astoria & Empire* (Lincoln: University of Nebraska Press, 1990) remain standard texts.

William H. Goetzmann's *Exploration and Empire: The Explorer and Scientist in the Winning of the American West* (New York: W. W. Norton, 1966) and *New Lands, New Men: America and the Second Great Age of Discovery* (New York: Viking, 1986) offer the best overviews of federal and scientific exploration in the early nineteenth-century West.

David J. Wishart's *The Fur Trade of the American West, 1807–1840: A Geographical Synthesis* (Lincoln: University of Nebraska Press, 1979) covers the northern Rockies and northern Plains. Barton H. Barbour, *Fort Union and the Upper Missouri Fur Trade* (Norman: University of Oklahoma Press, 2001) provides a more detailed portrayal of the latter. David J. Weber's *The Taos Trappers: The Fur Trade in the Far Southwest, 1540–1846* (Norman: University of Oklahoma Press, 1970) should be balanced with Gary Clayton Anderson's *The Indian Southwest, 1580–1830: Ethnogenesis and Reinvention* (Norman: University of Oklahoma Press, 2000) to understand the southern Rockies and southern Plains. The best one-volume source on the Santa Fe trade can be found in Stephen G. Hyslop, *Bound for Santa Fe: The Road to New Mexico and the American Conquest, 1896–1848* (Norman: University of Oklahoma Press, 2002).

For the Pacific Northwest, see James R. Gibson, *Otter Skins, Boston Ships, and China Goods: The Maritime Fur Trade of the Northwest Coast, 1785–1841* (Seattle: University of Washington Press, 1992); Elizabeth Vibert, *Traders' Tales: Narratives of Cultural Encounter in the Columbia Plateau* (Norman: University of Oklahoma Press, 1997); Alexandra Harmon, *Indians in the Making: Ethnic Relations and Indian Identities around Puget Sound* (Berkeley: University of California Press, 1998); and John Phillip Reid, *Peter Skene Ogden and the Snake River Expeditions* (Norman: University of Oklahoma Press, 2002).

Chapter 3

Anthony F. C. Wallace, *The Long Bitter Trail: Andrew Jackson and the Indians* (New York: Hill and Wang, 1993) provides a solid overview of Indian removal. For more on one family's experience of removal from the Southeast, see Tiya Miles, *Ties that Bind: The Story of an Afro-Cherokee Family in Slavery and Freedom* (Berkeley: University of California Press, 2005). Anders Stephanson, *Manifest Destiny: American Expansion and the Empire of Right* (New York: Hill and Wang, 1995) succinctly sums up the nature and origins of manifest destiny.

For more on Texas in the 1830s and 1840s, look to Paul D. Lack, *The Texas Revolutionary Experience: A Political and Social History, 1835–1836* (College Station: Texas A & M University Press, 1992) and, for a powerful corrective to pervasive myths, Gary Clayton Anderson, *The Conquest of Texas: Ethnic Cleansing in the Promised Land* (Norman: University of Oklahoma Press, 2005). See also Paul Foos, *A Short, Offhand, Killing Affair: Soldiers and Social Conflict during the Mexican-American War* (Chapel Hill: University of North Carolina Press, 2002).

For Indian, Spanish, and Mexican California, turn to Albert L. Hurtado's *Indian Survival on the California Frontier* (New Haven: Yale University Press, 1988) and *Intimate Frontiers: Sex, Gender, and Culture in Old California* (Albuquerque: University of New Mexico Press, 1999); James A. Sandos, *Converting California:*

Indians and Franciscans in the Missions (New Haven: Yale University Press, 2004); and Steven W. Hackel's *Children of Coyote, Missionaries of St. Francis: Indian–Spanish Relations in Colonial California, 1769–1850* (Chapel Hill: University of North Carolina Press, 2005). For the years after the American conquest, see Tomás Almaguer, *Racial Fault Lines: The Origins of White Supremacy in California* (Berkeley: University of California Press, 1994) and Miroslava Chávez-García, *Negotiating Conquest: Gender and Power in California, 1770s–1880s* (Tucson: University of Arizona Press, 2004).

Recent work on western pre-Civil War mining rushes includes Malcolm J. Rohrbough, *Days of Gold: The California Gold Rush and the American Nation* (Berkeley: University of California Press, 1997), Susan Lee Johnson, *Roaring Camp: The Social World of the California Gold Rush* (New York: W. W. Norton, 2000); Andrew C. Isenberg, *Mining California: An Ecological History* (New York: Hill and Wang, 2005); and Elliott West, *The Contested Plains: Indians, Goldseekers, and the Rush to Colorado* (Lawrence: University Press of Kansas, 1998).

Relationships among Mormons, Indians, and other Americans in Utah lay at the center of David L. Bigler, *Forgotten Kingdom: The Mormon Theocracy in the American West, 1847–1896* (Logan: Utah State University Press, 1998) and Will Bagley, *Blood of the Prophets: Brigham Young and the Massacre at Mountain Meadows* (Norman: University of Oklahoma Press, 2002).

Julie Roy Jeffrey's *Converting the West: A Biography of Narcissa Whitman* (Norman: University of Oklahoma Press, 1994) explores the Whitmans' story, while other emigrants get their due in John Mack Faragher, *Women and Men on the Overland Trail* (New Haven: Yale University Press, 1979) and John D. Unruh, *The Plains Across: The Overland Emigrants and the Trans-Mississippi West, 1840–1860* (Urbana: University of Illinois Press, 1979). For Indian–emigrant relations, see Michael L. Tate, *Indians and Emigrants: Encounters on the Overland Trails* (Norman: University of Oklahoma Press, 2006).

Michael A. Morrison, *Slavery and the American West: The Eclipse of Manifest Destiny and the Coming of the Civil War* (Chapel Hill: University of North Carolina Press, 1999) lays out the relationship between western territories and national political struggles over slavery. For the standard text on US–Indian confrontations in the pre-Civil War West, see Robert M. Utley, *Frontiersmen in Blue: The United States Army and the Indian, 1848–1865* (Lincoln: University of Nebraska Press, 1967). One example of the unraveling of Indian–white relations in the years leading up to the Civil War can be found in Gary Clayton Anderson, *Kinsmen of Another Kind: Dakota–White Relations in the Upper Mississippi Valley, 1650–1862* (Lincoln: University of Nebraska Press, 1984).

Chapter 4

The Battle of the Little Bighorn continues to spur historical controversy as well as reams of writing. Start with Richard Allan Fox Jr, *Archaeology, History, and Custer's Last Battle* (Norman: University of Oklahoma Press, 1993). For the military history of Indian displacement, see Paul Andrew Hutton, *Phil Sheridan's Army* (Lincoln: University of Nebraska Press, 1985). For the environmental history of the same, see Mark David Spence, *Dispossessing the Wilderness: Indian Removal and the Making of the National Parks* (New York: Oxford University Press, 2000).

Indian communities dealt with displacement and reservations in a variety of ways. For recent case studies, see David Rich Lewis, *Neither Wolf Nor Dog: American Indians, Environment, and Agrarian Change* (New York: Oxford University Press, 1994); Frederick E. Hoxie, *Parading Through History: The Making of the Crow Nation in America, 1805–1935* (New York: Cambridge University Press, 1995); Martha C. Knack, *Boundaries Between: The Southern Paiutes, 1775–1995* (Lincoln: University of Nebraska Press, 2001); Peter Iverson, *Diné: A History of the Navajos* (Albuquerque: University of New Mexico Press, 2002); Jeffrey Ostler, *The Plains Sioux and US Colonialism from Lewis and Clark to Wounded Knee* (New York: Cambridge University Press, 2004); Laura Woodworth-Ney, *Mapping Identity: The Creation of the Coeur D'Alene Indian Reservation, 1805–1902* (Boulder: University Press of Colorado, 2004); Paige Raibmon, *Authentic Indians: Episodes of Encounter from the Late-Nineteenth-Century Northwest Coast* (Durham: Duke University Press, 2005); and Gregory E. Smoak, *Ghost Dances and Identity: Prophetic Religion and American Indian Ethnogenesis in the Nineteenth Century* (Berkeley: University of California Press, 2005).

Attempts to assimilate Natives in the reservation era often fell to white women. Their complicated story is chronicled in Peggy Pascoe, *Relations of Rescue: The Search for Female Moral Authority in the American West, 1874–1939* (New York: Oxford University Press, 1990); Margaret D. Jacobs, *Engendered Encounters: Feminism and Pueblo Cultures, 1879–1934* (Lincoln: University of Nebraska Press, 1999); and Jane E. Simonsen, *Making Home Work: Domesticity and Native American Assimilation in the American West, 1860–1919* (Chapel Hill: University of North Carolina Press, 2006). Clyde A. Milner II's *With Good Intentions: Quaker Work among the Pawnees, Otoes, and Omahas in the 1870s* (Lincoln: University of Nebraska Press, 1982) and J. Henrietta Stockel's *On the Bloody Road to Jesus: Christianity and the Chiricahua Apaches* (Albuquerque: University of New Mexico Press, 2004) are fine studies of missionary work on reservations. Boarding schools proved an especially controversial form of attempted assimilation. Devon A. Mihesuah, *Cultivating the Rosebuds: The Education of Women at the Cherokee Female Seminary* (Urbana: University of Illinois Press, 1993) and Brenda J. Child, *Boarding School Seasons: American Indian Families* (Lincoln: University of Nebraska, 1998) offer comprehensive treatments, while Kathleen M. B. Osburn, *Southern Ute Women: Autonomy and Assimilation on the Reservation, 1887–1934* (Albuquerque: University of New Mexico Press, 1998) provides a clear picture of how some Native women reacted to these assimilation efforts.

Railroads revolutionized the West. Newer treatments include Claire Strom, *Profiting from the Plains: The Great Northern Railway and Corporate Development of the American West* (Seattle: University of Washington Press, 2003) and Richard J. Orsi, *Sunset Limited: The Southern Pacific Railroad and the Development of the American West, 1850–1930* (Berkeley: University of California Press, 2005). Late nineteenth-century American settlement is well handled in Nell Irvin Painter, *Exodusters: Black Migration to Kansas after Reconstruction* (New York: Knopf, 1976); Dean L. May, *Three Frontiers: Family, Land, and Society in the American West, 1850–1900* (New York: Cambridge University Press, 1994); Dee Garceau, *The Important Things of Life: Women, Work, and Family in Sweetwater County, Wyoming, 1880–1929* (Lincoln: University of Nebraska Press, 1997); and Brenda K. Jackson, *Domesticating the West: The Re-creation of the Nineteenth-Century American*

Middle Class (Lincoln: University of Nebraska Press, 2005). Peter H. Argersinger's, *The Limits of Agrarian Radicalism: Western Populism and American Politics* (Lawrence: University Press of Kansas, 1995) examines farmer-based populism that emerged from some western settlements.

In recent years, scholars refined and expanded their definitions of western violence, including social as well as personal conflict. Leading the way was Richard Maxwell Brown's, *No Duty to Retreat: Violence and Values in American History and Society* (New York: Oxford University Press, 1991). Also useful are Clare V. McKenna Jr, *Race, Homicide, and Justice in the American West, 1880–1920* (Tucson: University of Arizona Press, 1997); Anne M. Butler, *Gendered Justice in the American West: Women Prisoners in Male Penitentiaries* (Urbana: University of Illinois Press, 1997); and David Peterson Del Mar, *Beaten Down: A History of Interpersonal Violence in the West* (Seattle: University of Washington Press, 2002).

Chapter 5

For the rise of the urban West, see Carl Abbott, *The Metropolitan Frontier: Cities in the Modern American West* (Tucson: University of Arizona Press, 1993); Eugene P. Moehring, *Urbanism and Empire in the Far West* (Reno: University of Nevada Press, 2004); and Mark Wild, *Street Meeting: Multiethnic Neighborhoods in Early Twentieth-Century Los Angeles* (Berkeley: University of California Press, 2005). William Cronon, *Nature's Metropolis: Chicago and the Great West* (New York: W. W. Norton, 1991) and Kathleen A. Brosnan, *Uniting Mountain and Plain: Cities, Law, and Environmental Change along the Front Range* (Albuquerque: University of New Mexico Press, 2002) illustrate how western cities came to dominate hinterlands, while William Deverell, *Whitewashed Adobe: The Rise of Los Angeles and the Remaking of its Mexican Past* (Berkeley: University of California Press, 2004) notes the power of boosters and culture in remaking western cities and Matthew Klingle, *Emerald City: An Environmental History of Seattle and an Evolving Ethic of Place* (New Haven: Yale University Press, 2007) examines the environmental and social effects of the same.

For more on early twentieth-century laborers in the West, see

Elizabeth Jameson, *All That Glitters: Class, Conflict, and Community in Cripple Creek* (Urbana: University of Illinois Press, 1998); Gunther Peck, *Reinventing Free Labor: Padrones and Immigrant Workers in the North American West, 1880–1930* (New York: Cambridge University Press, 2000); John W. Heaton, *The Shoshone-Bannocks: Culture and Commerce at Fort Hall, 1870–1940* (Lawrence: University Press of Kansas, 2005); and Colleen O'Neill, *Working the Navajo Way: Labor and Culture in the Twentieth Century* (Lawrence: University Press of Kansas, 2005).

The powerful presence of the government in western life is elucidated in Joseph E. Taylor III, *Making Salmon: An Environmental History of the Northwest Fisheries Crisis* (Seattle: University of Washington Press, 1999); Karl Jacoby, *Crimes against Nature: Squatters, Poachers, Thieves, and the Hidden History of American Conservationism* (Berkeley: University of California Press, 2001); Stephen J. Pyne, *Year of the Fires: The Story of the Great Fires of 1910* (New York: Viking, 2001); María E. Montoya, *Translating Property: The Maxwell Land Grant and the Conflict over Land in the American West* (Berkeley: University of California Press, 2002); Karen R. Merrill, *Public Lands and Political Meaning: Ranchers, the Government, and the Property Between Them* (Berkeley: University of California Press, 2002); Nancy Langston, *Where Land and Water Meet: A Western Landscape Transformed* (Seattle: University of Washington Press, 2003); and Todd M. Kerstetter, *God's Country, Uncle Sam's Land: Faith and Conflict in the American West* (Urbana: University of Illinois Press, 2006).

Borderlands scholarship continues to blossom. Some of the best recent work includes Samuel Truett, *Fugitive Landscapes: The Forgotten History of the U.S.-Mexico Borderlands* (New Haven: Yale University Press, 2006); Charles Montgomery, *The Spanish Redemption: Heritage, Power, and Loss on New Mexico's Upper Rio Grande* (Berkeley: University of California Press, 2002); Benjamin Heber Johnson, *Revolution in Texas: How a Forgotten Rebellion and its Bloody Suppression Turned Mexicans into Americans* (New Haven: Yale University Press, 2003); Elliott Young, *Catrino Garza's Revolution on the Texas–Mexico Border* (Durham: Duke University Press, 2004); Pablo Mitchell, *Coyote Nation: Sexuality, Race, and Conquest in Modernizing New Mexico, 1880–1920* (Chicago: University of Chicago Press, 2005).

For the history of irrigation and the Bureau of Reclamation, see

Norris Hundley Jr, *The Great Thirst: Californians and Water, 1770s–1990s* (Berkeley: University of California Press, 1992); Mark Fiege, *Irrigated Eden: The Making of an Agricultural Landscape in the American West* (Seattle: University of Washington Press, 1999); and Donald J. Pisani, *Water and American Government: The Reclamation Bureau, National Water Policy, and the West, 1902–1935* (Berkeley: University of California Press, 2002).

For migration into the twentieth-century West, see James N. Gregory, *American Exodus: The Dust Bowl Migration and Okie Culture in California* (New York: Oxford University Press, 1989); George J. Sánchez, *Becoming Mexican American: Ethnicity, Culture, and Identity in Chicano Los Angeles, 1900–1945* (New York: Oxford University Press, 1993); Erika Lee, *At America's Gates: Chinese Immigration During the Exclusion Era, 1882–1943* (Chapel Hill: University of North Carolina Press, 2003); Dorothy B. Fujita-Rony, *American Workers, Colonial Power: Philippine Seattle and the Transpacific West, 1919–1941* (Berkeley: University of California Press, 2003); Douglas Flamming, *Bound for Freedom: Black Los Angeles in Jim Crow America* (Berkeley: University of California Press, 2005); and Eiichiro Azuma, *Between Two Empires: Race, History, and Transnationalism in Japanese America* (New York: Oxford University Press, 2005).

Understanding diverse western experiences during World War II demands close reading of Gretchen Lemke-Santangelo, *Abiding Courage: African American Migrant Women and the East Bay Community* (Chapel Hill: University of North Carolina Press, 1996); Shirley Ann Wilson Moore, *To Place Our Deeds: The African American Community in Richmond, California, 1910–1963* (Berkeley: University of California Press, 2000); Eduardo Obregón Pagán, *Murder at the Sleepy Lagoon: Zoot Suits, Race, and Riot in Wartime LA* (Chapel Hill: University of North Carolina Press, 2003); and Brian Masaru Hayashi, *Democratizing the Enemy: The Japanese American Internment* (Princeton: Princeton University Press, 2004).

Chapter 6

For the mythic West, see Robert G. Athearn, *The Mythic West in Twentieth Century America* (Lawrence: University Press of Kansas, 1986) and David M. Wrobel, *Promised Lands: Promotion, Memory, and the Creation of the American West* (Lawrence: University Press of Kansas, 2002). For the relationship between the Cold War and the Western genre, see Stanley Corkin, *Cowboys as Cold Warriors: The Western and US History* (Philadelphia: Temple University Press, 2004).

More on cities, suburbs, and the military-industrial complex in the West can be found in Ann Markusen, Peter Hall, Scott Campbell, Sabrina Deitrick, *The Rise of the Gunbelt: The Military Remapping of Industrial America* (New York: Oxford University Press, 1991); John M. Findlay, *Magic Lands: Western Cityscapes and American Culture after 1940* (Berkeley: University of California Press, 1992); Roger W. Lotchin, *Fortress California, 1910–1961* (New York: Oxford University Press, 1992); Becky M. Nicolaides, *My Blue Heaven: Life and Politics in the Working-Class Suburbs of Los Angeles, 1920–1965* (Chicago: University of Chicago Press, 2002); Stephen J. Pitti, *The Devil in Silicon Valley: Northern California, Race, and Mexican Americans* (Princeton: Princeton University Press, 2004); and Margaret Pugh O'Mara, *Cities of Knowledge: Cold War Science and the Search for the Next Silicon Valley* (Princeton: Princeton University Press, 2005). White flight, anti-tax movements, and black power are carefully linked in Robert O. Self, *American Babylon: Race and the Struggle for Postwar Oakland* (Princeton: Princeton University Press, 2003).

Donald Fixico, *Termination and Relocation: Federal Indian Policy, 1945–1960* (Albuquerque: University of New Mexico Press, 1986); Kenneth R. Philp, *Termination Revisited: American Indians on the Trail to Self-Determination, 1933–1953* (Lincoln: University of Nebraska Press, 1999); and R. Warren Metcalf, *Termination's Legacy: The Discarded Indians of Utah* (Lincoln: University of Nebraska Press, 2002) all examine the termination era.

On economic development in the post-World War II rural West, tourist or otherwise, see Hal K. Rothman, *Devil's Bargains: Tourism in the Twentieth-Century American West* (Lawrence: University Press of Kansas, 1998); Michael A. Amundson, *Yellowcake Towns: Uranium Mining Communities in the American West* (Boulder: University Press of Colorado, 2002); Bonnie Christensen, *Red Lodge and the Mythic West: Coal Miners to Cowboys* (Lawrence: University Press of Kansas, 2002); Julie Guthman, *Agrarian Dreams: The Paradox of Organic Farming in California* (Berkeley: University of California Press, 2004); and Annie Gilbert Coleman, *Ski Style:*

Sport and Culture in the Rockies (Lawrence: University Press of Kansas, 2004).

For political movements in the late twentieth-century West, see W. J. Rorabaugh, *Berkeley at War: The 1960s* (New York: Oxford University Press, 1989); R. McGreggor Cawley, *Federal Land, Western Anger: The Sagebrush Rebellion and Environmental Politics* (Lawrence: University Press of Kansas, 1993); Troy R. Johnson, *The Occupation of Alcatraz Island: Indian Self-Determination and the Rise of Indian Activism* (Urbana: University of Illinois Press, 1996); Joane Nagel, *American Indian Ethnic Renewal: Red Power and the Resurgence of Identity and Culture* (New York: Oxford University Press, 1996); Quintard Taylor, *In Search of the Racial Frontier: African Americans in the American West, 1528–1990* (New York: W. W. Norton, 1998); Lisa McGirr, *Suburban Warriors: The Origins of the New American Right* (Princeton: Princeton University Press, 2001); Ernesto Chávez, *"¡Mi Raza Primero!"* (*My People First!*) *Nationalism, Identity, and Insurgency in the Chicano Movement in Los Angeles, 1966–1978* (Berkeley: University of California Press, 2002); and Matthew C. Whitaker, *Race Work: The Rise of Civil Rights in the Urban West* (Lincoln: University of Nebraska Press, 2005).

Index

Page numbers in italics refer to illustrations

activism
  black, 198–200
  Catholic social activism, 137
  Chicana/o, 202–3
  environmental, 192, 207
  feminist, 199
  Hispana/o, 156
  labor movement, 106–7, 128,
    156–7
  Mexican American, 201–2
  Native American, 201, *202*
  rural, 134, 156, 157, 203
  student, 199
  Tejana/o, 156, 167–8
  urban, 157
aerospace industry, 186
African American women
  employment, 173, 174
  homesteaders, 140
  prostitution, 130
  urban life, 141–2, 173–4
African Americans
  civil rights movement, 198–9
  employment, 140–1
  fur trappers, 68
  journalism, 151, 152
  military service, 151, 153
  music, *141*
  segregation, 151, 152
  urban life, *141*, 141–2, 173
agribusiness, 134, 162, 163, 165,
    166, 191, 193, 203, 205

agriculture
  African American farmers, 140
  environmental degradation,
    132–3, 169, 205
  foreign introductions, 22
  Native American, 17, 18, 85,
    166
  organic farming, 205
  railroads, dependence on,
    133–4
  seasonal labor, 169
  slave labor, 36
aircraft production, 185–6
Alabama, 85
Alamo, 7, 89
Alamogordo, 176
Alaska, 50, 53, 189, 190, 201, 204
Albuquerque, 163, 190
Alcatraz Island, 201, *202*
Aleuts, 53
Algonquins, 32
alien introductions, 22, 132
  cattle industry, 132, 166, 168
Amarillo, 191
American Board of Commissioners
    for the Foreign Missions, 95–6
American Dream, 194
American Historical Association,
    150
American Indian Movement, 201
American Protective Association,
    128

American Revolution, 39–40, 84, 218
"Americanization," 85
Anaconda mine, 131
Anasazi, 135
Angel Island, 166–7
anti-Chinese sentiment, 106, 127–8, 142
anti-communism, 189, 194, 196, 197
anti-Indian sentiment, 116
anti-Mexican sentiment, 93, 145
anti-Vietnam War protests, 199
Apacheria, 40
Apaches, 19, 25, 41, 66
Arapahos, 47, 110, 116, 120
Arikaras, 47, 54, 55, 56, 60, 63, 67, 75, 76, 192
Arizona, 102, 167
Arkansas, 86
Arkansas River, 62, 65
arms manufacture, 177
army regiments, black, 151
Arness, James, 182
Article of Confederation, 42
Asian Americans, 189
Asian immigrants, 124, 167, 169, 204
    see also Chinese immigrants; Japanese immigrants
Asian women, 142, 143, 164
Aspen, 206
Assiniboins, 19, 47, 56, 67, 75
Astor, John Jacob, 63, 65
Astoria, 64
Astorians, 63–5
Austin, Moses, 87
Austin, Stephen, 87, 88
Aztecs, 20
Aztlán concept, 202
Azusa Street Mission, 156

back country people, 37, 39, 42, 43, 84
banking industry, 77, 124, 153
    and railroad construction, 124, 134
Bannocks, 107, 166
Baptists, 137

Bear Flag Revolt (1846), 102
Bear River Massacre (1863), 118
Bear River Range, 161
Beckwourth, James, 118
Beecher, Edward, 93
Berkeley, 199
big government, 152, 153, 158–9, 168–9, 174, 195, 198, 225
    see also federal bureaucracies
Bighorn Mountains, 67
Bighorn River, 63
Billings, 191
Billy the Kid, 123
Bisbee, 157, 206
bison, 69–70, 70
bison trade, 69–70, 71–2
Black Freedom Movement, 198, 199
Black Hawk, 84–5
Black Panthers, 199–200
black power, 198–200, 227
Blackfeet, 19, 23, 60, 61, 63, 67, 69, 75
Blew, May Clearman, 207
Bodmer, Karl, 74
Boise, 163, 208
Bonneville Dam, 172
Border Patrol, 167
borders, contested, 27, 42
Boston, 39, 48, 51
Bowie, Jim, 89
Bracero program, 174, 203
Braddock, Edward, 14
Brando, Marlon, 201
Brown, John, 109–10
Brown, Richard Maxwell, 123, 127
Brown Berets, 203
Brown vs Board of Education, 198
Buckley, William F., 195
buffalo, 23, 54, 135
Bunker Hill and Sullivan Mining Company, 128
Bureau of Indian Affairs, 112 n. 4, 121, 172, 201
Bureau of Reclamation, 162–3, 171, 191–2, 193, 225–6
Bush, George W., 1–4, 9, 210
Butte, 157, 163, 205–6

Cache National Forest, 161
Cache Valley, 69
Caddos, 40
Cahokia, 17
Calamity Jane (Martha Jane
    Canary-Burke), 125
California, 50–1, 103–4, 111, 159,
    188, 208, 220–1
  agriculture, 162, 169
  "alien labor" problem, 170
  California/os, 27
  Gold Rush, 103–5, 106
  immigrants, 164, 165, 167, 188
  Japanese Americans, 175–6
  migrant labor, 169, 203
  military bases, 185
  missions, 50–1, 136
  Native population, 101, 102,
    110
  Spanish presence, 50–1, 101
  statehood, 109
  universities, 186
  women's club movement, 142
Cameahwait, 57
Canada, 14, 100
canal building, 77, 82
Cannon, Lou, 197
capitalism, rise of, 6, 127
car culture, 187, 204
Cartier, Jacques, 28, 30
Carver, Jonathan, *13*
Cascades, 59
casinos, 206–7
Catawbas, 19
Catholicism, 26–7, 93, 136
  anti-Catholic sentiment, 93, 136
  and immigrant communities, 165
  laity, 136–7
  Native American adoption of,
    26–7
  social activism, 137, 203
  women religious, 136
Catlin, George, 73–4, 75
cattle industry, 132, 166, 168
Cayuses, 95, 96, 97, 98, 99, 100,
    110
centenary celebrations, 115
Central Arizona Project, 192
Central Pacific Railroad, 124

Central Valley, 162, 203
Centralia, 157
Centro de Acción Social
    Autónoma, 203
Chacon, Fernando de, 62
Champlain, Samuel de, 28, 29
Charbonneau, Toussaint, 56
Chardon, Francis, 76
Charleston, 38
Chávez, César, 203
Cherokees, 11, 38, 39, 85, 86
Cheyenne, Wyoming, 130, 191
Cheyennes, 19, 47, 67, 110, 116,
    118, 120
Chicago, 156
Chicana/o activism, 202–4
Chihuahua, 62
children
  mixed blood children, 24, 33, 144
  reservation schools, 121, 144–5,
    223
Chinese Americans, 163–4, 176
Chinese Exclusion Act (1882),
    127–8, 142, 163
Chinese immigrants, 106, *107*, 167
Chinese Telephone Exchange, 142,
    164
Chinese women, 164
Chinooks, 49, 54, 57, 59, 64
Chivington, John, 118
Choctaws, 11, 19
cholera, 76, 92
Church of Jesus Christ of Latter-
    day Saints *see* Mormons
civil rights, 146, 189, 198–9, 201
Civil War, 110, 111, 118
Clark, William, 48
  see also Lewis and Clark
    expedition
Clatsops, 59, 64
Clearwater River, 57
coal industry, 191
Colby, Mary M., 139
Cold War, 183, 189, 190, 191,
    194, 227
colonialism, 12–16, 150, 217–18
  see also English colonialism;
    French colonialism; Spanish
    colonialism

color line, 152
Colorado, 66, 91, 111, 139, 142,
    158, 184
Colorado River, 192
Colorado River Compact, 162,
    171, 192
Colorado School of Mines, *107*
Colorado Springs, 184
Columbia River, 49, 57, 58, 61,
    64, 157
Comancheria, 40
Comanches, 40, 56, 62, 66, 86, 87,
    90, 92, 120
commercial expansion, 82, 83,
    154, 155
    see also economic development
Committee of Indian Affairs, 85
communism, 191, 194, 195
community newspapers, 151, 152,
    164, 165
Company of 100 Associates, 34
Compromise of 1820, 109
Compromise of 1850, 109
Congregationalists, 137
conquest rhetoric, 110
conquistadors *see* Spanish
    colonialism
conservative hegemony, 127
consumer consumption, 193, 208
Continental Divide, 59
Conway, Jennie, 130
Cooper, James Fennimore, 82
corridos, 166
Cortés, Hernando, 20
Corwin, Thomas, 103
cotton cultivation, 77, 88, 91
Council Bluffs Indian Agency, 75
cowboys, 132, 207
Crawford, Texas, 1, 3
Creeks, 11, 19, 39
Crees, 47, 56
Cresap, Thomas, 14
Crockett, Davy, 89
Crows, 19, 47, 63, 67, 71
cultural forms, new, 155–6, 187
cultural identities, 27, *98*
    women, 145
Custer, George Armstrong,
    General, 7, 115, 116

Dallas, 173
Dalles, 58, 59
dam-building, 161, 162, 171–2,
    177, 186, 191–2, 193
defense industries, 174, 194
Delawares, 11, 19, 39
Democrats, 83, 100, 189, 196, 197
demographic diversity, 153
demographic shifts, 173, 184, 188
Denver, 130, 138, 140, 153, 163,
    173, 191, 201
desegregation, 199
DeVoto, Bernard, 190–1
dietary habits, changing, 134
Dinosaur National Monument,
    192
diplomacy
    intertribal, 19, 32, 51
    Native–white, 20, 30, 54–5, 58,
        60, 117, 118, 121
    trade as conduit for, 51, 61
disease, 23, 30, 34, 52, 75–7, 100,
    102, 130
Distant Early Warning Line
    (DEW), 189
domestic violence, 130
Dominy, Floyd, 192
drought, 168
Durango, 190
Dust Bowl, 169

Earp, Wyatt, 123
Echo Park, 192
economic depressions, 77, 82, 168
economic development, 77, 227–8
    indigenous economies, 122
    see also commercial expansion
economic displacement, 156
economic hegemony, 154
education, 82
    post-war programs, 188
    reservation schools, 121, 144–5,
        223
    school segregation, 198
El Paso, 26, 163, 165
empresarios, 87, 88
energy economy, 177, 204
English colonialism, 35–40, 218
    American Revolution, 39–40

Native–white domestic relations, 37
Native–white warfare, 38
entrepreneurialism
  collaborative, 105
  Native, 85, 173, 206–7
environmental degradation, 22, 99, 205
  agriculture and, 132–3, 169, 205
  economic expansion and, 154
  mining and, 131–2
environmental regulation, 207
Episcopalians, 137
Esteban, 20
ethnography, 61, 73–4
Evanston, 163
Everett, 157
Exodusters, 140
expansionism, 6, 37, 77, 81, 83, 87, 91, 92, 94, 102, 103, 134–5, 166, 190
exploration
  French, 28–30
  Lewis and Clark expedition, 48–61
  scientific expeditions, 65–6
  trade expeditions, 61–5, 66–7
extraction industries, 158, 173, 184, 190, 191, 205
  see also gas extraction; mining industry; oil industry; uranium mining

farming *see* agriculture
Farmington, 190
Federal Bureau of Investigation (FBI), 175
federal bureaucracies, 158–9, 160–3, 171, 191–3
  see also big government
Federal Housing Administration, 188
Filipina/os, 165
filles du roi, 33
fishing
  industrial, 28, 157, 159
  Native, 18, 57, 201
  sport fishing, 157
Five Civilized Tribes, 85

Five Nations confederacy, 32
Florida
  missions, 21
  Spanish Florida, 16, 20
forest fires, 160
Fort Berthold, 192
Fort Cass, 71
Fort Clark, 71, 75, 76
Fort Clatsop, 49, 59
Fort Douglas, 151
Fort Fauntleroy, 117, 120
Fort Laramie, 110
Fort Lemhi, 108
Fort Pierre, 71, 75
Fort Ross, 51
Fort Union, 71, 75
Fort Vancouver, 67, 95, 96
Fort Worth, 153, 173
49th parallel, 100
Four Square Gospel Church, 156
Franciscan friars, 21, 26
Free Speech Movement, 199
Frémont, John C., 102
French Canadians, 35
French colonialism, 28–35, 218
  Native–French economic relations, 29–30, 31, 35
  Native–French familial relationships, 31, 33
French and Indian War (1754–63), 12, 14, 40
frontier, 5, 150–1, 152
frontiersmen, 84
fur trapping and trading, 31, 32, 49, 50, 51, 59, 63, 66, 67, 68–9, 71, 77
  over-trapping, 69
  trading posts, 51, 63, 69, 71

Garrison Dam, 192
gas extraction, 190, 204, 205
gender practices, changing, 104, 118, 144, 145
General Land Office, 159
George III, 14, 15–16
Georgia, 85, 86
German Jewish immigrants, 98
Ghost Dances, 136
GI Bill (1944), 188

Gist, Christopher, 14
Glen Canyon Dam, 192
Gold Rush, 103–5, 106, 111, 138
Goldwater, Barry, 195–6, 197
Gonzalez, Rodolfo, 202
Goshutes, 107
Grand Canyon, 192
Grand Coulee, 172
Granger laws, 134
Grant, Ulysses S., 120
Grants, New Mexico, 190
Gray, Robert, 49
Great Basin Kingdom, 108
Great Depression, 168, *170*, 171
Great Falls of the Missouri, 59–60
Great Lakes, 47
Great Plains, 52, 62, 66, 73, 124
    division of, 110
    Dust Bowl, 169
    see also Plains Indians
Great Salt Lake, 67, 107–8
Great Society program, 198, 200
Green River, 63, 69
Greensboro, 198
Gregory, Dick, 201
Grenada Relocation Center, *175*
Gros Ventres, 19, 110
"Gunsmoke," 182
Guthrie, Woody, 172

Hardin, John Wesley, 123
Harper's Ferry raid, 110
Hawai'i, 51, 63, 154, 164, 165,
    189, 190
    statehood, 189, 190
Haywood, William (Big Bill), 128
heritage tourism, 206
Hermitage, 84
Hetch Hetchy Valley, 162
Hidatsas, 47, 54, 56, 60, 63, 67,
    75, 192
Hill, Joe, 128
hippies, 200
Hispana/os, 27, 66, 156
Homestead Act (1862), 139, 140
Honolulu, 165
Hoover, Herbert, 171
Hoover Dam (Boulder Dam), 171,
    172

Hopis, 173
horse culture, 22–3, 24, 52–3
horse trade, 47, 52, 57, 99
House of Burgesses, 36
housing segregation, 173, 188
Houston, 173, 204
Houston, Sam, 89, 90
Hudson's Bay Company, 94
Huerta, Dolores, 203
hunting, hunting grounds, 17, 84
Hurons, 11, 30, 31, 32
Hutchinson, Hannah S., 140

Idaho, 57, 111, 128, 154, 158,
    171
Illinois, 84
immigration, 82, 93, 106, 167
    anti-immigration legislation,
        127–8, 142, 163
    controls, 167
    illegal immigration, 167
    repatriation programs, 170–1
    see also specific groups
Immigration and Naturalization
    Service (INS), 167, 170
imperialism, 75
indentured servants, 34
Indian Department, 84, 112 n. 4
    see also Bureau of Indian Affairs
Indian Reorganization Act (IRA)
    (1934), 172
Indian Territory, 85
Indian Wars, 108, 120, 122
individualism, 198
Industrial Workers of the World
    (IWW), 107, 156–7
industrialization, 127, 131
industries
    wartime, 173
    see also specific industries
influenza, 76
inner city poverty, 208
intellectual centers, 186–7
international boundaries, 100
international financial cooperation,
    105
Irish immigrants, 124, 128
Iroquois, 11, 32
Iroquois League, 32

irrigation, 29, 120, 145, 161, 171, 225–6
Irving, Washington, 82
Italian Americans, 175

Jackson, Andrew, 83–4, 85
James, Jesse, 123
Jamestown, 35, 36
Japanese Americans, 164–5, 189
  internment, 175–6, *175*
Japanese immigrants, 143, 164, 167
Jefferson, Thomas, 42, 48, 50, 61, 63, 81, 83
Jewish immigrants, 98, 138
Jocques, Isaac, 32
Johnson, Lyndon Baines, 3, 198, 200
journalism
  African American, 151, 152
  Asian, 164
  Mexican American, 165
judicial system, women and the, 125–6

Kakawissassa, 55
Kansas, 20, 62, 109, 140, 142, 169
Kansas City, 153
Kansas-Nebraska Act (1854), 109
Kelley, Hall Jackson, 95
Kelley, Oliver Hudson, 134
Kennecott mine, 131
King Philip's War (1675–6), 38
Kiowas, 19, 47, 86, 98, 120
Kittredge, William, 207
kivas, 17
Klamaths, 200
Kootenais, 200

La Raza Unida, 203
labor conflict, 106, 124, 127, 157
labor migrants, 132, 163, 165, 169
labor movement, 107, 128, 156–7
labor recruitment, 165, 167
Lake Michigan, 29
Lakotas, 47, 49, 54–5, 56, 60, 61, 63, 64, 67, 71, 75, 122
land distribution, 42–3

land grants
  colonial, 13, 34
  Mexican, 87
Land Ordinance (1785), 42–3
land speculation, 42, 43
Lange, Dorothea, *170*
las Casas, Bartolomé de, 25
Las Vegas, 171, 208
LaSalle, René-Robert Cavelier, Sieur de, 29
Lee, Jason, 95
Lewis, Meriwether, 48
  see also Lewis and Clark expedition
Lewis and Clark expedition, 48–61
liberal Democratic consensus, 198
libertarianism, 194, 198
Lisa, Manuel, 62–3, 71
literary depictions of the West, 82
Little Bighorn River, Battle of (1876), 115, 116, 117, 222
living standards, improved, 134
Lolo Pass, 49, 57, 59
lone prospector myth, 105
Long, Stephen, 65–6
Long Walk, 117
Los Alamos, 176
Los Angeles, 154, 155, 165, 173, 185, 201, 203
  Azusa Street Mission, 156
  multiculturalism, 173
  repatriation programs, 170–1
  riots, 199, 208
  water shortages, 155
  Zoot-Suit riots (1943), 174
Los Hermanas, 203
Los Hermanos, 137
Louisiana, 29, 40
  Spanish administration, 40
Louisiana Purchase, 1803 48
Louisiana Territory, 48
Lumbees, 19
lumber industry, 132, 159–60, 206
lynch law, 126, 127

McCarran–Nixon Internal Security Act (1950), 189
MacKenzie, Alexander, 49, 50
McLean, William, 85

McLoughlin, John, 94, 95, 96
McPherson, Aimee Semple, 156
Maine, 159
male-centered perspective, 8, 41, 122, 125, 126, 145
Mandans, 19, 47, 49, 54, 56, 60, 63, 67, 71, 75, 76, 110, 192
Manhattan Project, 176–7
Manifest Destiny doctrine, 110, 220
maritime trade, 51
Marquette, Jacques, 29
masculinity, stylized, 198
Massachusetts Bay Colony, 37
materialism, 193
matrimony
    arranged marriages, 143
    Native–white unions, 24, 31, 72
Maximilien of Wied, Prince, 74, 75
Maxwell, Martha, 140
Mayflower, 37
measles, 100
meat-packing industry, 153
Mesa Verde, *18*
Mesquakies, 84
mestizos, 24, 26, 202
Methodism, 95, 137
métis, 33
Mexican American women, 145
Mexican Americans, 165, 171
    activism, 201–2
    culture, 165–6
    military service, 174
    repatriation, 171
Mexican Revolution (1821), 102, 167
Mexican War (1846–8), 91, 102, 103, 109
Mexico, 66, 87–9
    Immigration Law (1830), 87
    labor migrants, 167, 168, 169–70, 171, 174, 203
    Mexican–Texan relations, 90–1, 167
    missions, 21
    "no slavery" dictate, 87
    settlement conditions, 87–8, 93
    sovereignty issues, 7
    Spanish Mexico, 20, 87

Mexico City, 26, 66, 91
Michigan, 159
middle class, growth of, 188
military bases, 176, 177, 184, 185, 189
military-industrial complex, 177, 182–3, 184, 185, 187, 189, 190, 191, 194, 198, 204, 208, 209, 227
Milk River, 161
Mineral Leasing Act (1920), 159
minimum wage laws, 203
Mining Act (1872), 159
mining industry, 103–7, 127, 131–2, 156, 166, 205, 221
    environmental degradation, 104–5, 131–2
Minneapolis, 153, 157, 173, 201
Minnesota, 157, 159
Minot, 185
missionary work
    Catholic, 21, 26, 30, 85, 95, 101, 102, 111, 136
    Mormon, 108, 111
    Protestant, 95–8, 99, 111, 137, 164
Mississippi River, 29, 40, 42
Mississippi River Valley, 54
Missouri Compromise (1820), 65
Missouri River, 18, 47, 49, 50, 54, 56, 60, 63, 67, 69, 70, 71, 74, 191
Miwoks, 19
Moab, 190, 206
Moderator Movement, 39
Mogolon, 17
Mohawks, 11
Mojaves, 67
Montana, 56, 111, 139, 142, 153, 158
Montcalm, Marquis of, 14
Montez, Lola, 140
Montreal, 33, 63
Morgan, Neil, 188, 198
Mormons (Church of Jesus Christ of Latter-day Saints), 108–9, 111, 137, 152, 153, 221
Moundbuilders, 17
Mountain Meadows massacre, 109

mountain men, 68–9
movies *see* Westerns
Muckleshoots, 201
Muir, John, 162
Mulholland, William, 155
multiculturalism, 166, 173
mythic West, 9, 183, 187, 188, 197, 206, 207, 208, 210, 226–7

Nacogdoches, 62
Narragansetts, 38
Narváez, Panfilo de, 20
Nashville, 198
Natchitoches, 41
nation building project, 6
National Association for the Advancement of Colored People, 199
national confidence, 81, 83
National Congress of American Indians, 201
national identity, 4
National Indian Youth Council, 201
National Interstate and Defense Highways Act (1956), 187
National Museum of the American Indian, 210
National Park Service, 162
national parks, 158
National Road, 83
Native American women
  cross-cultural interpreters, 23, 31, 118, 143
  interracial relationships, 31, 68, 72, 118, 143
  matriarchal power, 31, 32, 41, 144, 145
  sexual exploitation, 24, 30, 41, 101, 143
  slavery, 41, 53
  trading activity, 72
Native Americans
  activism, 201, 202
  assimilation, 85–6, 121, 223
  Christian conversion *see* missionary work
  colonial experience, 12, 19–40

cultures, 19
  death toll (military engagements), 119
  decimation by disease, 52, 75–7, 92, 102, 122
  displacement, 85–7, 117, 158, 220, 222
  enslavement, 25
  farming, 17, 18
  indigenous economies, 122
  intertribal politics, 47–8, 55, 60, 97, 121–2
  kinship relations, 31, 72
  languages, 19, 23
  Native–colonial relations *see* colonialism
  pan-Indian identity, 120, 166
  population decline, 122
  pre-contact history, 11–12, 16–19, 217
  religious systems, 135–6
  reservations *see* reservations
  sovereign status, 172, 173, 201
  treaties, 67, 86, 110, 120, 121
  tribal history records, 52
  tribal identity, 19, 51, 136, 172
  US military service, 172–3
  and US peace policy, 120–1
Navajos, 19, 117–18, 145, 166, 172
Nebraska, 158
Nevada, 102, 111, 154
New Deal politics, 171, 193, 197–8
New France, 15, 28, 29, 33–5
  see also French colonialism
New Left, 198, 199
New Mexico, 61–2, 90, 109, 111, 206
  Hispana/os, 27, 156
  immigrant control, 167
  missions, 21
  Texan land claims, 91
New Right, 194, 195, 196, 197
New Spain, 24, 26, 66
  see also Spanish colonialism
new western history, 7, 8
New York City, 63
Newlands Act (1902), 171

Newlands, Francis G., 161
Nez Perces, 49, 57, 59, 60, 61, 95, 96
Nicodemus, 140
Nicolet, Jean, 29
Nisquallys, 201
Nixon, Richard M., 197
Nonpartisan League (NPL), 157–8
North American Air Defense Command (NORAD), 184
North Carolina, 84
North Dakota, 47, 111, 153, 157, 169
North Platte River, 161
Northwest Ordinance (1787), 43, 219
nuclear testing, 176–7, 185, 190

Oakland, 199–200
Ogallala aquifer, 191
Ohio Valley, 14, 15, 40
oil industry, 190, 204, 205
oil spills, 205
Oklahoma, 85, 86, 120, 139, 169
Oklahoma City, 154, 191, 199
Omaha, 153, 184
Oneidas, 11
oral tradition, 33–4
Order of the Patrons of Husbandry, 134
Oregon, 94, 95, 100, 110, 111, 157, 159
and slavery, 100–1
Oregon Trail, 98
organic farming, 205
Osages, 19, 86
O'Sullivan, John L., 81, 83
other, voice of the, 8
outlaws, 123, 124–5, 126
female, 124–5
Owens Valley, 155

Paiutes, 67, 107, 120
Palo Alto, 187
Panama Canal, 166
Panic of (1837), 77, 82
Papagos, 17, 19
Park City, 206
Parker, Ely S., 121

Parkman, Francis, 82
patriotism, 7, 9, 172
Pawnees, 19, 75
peace policy (US/Native), 120–1
Pearl Harbor, 175
Pentecostal movement, 156
Pequots, 19, 38
Philadelphia, 14, 39, 48
Philippines, 165
Phoenix, 186, 208
Pick-Sloan Plan, 192
piedmont communities, 37–8
Pike, Zebulon, 61–2, 66
Pike's Peak, 62
Pilcher, Joshua, 75
Pim Indians, 17
Pinchot, Gifford, 160, 162
Pine Ridge Reservation, 201
Pinkertons agency, 128
pioneer families, 111, 138–9
Plains of Abraham, 14
Plains Indians, 40, 41, 47, 52, 54, 120, 135
Plan de San Diego uprising (1915), 167
Pocahontas, 37
political movements, 184, 194–7, 198, 199, 228
Polk, James, 91
polygamy, 108, 114 n. 31, 152, 153
Poncas, 67
Popé (Pueblo holy man), 26
Portland, 154, 173, 208
potlatch, 19
Potomac River, 14
Pottawatomie Creek, 110
Powhatans, 35
pow-wow circuit, 166
Presbyterianism, 137
presidios, 24, 101
prisons, 126
women prisoners, 126
Proclamation of 1763, 15, 16, 38, 39, 88, 218
prostitution, 103, 104, 128–31
African American women, 130
Asian women, 142, 143
violence, 130

Protestantism, 88, 93
  missionary work, 137
Prudhoe Bay, 204
public lands
  federal management, 168–9
  projects on, 161
  sale of, 159
Pueblo Revolt (1680), 25–6
Pueblos, *18*, 20, 25, 26, 135
Puget Sound, 51, 172, 201
Puritans, 37, 38
Puyallups, 201

Quebec, 14, 15, 16, 33–4

race relations, 4, 20, 128, 167
racial control issues, 24
racial integration, 200
racism, 4, 68, 88, 93, 106, 116,
  127–8, 142, 145, 153, 163,
  164, 168, 175, 210
railroad construction, 77, 82, 111,
  153, 154, 167, 223
  and agriculture, 133–4
  banking alliances, 124, 134
  trans-continental railroad, 124
Rayburn, Sam, 197–8
Reagan, Ronald, 3, 196–7, 207,
  209
Reclamation Service, 161–2
Red Horse, 116–17
Red Power movement, 201
Red River, 62, 65
Regulator Wars (1763–73), 38–9,
  123, 126
religion
  and female activism, 195
  female pastors, 137, 156
  Jewish, 138
  Methodism, 95, 135–7
  Native American spirituality,
  135
  new religious movements, 156
  see also Catholicism; Mormons;
  Protestantism
repatriation programs, 170–1, 174
Republican Party, 195, 196, 197
reservations, 118, 120, 121, 158,
  222

Christian missions, 137
  sale of, 200–1
  schools, 121, 144–5, 223
  termination era, 200–1, 227
resources, distribution of, 134–5
Rio Grande, 62, 92, 161
Rocky Mountains, 49, 56, 57, 59,
  62, 65, 73, 160, 219
Rolfe, John, 37
Roosevelt, Franklin D., 168, 175,
  176
Roosevelt, Theodore, 3
Ross, John, 86
Russian traders, 50, 51, 53
Ryan, Annie, 130
Ryan, Jane Elizabeth, 130

Sacagawea, 56–7
Sacramento, 103, 140
Sagebrush Rebellion, 207
St Cloud, 140
St Lawrence River, 28
St Louis, 49, 54, 60, 66, 69
St Paul, 153
Sakakawea, Lake, 192
Salish, 57, 95, 200
Salt Lake City, 115, 151–2, 153,
  154, 163, 173, 190, 201, 208
Salt River, 161
San Antonio, 62, 165
San Diego, 173, 185
San Francisco, 51, 103, 111, 140,
  154, 162, 165, 173, 185, 199,
  200–1
  Chinese community, 163–4
  Chinese Telephone Exchange,
  142, 164
  Jewish community, 138
  water supplies, 162
San Jacinto River, 89
Sanchez, Adelle, 130
Sand Creek Massacre (1864), 118,
  120
Sangre de Cristos, 62
Santa Ana, Antonio López de, 88,
  89, 90
Santa Barbara, 205
Santa Fe, 26, 61–2, 65, 66, 90,
  206, 219–20

Santa Fe Trail, 66, 68, 111
Sauks, 84
school segregation, 198
scientific expeditions, 61, 73, 74–5, 219
Seattle, 154, 155, 165, 173, 185–6, 208
segregation, 151, 152, 173, 198
self-reliance, 194
Seminoles, 19
Senate, 83
Senecas, 11, 32
sentimental populism, 197
service economies, 206
Seward, 205
sharecropping, 156
Shawnees, 11, 39
Shoshones, 19, 56, 57, 60, 61, 63, 64, 107, 118, 166
Sierra Club, 192
Sierra Nevadas, 67, 155
Silicon Valley, 186, 208
Singleton, Benjamin, 140
Sioux, 19, 110, 116
Sitka, 51
Sitting Bull, 7
ski industry, 206
Skilloots, 59, 61
slavery, 100–1, 221
    abolitionists, 91, 109–10
    black slavery, 22, 36, 83, 88, 93–4
    and the cotton industry, 91
    gendered, 40–1, 53
    Missouri Compromise (1820), 65
    Native Americans, 25, 40, 41, 83
    Native slave owners, 85
smallpox, 23, 34, 52, 75–6, 77, 92
Smith, Jedediah, 66–8
Smith, Joseph, 108
Smith, Truman, 91
Snake River, 57
Snake River Valley, 64
Snakes, 120
social activism, Catholic, 137
Society of Friends (Quakers), 120
sod-houses, 140

Soil Conservation Service, 169
Soto, Hernando de, 20
South Carolina, 38
South Dakota, 29, 111, 139, 153, 158, 169
South Pass, 67
Spanish colonialism, 19–27
    resistance to, 25–6, 27, 66
spirituality, 135
    see also religion
Spokane, 95, 154
Stanford University, 187, 208
Starr, Belle, 125
Stegner, Wallace, 188
stereotyping, 2, 3–5
    see also mythic West
Strauss, Levi, 138
Strawberry River, 161
strikes, 128
suburban living, 187
suffrage, female, 146, 157
Sun Valley, 206
Susquehannocks, 19
Swisshelm, Jane Grey, 140

Tacoma, 173
Taos, 65
taxation, colonial, 34, 36
Taylor, Julius, 152
Taylor, William, 151
Taylor Grazing Act (1934), 168
technocracy, 186, 187, 188
technological revolution, 208
Tejana/os, 27, 87, 88, 89, 90, 91, 112 n. 11, 156, 167
Tennessee, 84
Tetharsky, 57
Teton Dam, 193
Texas, 1, 87, 111, 161, 220
    declaration of independence, 89
    immigrant control, 167
    Mexican–Texan relations, 90–1, 167
    Spanish Texas, 40
    Tejana/os, 27, 87, 88, 89, 90, 91, 112 n. 11, 156, 167
    Texas Revolution, 89–90
    women's club movement, 142
Texas Ranger Hall of Fame, 1

Texas Rangers, 167
tick fever, 132
tidewater communities, 37, 38
Tlingits, 19, 51
tobacco cultivation, 88
tourism, 184, 206, 207, 210
trade, 30, 41
  bison trade, 69–70, 71–2
  female slaves, 41
  Native American, 12, 30, 47, 58
  Native–European, 50–1, 54, 55,
    56, 57, 58, 59, 61, 64
  treaties, 67
  see also fur trapping and trading
trade agreements, 61
trading posts, 63, 64, 71
Trail of Tears, 86
transnational ideology, 165
transportation infrastructure,
  77–8, 82, 153
  see also canal building; railroad
    construction
Travis, William, 89
treaties, 86, 110, 121
  abrogation of, 200
  trade, 67
Treaty of Guadalupe-Hidalgo
  (1848), 91, 103
Treaty of Medicine Creek Lodge
  (1867), 120
Treaty of New Echota (1836), 86
Treaty of Paris (1763), 15
Treaty of Paris (1783), 39
Truckee River, 161
Truman, Harry, 176
Tulalips, 201
Tulsa, 173
Tulsa riot (1921), 168
Turner, Frederick Jackson, 150–1,
  152
Twisted Hair, 57

Umatilla River, 161
Umatillas, 57
Uncompahgre River, 161
Underhill, Professor James, *107*
Union Pacific Railroad, 124
United Farm Workers (UFW), 203
Untongarabar, 54, 55

uranium mining, 190
urban design and renewal, 155
urban population growth, 173
urban–rural dynamics, 82, 154,
  157, 158, 184, 191, 205
urbanization, 152–4, *209*, 224
US Air Force Strategic Air
  Command, 184
US Army Corps of Engineers, 171,
  191
US Forest Service (USFS), 159–61
Utah, 66, 102, 108, 109, 111, 190
  statehood, 152
Utes, 66, 107, 108, 200

Vancouver Island, 51
Vargas, Diego de, 26
venereal disease, 23, 130
Veterans Administration programs,
  188
Victorian sexuality, 108
vigilantism, 39, 123, 126–7, 167
  economic outcomes, 126–7
violence, 4, 6, 106, 122–4, 224
  against the land *see*
    environmental degradation
  labor conflict, 157
  military, 120
  outlaws, 123, 124–5, 126
  racist, 168
  sexual, 24, 31, 101, 130
  vigilantism, 39, 123, 126–7, 167
Virginia, 35–6
Virginia City, 163, 206

Waiilatpu Mission, 96
Walkara, 108
Walla Walla River, 96
Walla Wallas, 57
Wampanoags, 38
Wanapams, 57
War of (1812), 64, 84
Wascos, 58
Washington, 84, 94, 154, 158,
  159, 171
Washington, DC, 210
water supplies, 155, 161, 162,
  191–3, 205
Wayne, John, 5, 182

Western Federation of Miners, 107
Western identity, 4, 8
Western Negro Press Association, 151
Westerns, 5, 182, 183, 193–4, 204
Wheatland, 157
Whigs, 83
White, Richard, 123
white flight, 188, 227
Whitman, Marcus, 95–8, 100, 137, 221
Whitman, Narcissa, 96–8, 99, 100, 137, 221
Wichita, 173, 199
Wichitas, 40
Wilderness Society, 192
wilderness tourism, 206
Willamette Valley, 95, 96
Winnebagos, 19
winter count, 52, 96
Wisconsin, 159
Wise Use movement, 207
Wishrams, 57, 58
Wolfe, James, 14
women
  Asian women, 142, 143, 164
  as civilizers, 97
  club movement, 141–2
  colonial, 33, 36–7
  criminals, 125–6
  cultural expectations, 97
  division and hostility between, 146
  employment, 140, 173
  and the Gold Rush, 103–4
  Mexican American women, 145
  middle-class white women, 104
  missionary workers, 96–8, 99, 100, 137, 221
  and the New Right, 195
  outlaws, 124–5
  pastors, 137, 156
  pioneer women, 138–9
  prostitution, 103, 104, 128–31
  religious orders, 136
  single women pioneers, 139
  suffrage, 146, 157
  urban life, 139–40, 141–2
  women's movement, 199
  see also African American women; Native American women
Wool, General John E., 86
World War II, 172–3, 174, 175–6, 189, 226
Wounded Knee massacre (1890), 122
Wyandotte, 95
Wyeth, Nathaniel, 95
Wyoming, 29, 64, 139, 140

Yakima River, 161
Yakimas, 57, 173
Yellowstone National Park, 158
Yellowstone River, 60, 63, 71
York (African slave), 55
Yosemite National Park, 158, 162
Young, Brigham, 108, 109
Younger, Cole, 123

Zoot-Suit riots (1943), 174
Zunis, 19, 20, 173

Made in the USA
Las Vegas, NV
19 January 2023